Women's Studies

Women's Studies
A Recommended Core Bibliography

Esther Stineman

Women's Studies Librarian-at-Large
The University of Wisconsin System

with the assistance of
CATHERINE LOEB

Libraries Unlimited, Inc. - Littleton, Colo. -1979

LIBRARIES UNLIMITED, INC.
P.O. Box 263
Littleton, Colorado 80160

Library of Congress Cataloging in Publication Data

Stineman, Esther, 1947—
    Women's studies.

    Includes indexes.
    1. Women--Bibliography. 2. Women's studies--
Bibliography. I. Loeb, Catherine. II. Title.
Z7961.S75   [HQ1180]   016.30141'2   79-13679
ISBN 0-87287-196-7

This book is bound with Scott Graphitek®–C Type II nonwoven material.
Graphitek–C meets and exceeds National Association of State Textbook Administrators' Type II nonwoven material specifications Class A through E.

EPIGRAPHS

Scholarship about women is not new. They have long been subject to investigation. Some of it has been serious or sympathetic; some, trivial or hostile. What is novel is the amount of intellectual energy men and women are now spending on such scholarship and the consciousness that often frames their efforts. That charged, restless consciousness respects many of the concepts, tools, and techniques of modern study. It uses them to compensate for old intellectual evasions and errors, to amass fresh data, and to generate new concepts, tools, and techniques. It also tends to question the social, political, economic, cultural, and psychological arrangements that have governed relations between females and males, that have defined femininity and masculinity. It even suspects that those arrangements have been a source of the errors that must be corrected.

Editors of *Signs: Journal of Women in Culture and Society*,
Volume I, No. 1

A: I came here to see you because I want to do a paper about feminism.

B: Any particular period of feminism? any specific aspect or theory?

A: No, not really. I just want to do the whole thing.

Conversation between librarian and student,
October 1978

One went to the counter; one took a slip of paper; one opened a volume of the catalogue, and ..... the five dots here indicate five separate minutes of stupefaction, wonder and bewilderment. Have you any notion how many books are written about women in the course of one year. ... Here had I come with a notebook and pencil proposing to spend a morning reading, supposing that at the end of the morning I should have transferred the truth to my notebook. But I should need to be a herd of elephants, I thought, and a wilderness of spiders, desperately referring to the animals that are reputed longest lived and most multitudinously eyed, to cope with all this.

Virginia Woolf, *A Room of One's Own* (1929),
p. 26

I *believe* in reading unsystematically and taking notes erratically. Any effort to form a rational policy about what to take in, out of the inhuman flood of printed human utterance that pours over us daily, feels to me like a self-deluded exercise in pseudomastery.

Dorothy Dinnerstein, *The Mermaid and the Minotaur*,
p. ix

5

For

J. B. S. and C. L. H.

PREFACE AND ACKNOWLEDGMENTS

When I arrived at the University of Wisconsin in 1977 to take the newly created position of System Librarian-at-Large for Women's Studies, I faced two major questions in defining what constitutes library support for women's studies: what is women's studies? and how can library collections respond to women's studies in their collection building policy? Other questions clustered around specific problems such as trying to identify the best sources on the history of the suffrage movement in the United States, say, or general bibliographic issues such as whether or not all women novelists' works might be said to support a women's studies literature curriculum.

Miriam Allman and Dorothy Schultz's *Women's Studies Resources* (1977), a list compiled at Madison and distributed throughout the System, was of great help to me, as it provided titles and bibliographic information for over 900 books relevant to women's studies. Their effort had tapped the suggestions and expertise of women's studies faculty and librarians from the 14 campuses in the University cluster, and to some extent, the present list reflects its Wisconsin genesis. Users will find materials emanating from various Wisconsin groups sprinkled throughout.

Though many campuses began filling gaps in their collections by using Allman and Schultz's list, something more was needed. To list books under broad headings represented a fine beginning. Yet, many people wanted to know the specific approach or content of a given book; students and faculty often requested annotated bibliographies; librarians needed to identify major reference books on women and to recognize the comparative differences between titles. The larger problem remained of advising libraries on the formulation of collection policies responsive to women's studies when the field is, by definition, interdisciplinary, controversial, and political in its connection to the women's movement and is subjectively defined (as, after all, all disciplines are). On many campuses in the United States, these attributes deny women's studies legitimacy as a "proper" subject area. However, the identification of books that illuminate women's experiences and contributions to society, whether they be books by or about women, or both, has been and continues to be a priority in women's studies and in the women's movement. The commitment of the University of Wisconsin System to library support in the area of women's studies is informed by the recognition that the problems of resource identification and collection development loom as substantial ones for students, faculty, librarians—indeed for everyone interested in seeing libraries respond to the information needs and contributions of over one-half the world's population.

It is a pleasure to say that collaborative effort saw this bibliography through from its initial idea to its final form. Thanks go to Dorothy Schultz and Miriam Allman and to the women of the University of Wisconsin System who assisted in the preparation and publication of *Women's Studies: A Recommended Core Bibliography.*

The present bibliography would not exist if not for the massive efforts of Catherine Loeb, research assistant on the project for more than one year. She annotated a substantial number of entries, assisted in editing, and performed many of the most painstaking and difficult tasks that characterize all bibliographic work—searching and verifying information. Without her assistance and her knowledge of the social sciences, this bibliography would be missing much. Her good cheer and good sense up to the eleventh hour and the ninth month (for she was expecting the birth of her first child as she worked on final details before this book went to the publisher) have made this project a reality in major and minor ways too numerous to detail here.

Barbara Rohland creatively searched out books hiding in the many nooks and crannies of the complex Madison campus library system, and worked on many of the time-consuming and important clerical details of the project. Susan Looper, before leaving for law school, assisted us for several months.

For heroic typing efforts, thanks go to librarian Jan Behn, who carefully typed and retyped most of the entries. Whitney Walton's expertise in typing and her contribution of many extra hours during the last stages of this project, even as she was engaged in her own substantial projects, saved us in many ways on many days. Thanks to Carolyn Wilson for assisting with proofreading and general encouragement.

The following people and organizations should be singled out for the assistance they gave: Mary Williamson, Sylvia Adrian, and Gerry Hurley of Wisconsin Interlibrary Loan (WILS), who assisted in coming up with a strategy for handling the large volume of interloan that this project entailed; Tamara Miller of Wisconsin Library Consortium who provided OCLC computer time for the verification of entries; Joseph Treyz of Memorial Library who supported this project by providing additional office space and staff money during the duration, and to library staff at Memorial Library and many branch libraries on the Madison campus, who accommodated us both by buying books involved in the project and in many other gracious ways.

Miriam Allman (UW-Madison), Edi Bjorklund (UW-Milwaukee), Karen Merritt (UW-Central Administration), Nancy Marshall (Director, WILS/WLC), Alice Randlett (UW-Stevens Point), Joseph Boisse (UW-Parkside), Agate Krouse (UW-Whitewater) and Jacqueline Ross (UW-Platteville)—members of the advisory panel to the University of Wisconsin System Librarian-at-Large for Women's Studies—supported this project from the beginning.

Finally, the suggestions and encouragement from women's studies faculty and librarians on every campus of the University of Wisconsin System, and from women involved in women's studies all over the United States, have made this a truly collaborative enterprise and have helped to give this bibliography scope and depth. Though the project has benefitted from the assistance of many people, any errors in judgment and in fact are mine alone.

Esther Stineman
Madison, Wisconsin
December 1978

TABLE OF CONTENTS

INTRODUCTION

Women's studies has been defined variously—the study of traditional disciplines from a feminist perspective; courses that focus on the contributions of women only; a curriculum that seeks to overthrow traditional knowledge paradigms with the intent of exploring the behaviors and contributions of both men and women in new ways. Typical course titles in women's studies reflect this diversity: "Black Women in American Society," "Women and Literature," "Women and Politics," "Sexism and Social Work Practice," "Aging Women." Those who teach women's studies courses agree that their field is interdisciplinary, feminist, and collaborative by definition.

Underlying this bibliography is the intent to provide an annotated and indexed collection, organized around traditional disciplines, of English-language, mainly in-print publications that support research on women. This is a bibliography of women's issues—of displaced homemakers, alcoholism among women, rape, abortion, battered women, and day care—as much as it is a bibliography of the intellectual concerns of radical feminism, lesbian literary movements, feminist criticism, women's language, and feminist historical method. Such a core collection of women-related materials will support a women's studies curriculum comprising courses heavily taken by undergraduate students—courses that reflect a sweep of subject possibilities from "The Life Cycles of Women" to "Women and Sport."

A bibliography that seeks to give broad-based support to women's studies curricula must survey the traditional disciplines for the new women-related literature, but it must look to literature outside of narrowly defined disciplinary boundaries, too. In undertaking this project, I have tried to keep in mind the varying definitions of women's studies that exist, and the vast array of courses being offered under the heading "women's studies" have been borne in mind. The books here are recommended as essential items that should be available to users, if not in their own institutions and libraries, then in the resource centers that serve them for interlibrary loan.

A few specifics should be given as to what this bibliography does and does not do. It assumes that scholarly attention to women's points of view has been, until quite recently, negligible. It stresses the importance of subjects related to a woman's daily life from *her* perspective—childbearing, childrearing, traditional and non-traditional work roles, education, political participation, and cultural achievements. Such subjects have been considered in the past less worthy for study than, for example, male-dominated activities such as war and political history. This bibliography begins, then, on the premise that all women, whatever their personal arrangements and economic status, are important. Therefore, I have responded strongly to works by and about doubly-excluded women—lesbians; minority and Third World women; ordinary, poor, aging, underemployed, and unemployed women—as essential, not peripheral collection priorities.

I have not followed a carefully circumscribed collection policy or a specialized focus in selecting materials for inclusion. This differs from the approach taken in recent, excellent, but more selective bibliographies of note—for example Barbara Haber's *Women in America: A Guide to Books* (1978), based on the existing collection policy at Radcliffe's Arthur and Elizabeth Schlesinger Library, or the Women and Literature Collective's *Women & Literature: An Annotated Bibliography of Women Writers* (3rd ed., 1976). Nor are there annotations of individual periodical articles or special issues, as Elizabeth Oakes and Kathleen Sheldon included in their splendid *Guide to Social Science Resources in Women's Studies* (ABC-Clio, 1978).

Identification of non-traditional materials implies non-traditional bibliographic methods and evaluation sources. The books and authors that appear in this bibliography have come to my attention through a variety of sources: syllabi, bibliographies, informal recommendations, reviews, women's bookstores, citations, professional meetings. All of these sources have been related to or directly involved in women's studies or the women's movement. After a book was read and compared with other possibilities on the subject, the item was either accepted or rejected for inclusion. Many books receive mention within the context of an annotation on another book when the work either was significant but could not be examined readily; did not offer a discernibly different approach from another selected entry; was not in print; was very new; or was poorly written, argued, or documented. Linking of sources to one another, both in the annotations and through the subject index, will emerge, I hope, as a major strength of this bibliography.

The annotations have been written to give individuals who use them full bibliographic information and a firm idea of what they can expect from books in terms of content. Much thought has gone into assisting librarians, especially reference librarians, in the work of recommending titles to those they serve and of building collections hospitable to women as authors and subjects. As a result, each entry reflects attention both to the questions that faculty and students may likely ask first (what does the book cover?) and to the questions that librarians often ask first (is the book indexed well? does it have a good bibliography? how much does it cost?). The annotations are both evaluative and descriptive, frankly stating whether a work is feminist or not, relating books to other similar or contrasting works, sketching the author's point of view. If objective description can be defined as avoiding controversial issues, the approach here has been decidedly lacking in objectivity. Controversy is at the root of many of the titles listed here; sidestepping will not do for a list such as this one.

Teachers and librarians often shape what others will come to know simply by directing them to familiar sources. I have taken into account here the gaps in existing media and tried to touch upon sources that surface in lesser-known, women-oriented media that note works by women either underrated or only recently recognized. At the same time, books written by well-known established writers, both male and female, that appear on standard lists have been included. All decisions for inclusion reflect an effort to make this bibliography as richly textured and comprehensive a source in the area of women's studies collection building as possible without violating the notion of a *core* listing, and recognizing the ever-expanding range of titles from which to choose. Thus, Mailer appears here as well as Millett, D. H. Lawrence as well as Rita Mae Brown, Emma Goldman as well as Anita Bryant.

Older materials appear frequently in the bibliography, though publishing trends favorable to women account for the principal emphasis on 1970s imprints. Major topics in women's studies—the rediscovery of previously forgotten women, for example—accounts for the heavy concentration of biographies, autobiographies, letters, diaries, journals, and memoirs. Such items provide the raw materials from which we can interpret women's lives and often represent the fruits of women-related scholarship.

With the awakened interest in identifying out-of-print and lost materials by and about women have come a number of new resources in both book and microform format. On occasion, these will present collection developers with difficult and very costly decisions. Large microform collections related to women, such as the *Gerritsen Collection* (Microfilm Corporation of America) and the *History of Women Collection* (Research Publications, Inc.), appear in this bibliography in some form, not because every library should purchase (in the case of the $25,000-plus microform collection), but because access to these important sources on women is possible only through their indexes. Expensive reprint series on women—for example, projects by Garland, Arno, and Greenwood presses—can be costly, and in many cases, the introductory material announced by the reprint publishers is insubstantial. Libraries and individuals must weigh the cost of obtaining available reprints in attractive format against the problematic aspects of picking up older editions. The important and costly forthcoming Bowker project, *Women's History Sources: A Guide to Archives and Manuscript Collections in the United States*, edited by Andrea Hinding, has been purposely included in this bibliography despite its high prices ($100+) because of its vast scope and its importance in bringing to light buried and forgotten materials, the primary sources of women's history, which are the root and ground of women's studies.

Although much material generated by well-established presses has been included, the women's movement has provided the impetus for exciting alternative ventures that speak to women's diverse information needs in ways that are innovative, cooperative, and supportive of women's lives and work. Two such separate enterprises are the non-profit Feminist Press and the Women's Educational Equity Communications Network (WEECN). The Feminist Press is run by feminists working on books that illuminate the experiences of women and on projects designed to change stereotyped education patterns in the classroom. WEECN, established and supported by the U.S. Office of Education, develops services and communications systems to facilitate information exchange and resource sharing on the myriad issues that surround women's educational equity. Many materials by the Feminist Press and WEECN appear here.

As noted, small press items surface in this bibliography, while ongoing assistance in collecting materials from women's presses is available from the catalogs of Women in Distribution (P.O. Box 8858, Washington, DC 20003). A useful directory called *Guide to Women's Publishing*, by Polly Joan and Andrea Chesman (1978), summarizes the state of the art in feminist publishing. Those involved in ongoing collection development for women's studies also will want to regularly check feminist press and project sources as well as more traditional information and media announcement channels.

Government documents are not emphasized here, but they do appear selectively in the form of major reference sources for statistical information on women and specially commissioned reports on women's status. A gold mine of information is to be found in transcripts of hearings, though they will only be found here when they have been commercially reprinted, as in the case of *Discrimination against Women: Congressional Hearings on Equal Rights in*

Education and Employment (1973), edited by Catharine R. Stimpson. The Congressional Information Service (CIS) indexes provide fine access for those who are discouraged by the difficulties imposed by the *Monthly Catalog.*

Ideally, this bibliography would encompass in one convenient package the full range of feminist scholarship. This, of course, is impossible. However, librarians, students and teachers will find here a road map to the literature that exists, marked with specific comments on what they are likely to find upon reaching their destination. The annotations themselves serve as a running commentary on trends in publishing by and about women in the fields of sociology, anthropology, the fine arts, and philosophy, for example.

Finally, this bibliography speaks to the issue of total collection improvement. The study of women and scholarship by women cannot be accomplished in a vacuum nor contained in a small corner of an existing curriculum. Just so, the acquisition of materials by and about women cannot remain a closeted, contained collection issue. It is a mistake to think of women's studies collection building as the concern of a ghettoized few or as a scavenger hunt for fringe items. All libraries need to think in terms of reshaping their existing collection policies to reflect the reality that the selection and purchase of women-related materials will improve the total collection.

NOTES ON USING THIS BIBLIOGRAPHY

ANNOTATIONS

The writing of annotations followed the process of identification, verification, and examination of each book. The intent of the annotations is to convey the specific content of the work, its applicability to women's studies, and its relationship to other books on similar topics. The limitations in this approach are obvious. The reading of each book reflects the viewpoint of the common reader rather than the specialist. Since many of the items are political in content, the interpretation of the annotations may be questioned or disputed by some. However, after examining numbers of existing bibliographies, it seemed that the decision to take a position in the annotations was preferable to the familiar, vague, and often unhelpful annotational out—"good source" or "recommended."

BIBLIOGRAPHIC INFORMATION

The authority for all bibliographic information is Library of Congress cataloging. All entries have been verified using the OCLC data base to obtain Library of Congress copy. Because we have consistently followed LC, biographical dates for authors appear only when LC has provided this information. Though the result is an inconsistent appearance, we believe that users will prefer to have date information when it is readily available than none at all. For uniformity, each entry uses LC cataloging data for the main entry, however sexist this may be in handling the personal names of women. "Ossoli," for example, is the entry used for Margaret Fuller, because this is how the Library of Congress designates her name (Fuller's work appears under Ossoli in almost every library). By using the author index, the user who looks under Fuller will be led to Ossoli. Full titles including subtitles are used for all entries.

IN-PRINT, OUT-OF-PRINT, AND REPRINTS

Each entry has been verified for in-print status using *Books in Print* (1977). An asterisk (*) following an entry means that the book did not appear in *Books in Print* (1977). In some cases, this means that the book was not in print; in others, the asterisk indicates that a book has been published by a publisher not indexed in BIP (e.g., small press materials and government documents).

Out-of-print books have been included for a number of reasons. Classic studies may be reprinted in the future; students, teachers and librarians need to know that they exist, however. Books by black women on recommended bibliographies (e.g., those identified by Gerda Lerner's *Black Women in White America*, 1972) have often been allowed to go out of print because of racist/sexist priorities. In many cases, specific works by black women were not available in any of the libraries in the University of Wisconsin System or among the libraries in the Wisconsin Interlibrary Loan network.

For reprints, information has been provided about the original edition to the extent that this information was readily available. Sometimes an entry includes place of publication, publisher, and date (e.g., New York: Macmillan, 1946; repr. New York: Praeger, 1977); at other times, only the date (e.g., New York: Praeger, 1977 [repr. of 1946 ed.]).

PRICING AND ISBN AND LC NUMBERS

Prices reflect hard cover pricing because most libraries purchase in hard cover format. The book may be available in paper cover. If it was unavailable *except* in paper, the price indicates the paper pricing. ISBN numbers and LC numbers are given to facilitate interlibrary loan and purchasing. This information is based on available LC and BIP data.

EDITIONS

In the case of well-known works of literature, editions were chosen on the basis of what was available for verification and examination in some cases but on the basis of a particular editor or publishing house in other instances. In all cases, the choice reflects the priority of obtaining an in-print edition. Annuals are listed by their latest in-print edition (e.g., Marquis Publications, *Who's Who of American Women*, 1977).

SUBJECT INDEXING

Subject indexing provides access by employing the headings used in current bibliographical sources for women-related materials. We have surveyed existing terminology in numerous bibliographies and indexes and looked to feminist indexing and abstracting sources (e.g., Joan K. Marshall's *On Equal Terms: A Thesaurus for Nonsexist Indexing and Cataloging*) to arrive at a subject index that complements the chapter arrangement and gives good access to the materials contained in anthologies and essay collections, as well as to books treating a single topic.

ANTHROPOLOGY

This section illustrates the interdisciplinary aspects of women's studies materials, since many of the books might also fit comfortably in the other chapters dealing with social science materials. The authors and researchers whose work is represented here, however, have taken a specifically anthropological approach. Selected for this chapter are the classic and contemporary studies of pre-industrial societies (see entries for Kaberry, Landes, and Mead); contemporary ethnographies of women's lives and work (see Newton and Spradley); classic and contemporary theoretical works that often address the origins of sexual inequality (see Engels, Briffault, and Reed); comparative cross-cultural studies (see Schlegel) and the newer anthologies of feminist research (see Reiter, and Rosaldo and Lamphere). Contemporary and historical studies of developed countries are more likely to be in the Sociology, Business or History chapters. Bibliographies rich in anthropological material will be found in the Reference chapter. For an excellent listing of special periodical issues useful in gaining women's studies anthropological perspective, see Oakes and Sheldon's *Guide to Social Science Resources in Women's Studies* (1978) and the special issues bibliographies issued by the *Canadian Newsletter of Research on Women*. The Human Relations Area Files (HRAF) provide a continuing, rich array of anthropology materials.

1 Andreski, Iris. **Old Wives' Tales: Life-Stories from Ibibioland.** New York: Schocken Books, 1970. 190p. index. $8.00. ISBN 0805233423. LC 77-107613.

Andreski presents a series of brief life histories collected in Eastern Nigeria and rendered "in a form of English which is as near as possible to the vernacular in which they were told, while being intelligible to the ordinary English reader." She chose the oldest available women in order "to obtain a first-hand record of a pattern of human life which the impact of a foreign civilization had nearly erased and which has been much less publicized than its masculine counterpart." The life histories are preceded by a long introduction in which Andreski gives the reader some rudimentary understanding of the social and cultural context of these women's lives. Some of the histories are followed by brief explanatory commentaries.

2 Ardener, Shirley, ed. **Perceiving Women.** New York: Wiley, 1975. 167p. bibliog. index. $17.50. ISBN 0470033096. LC 75-12662.

The papers in this collection share two major concerns: "how groups of women perceive themselves and the world around them, and how we as observers (whether male or female) are to perceive them" (from the editor's introduction). Included in the volume are reprints of Edwin Ardener's "Belief and the Problem of Women" (1968) and of Shirley Ardener's "Sexual Insult and Female Militancy" (1973), plus articles on Gypsy women, diplomats' wives, nuns in a Carmelite Order, and a women's uprising in Nigeria in the 1920s.

3   Bachofen, Johann Jakob, 1815-1887. **Myth, Religion, and Mother Right**: **Selected Writings of J. J. Bachofen.** Princeton, NJ: Princeton University Press, 1967. 309p. bibliog. $14.00. ISBN 0691097992. LC 67-22343.

Bachofen is perhaps best remembered for his theory of "mother right," positing that human history's first period was matriarchal, in which the mother was the dominant societal, familial, and religious figure (a theory largely discredited today). Joseph Campbell provides an excellent introduction to Bachofen and his work as anthropologist and mythographer, explaining the procedures that Bachofen used to arrive at an interpretation of culture: "religious beliefs, laws and customs, family structures, political practices, philosophies, sciences, crafts and economics, are all viewed as related manifestations of implicit informing ideas, and it is to the recognition and naming of these that his attention is addressed." Bachofen is essential reading in conjunction with Engels's *Origin of the Family, Private Property and the State.*

4   Beck, Lois, 1944- , and Nikki R. Keddie, eds. **Women in the Muslim World.** Cambridge, MA: Harvard University Press, 1978. 698p. bibliog. index. $30.00. ISBN 0674954807. LC 78-3633.

Beck and Keddie have gathered together a splendid sample of essays tracing the history, institutions and traditions that have created the male-dominated societies of the Middle East—noting from the outset the profound variations that exist between and within these societies in class structure, marriage customs, and family organization. Authorities on Muslim culture offer 33 perspectives on the lives of women, arranged around the following broad topics: legal and socioeconomic change; historical roles; nomadic, village, and urban case studies; and religious roles. The essays move from the general overview (Elizabeth White's "Legal Reform as an Indicator of Women's Status in Muslim Nations") to the finely focused (Erika Friedl's "Women in Contemporary Persian Folktales"). In their helpful introduction, the editors argue that it is only by understanding the powerful religious and social significance placed on woman's sexual functions— her virginity before marriage, her wifely role as breeder of sons, and her constricted sexual role as passive recipient of male attention—that some notion of the intricacy of family interrelationships in Muslim culture can be achieved.

5   Beidelman, Thomas O. **The Kaguru: A Matrilineal People of East Africa.** New York: Holt, Rinehart and Winston, 1971. 134p. bibliog. $3.95. ISBN 0030767652. LC 71-144053.

This book will be of interest generally as an account of a matrilineal society—that is, one that traces primary relations through women—which is in the process of moving toward patriliny as part of a larger social, economic and political transformation. The study may be of more particular interest within women's studies due to the author's attention to the sexual division of labor, Kaguru concepts of sex differences, marriage arrangements, and so on.

6   Benedict, Ruth Fulton, 1887-1948. **An Anthropologist at Work: Writings of Ruth Benedict.** New York: Houghton Mifflin, 1959; repr. Westport, CT: Greenwood Press, 1977. 583p. bibliog. index. $29.50. ISBN 0837195764. LC 77-3017.

Margaret Mead has drawn a portrait of Ruth Benedict, the woman and the anthropologist, by bringing together in this volume a collection of Benedict's published and unpublished papers, poetry, diaries and correspondence, which Mead has ordered and set within their biographical context in a series of her own essays. Mead was one of three anthropologists considered primary by Benedict in her work—the other two were Franz Boas, their teacher, and Edward Sapir, a contemporary—and their 25-year friendship and professional relationship provide a rich basis for Mead's recreation of Benedict's life, work, and the intellectual milieu within the merging field of anthropology. Part 1 brings together materials from Benedict's early years, 1920-1930 (she only embarked upon her graduate career at the age of 33); part 2 deals with her humanist and poetic side, which she kept strictly apart from her anthropological identity during most of her life, publishing only under the pseudonym Anne Singleton. Part 3 concerns the period during which she wrote her classic work, *Patterns of Culture*; part 4, her years as Boas's "left hand." Part 5 covers the period between World War II and her death in 1948; and part 6 presents selected poems from 1941 and a previously unpublished short study of Mary Wollstonecraft—one of three such studies that Benedict embarked upon (the others dealt with Olive Schreiner and Margaret Fuller) and the only one she completed.

7   Biggs, Bruce, 1921- . **Maori Marriage: An Essay in Reconstruction.** Wellington, New Zealand: A. H. and A. W. Reed Books; distr. Rutland, VT: Charles E. Tuttle, 1970. (Repr. of 1960 ed.). 108p. bibliog. index. $5.25. ISBN 0589004735.

The Maori of New Zealand are one of the most extensively documented of the world's "primitive" peoples. Problems of interpretation crop up, however, due to the limitations of the early observers, on the one hand, and to the extensive changes that came in their wake, on the other, transforming traditional Maori society. This study is an attempt "to present a coherent, systematic account of marriage in indigenous Maori culture." Topics include: Maori Attitude to Sex; Personal and Social Factors Determining Marriage; Some Social and Economic Aspects of Marriage; and Marriage as a Procreative Institution.

8   Borun, Minda, et al. **Women's Liberation: An Anthropological View.** Pittsburgh, PA: Know, 1971. 42p. bibliog. $1.75. ISBN 0912786191.

This pamphlet was written by five feminist anthropologists in response to what they saw as the distortion of anthropological evidence by proponents and opponents of women's liberation eager to give their opinions "scientific" legitimacy (their examples are Lionel Tiger's *Men in Groups* and Evelyn Reed's article, "The Myth of Women's Inferiority"). There is much to recommend this brief work as an introduction to key issues in the anthropology of women, written in a very non-technical and accessible style. However, readers with a further interest in the subject should note that the pamphlet is now quite dated; the bibliography at the end predates almost entirely the new work by feminist anthropologists. Rayna Reiter's *Toward an Anthropology of Women* (1975) and Rosaldo and Lamphere's *Woman, Culture and Society* (1974) are more up-to-date collections.

9   Briffault, Robert, 1876-1948. **The Mothers: A Study of the Origins of Sentiments and Institutions.** New York: Macmillan, 1927; repr. New York: Johnson Reprint, 1969. 3v. $105.00. ISBN 0384058000. LC 70-47212.

Briffault's *The Mothers* is one of the classic works in the old and continuing debate over the matriarchal or patriarchal character of earliest human societies (other key figures in this debate are Lewis Morgan, Friedrich Engels, Johann Bachofen, and, more recently, Helen Diner and Elizabeth Gould Davis). Briffault writes in his preface that his research led him to conclude that "the social characters of the human mind are, one and all, traceable to the operation of instincts that are related to the functions of the female and not to those of the male. That the mind of women should have exercised so fundamental an influence upon human development in the conditions of historical patriarchal societies, is inconceivable. I was thus led to reconsider the early development of human society, or its fundamental institutions and traditions, in the light of the matriarchal theory of social evolution." Among the many topics he discusses are: the evolution of motherhood, the origin of love, the matriarchal phase in civilized societies, primitive division of labor between the sexes, the institution of marriage, group marriage and sexual communism, promiscuity and individual marriage, primitive jealousy and love, the social evolution of monogamic marriage, tabu, the witch and the priestess, the great mothers, modesty, purity, and romance. There is an abridged edition of *The Mothers* in print (Gordon Taylor, ed.; Atheneum, 1977; $5.95), but we were unable to consult it to judge its quality.

10   Briffault, Robert, 1876-1948, and Bronislaw Malinowski, 1884-1942. **Marriage, Past and Present.** Boston: Sargent, 1971. 90p. $3.95. ISBN 0875580270.

The six chapters of this slim volume reflect talks delivered by anthropologists Robert Briffault and Bronislaw Malinowski in the form of a debate in a 1931 British Broadcasting Corporation series on the topics of marriage and the family. Briefly, Robert Briffault's three-volume work, *The Mothers* (1927), posited that the functions of motherhood had largely shaped many human institutions. He defended in *The Mothers* and also in his dialogue with Malinowski the matriarchal theory of social evolution. Briffault rejected Bachofen's thesis that women had ruled as the dominant sex in certain early societies, but he embraced the theory that women played more significant roles in earlier societies than in civilized societies. Briffault argued that social anthropologists had overlooked the considerable influence women wielded in influencing the social organization of human societies. Malinowski disagreed with many of Briffault's theories of the family, especially with Briffault's assessment that human institutions have been economically determined. Malinowski's basic position was that the family has been and will continue to be the essential institution of society, and he found no reason to believe that marriage will evolve more and more into a private contract situation. Neither anthropologist could be considered a champion of feminism, but both have formulated significant and controversial positions on the institution of marriage and the position of woman in marriage. Reading these positions in debate form is useful even 45 years after the debate. Ashley Montagu writes a helpful introductory essay sketching the history of the debate and championing Malinowski's scientific position.

11   Chagnon, Napoleon A., 1938- . **Yanomamo: The Fierce People.** (2nd
       ed.). New York: Holt, Rinehart and Winston, 1977. 174p. bibliog. index.
       $3.95. ISBN 0030710707. LC 76-46431.
This is a case-study of the culture and social organization of the Yanomamo
Indians of southern Venezuela and northern Brazil, a people with cultural norms
dictating violent behavior and interaction and chronic warfare. While there is
no real focus on women by the author, the volume includes material relevant to
a feminist approach: for example, on the sexual division of labor; the function of
women as property and political currency and the exchange of women in alliances;
the treatment of women by their husbands and the protection they receive from
their brothers; and childcare and the socialization of children. Chagnon has written
an additional chapter for the second edition on cultural penetration of Yanomamo
society by outside influences.

12   Chiñas, Beverly. **The Isthmus Zapotecs: Women's Roles in Cultural
       Context.** New York: Holt, Rinehart and Winston, 1973. 122p. bibliog.
       $3.95. ISBN 0030803012. LC 73-3945.
Designed as case studies to be used in beginning and intermediate anthropology
courses, the material here is easily accessible to the non-professional. The author
corrects the mistaken assumption that the Isthmus Zapotecs of Tehuntepec have
a matriarchal society. Chiñas examines the infrastructure of the society to demonstrate how men dominate the public sphere of society in roles as public and religious leaders as well as family heads, while women deliberately call themselves
homemakers because homemaking roles carry with them a measure of status and
economic prestige. It is the market vending role that has distinguished the
Zapotec women as being economically independent, but Chiñas points out that
Zapotec women disparage that role, considering the work hot and tiring and the
exposure in the marketplace as publicly humiliating because it indicates a lower
economic status. Chiñas's chapter, "Women and Men: Women's Roles," is particularly interesting as she compares the submerged roles of women, so important
to Zapotec culture, to the hidden mass of an iceberg. Much of the Zapotec
woman's interaction in the marketplace grows out of an unstated social code in
which men are unable to relate to each other socially and are dependent on women
to establish an acceptable social flow in the marketplace context. Chiñas makes
the important point that there can be no cross-cultural definition of equality
for women that wouldn't be simplistic.

13   Cornelisen, Ann, 1926- . **Women of the Shadows.** Boston: Little, Brown,
       1976. 228p. $8.95. ISBN 0316157457. LC 75-28345.
Cornelisen perceptively writes of the peasant women of southern Italy, where
the Marian cult shapes the roles of women in a life that is brutally hard, but over
which women exert a good amount of familial power and control. Overpopulation,
illiteracy, religious superstition, primitive housing, medical and sanitary conditions,
and physical violence are the commonplace realities of a lifestyle that appears to
be permanently time warped in the nineteenth century. Pointing to the paradox
that men and women appear to live separate lives despite the biological reality
of large families, Cornelisen examines the lives of five women, all of whom seem
isolated. Though lip service is paid to the male's superiority in the family, the
author believes that southern Italy is essentially matriarchal and is not likely

to change. Several fine photographs of the life cycle of southern Italian women accompany the text.

14   Davis, Elizabeth Gould, 1910- . **The First Sex.** Baltimore, MD: Penguin
     Books, 1972. 382p. bibliog. index. $2.95. ISBN 0140035044.
"We must repudiate two thousand years of propaganda concerning the inferiority of women," writes Elizabeth Gould Davis in her introduction to *The First Sex.* This book follows in a tradition of writers who have argued that a matriarchal or female-dominated order preceded the patriarchal societies known to us (others in this tradition include Lewis Morgan, Friedrich Engels and J. J. Bachofen); Davis's approach is distinguished by its contemporaneousness (1971) and by the strength of feminist sentiment which combines with extensive research to inform her work. She writes, "the implacability with which Western man has . . . retaliated against woman serves only to confirm the truth of her former dominance—a dominance that man felt compelled to stamp out and forget. . . . Recorded history starts with a patriarchal revolution. Let it continue with the matriarchal counterrevolution that is the only hope for the survival of the human race." Major topics in the study are as follows: The Gynocratic World; The Patriarchal Revolution; Pre-Christian Women in the Celto-Ionian World; and The Tragedy of Western Woman.

15   Elam, Yitzchak. **The Social and Sexual Roles of Hima Women: A Study
     of Nomadic Cattle Breeders in Nyabushozi County, Ankole, Uganda.**
     Manchester, England: Manchester University Press; distr. New York:
     Humanities Press, 1973. 243p. bibliog. index. $12.75. ISBN 0719005345.
     LC 75-327378.
Noting that the social system of the nomadic Hima of Ankole had been studied and analyzed by a number of writers prior to his own research, Elam states at the outset that his work has a limited focus. He wanted to understand why it is that Hima women, unlike women in most other pastoral societies, are denied access to the livestock herds that constitute the main property of the Hima. He concluded that women's reproductive functions are considered threatening to those of the cattle, and consequently every effort is made to ensure "the separation from cattle of wives whose mission is to bear children: the separation is regarded as a means of averting the danger." Elam goes on to argue, "given a tribal society in which familistic institutions predominate and in which cattle serve as almost the only source of subsistence, the separation of wives from the family herd is a rule that must affect the entire social structure." Elam discusses this key organizing principle of Hima society in its socio-economic aspects, in its connection with the successive stages of the life-cycle of women, and in its relation to some of the symbolic aspects of relationships between men and women.

16* Elmendorf, Mary Lindsay. **Nine Mayan Women: A Village Faces Change.**
     Cambridge, MA: Schenkman, 1976. 159p. bibliog. ISBN 0470238623.
     LC 74-12464.
Mary Elmendorf's interest in Mexico and Mayan women dates back to the 1950s. This study is based on field work conducted in the village of Chan Kom during the early 1970s. Chan Kom had already previously been the focus of well-known

studies by Robert Redfield (*Chan Kom: A Maya Village*, 1934; *A Village That Chose Progress: Chan Kom Revisited*, 1950). Elmendorf's approach was to undertake an intensive examination of the lives of nine peasant women, aged 17 to 65, all members of one of the leading families of the village. She follows her series of vignettes of the women with a discussion of the following topics: self-image; marriage and children; economy, property, and income; and work, religion, and nature. One of Elmendorf's chief concerns is to assess the nature of the changes occurring in the village as a result of cultural and economic penetration from the outside—particularly the impact of these changes on women in the context of the transformation of the traditional pre-Columbian corn culture. Sensitive photographs accompany this revision of the author's thesis, Union Graduate School, 1972, published under the title, *The Mayan Woman and Change.*

17   Engels, Friedrich, 1820-1895. **The Origin of the Family, Private Property, and the State, in the Light of the Researches of Lewis H. Morgan.** New York: International Publishers, 1972. 285p. bibliog. $7.50. ISBN 0717803384. LC 79-184309.

Very few books spark as much heated debate, for so long a period of time, as this one has. While much of the debate has occurred within the field of anthropology and has concerned the relative accuracy of Engel's theory, the work's lingering influence must be attributed more to the questions it poses than to the answers it provides—namely, how were the development of kinship and family systems, male supremacy, class, and ultimately the state, historically connected? Eleanor Leacock's introduction to the International Publishers edition provides an overview and critical analysis of the historical debate over Engels. This is a translation of *Der Ursprung der Familie.*

18   Evans-Pritchard, Edward Evan, 1902-1973, ed. **Man and Woman among the Azande.** New York: Free Press, 1974. 197p. bibliog. index. $9.95. ISBN 002909920X. LC 73-22630.

"It has seemed to me that anthropologists (include me if you wish) have, in their writings about African societies, dehumanized the Africans into systems and structures and lost the flesh and blood. It may be somewhat of an experiment, but in these texts I am asking Azande to say in their own way what they want to say" (from the preface). These direct transcriptions of interviews with the Azande on subjects pertaining to relations between men and women make for fascinating reading and recommend this book over more analytic and abstract accounts by anthropologists. The key limitation is one common to ethnographic materials—all of the informants in the collection are men. As long as this fact is kept in mind, the material provides vivid glimpses into Azande men's ideas, customs and folklore concerning, for example, intercourse, pregnancy and childbirth, fatherhood and motherhood, marriage, men's work and women's work, kinship relations, love affairs and adultery, the "stupidity of women," lesbianism, bridewealth, and divorce. Materials were collected at two different times (part 1, 1927-1930; part 2, 1961-1964), thus permitting some historical comparison. A brief subject index helps direct the reader to passages on particular topics.

19   Fernea, Elizabeth Warnock. **Guests of the Sheik: An Ethnography of an Iraqi Village.** Garden City, NY: Doubleday, 1969. 346p. $2.95. ISBN 0385014856. LC 65-13098.

Fernea's book is a personal narrative of her first two years of marriage in a village in southern Iraq to which she had come with her anthropologist husband. Hers is a chronicle of reactions to life in an alien culture among the veiled women. Although she is not trained as an anthropologist, she provides a vivid and open view of life in the village and carefully drawn, non-judgmental observations of its inhabitants. Her chapters on purdah, harems, weddings, and interactions among the women are especially interesting; Fernea is clearly present as a participant in all that she describes.

20   Ford, Clellan Stearns, 1909- , and Frank Ambrose Beach, 1911- . **Patterns of Sexual Behavior.** New York: Harper and Row, 1970. 318p. bibliog. index. $3.25. ISBN 0061319139.

The value of this treatise on sexual behavior (originally published in 1951) lies in its comparative approach: human sexual behavior is examined for cross-cultural variation and is additionally compared to sexual behavior among animal species. This approach is closely related to and provides a foundation for the authors' commitment to distinguishing biological, psychological, sociological, and moral issues. A key focus of concern is the exploration of hereditary and social dimensions of sexuality and the authors state their belief that sexual behavior *is* primarily social, learned behavior. Chapter topics are as follows: The Nature of Coitus; Types of Sexual Stimulation; Circumstances for Coitus; Attracting a Sex Partner; Sexual Partnerships; Homosexual Behavior; Relations between Different Species; Self-Stimulation; Development in the Individual; Feminine Fertility Cycles; Other Physiological Factors in Sex Behavior; and Human Sexual Behavior in Perspective.

21   Friedl, Ernestine, 1920- . **Women and Men: An Anthropologist's View.** New York: Holt, Rinehart and Winston, 1975. 148p. bibliog. $4.25. ISBN 0030915295. LC 74-32308.

Beginning from the premise that biology is not the determinant of gender roles, Friedl explores and analyzes cross-cultural variations in the status of women. She divides her attention between hunting and gathering societies and horticultural societies, examining variations in the sexual division of labor (including men's and women's roles in production, distribution, and child care) and kinship organization in each. Using an ecological and structural-functional theoretical approach, Friedl concludes that power in society is rooted in control over production and distribution—giving less importance to the question of control over reproduction. This is a useful introduction to the cross-cultural study of women and the sexual division of labor.

22   Giffen, Naomi Musmaker. **The Roles of Men and Women in Eskimo Culture.** Chicago: University of Chicago Press, 1930; repr. New York: AMS Press, 1975. 113p. bibliog. $10.00. ISBN 0404116426. LC 74-5837.

Consideration is given here to Eskimo men's and women's roles in procuring and preparation of food, transportation, building and care of houses, manufacturing, property and inheritance, clothing and ornament, and non-material culture. This study appeared in 1930; hence, the researcher will clearly need to look to other sources for more recent documentation.

23   Golde, Peggy, 1930- , comp. **Women in the Field: Anthropological Experiences.** Chicago: Aldine, 1970. 343p. bibliog. $11.95. ISBN 0202010759. LC 68-8149.
This collection of writings by women anthropologists explains not only the experience of the researcher, her techniques, the impact of her sex on her role, but also cross-cultural attitudes toward women. Contributors are Peggy Golde, Jean Briggs, Laura Thompson, Laura Nader, Ruth Landes, Helen Codere, Gloria Marshall, Ernestine Friedl, Cora Du Bois, Hazel Hitson Weidman, Ann Fischer, and Margaret Mead. Their diverse experiences reflect work in Greece, Brazil, Rwanda, and many other cultures.

24   Goodale, Jane Carter, 1926- . **Tiwi Wives: A Study of the Women of Melville Island, North Australia.** Seattle: University of Washington Press, 1974. 368p. bibliog. index. $10.00. ISBN 0295950897. LC 72-117728.
This is a study of Tiwi aboriginal culture as revealed through an examination of the life cycle of Tiwi women, based primarily on eight months' field work undertaken by Goodale in 1954. Goodale relied for the most part on female informants in the field, a departure from the conventional androcentric approach in anthropology. Topics discussed include a variety of rituals associated with the female life cycle; Tiwi social structure and marriage, pregnancy and mother-hood; the economic role of the Tiwi wife; old age, sickness, and death; and the Tiwi's world view and values.

25   Hafkin, Nancy J., and Edna G. Bay, eds. **Women in Africa: Studies in Social and Economic Change.** Stanford, CA: Stanford University Press, 1976. 306p. bibliog. index. $15.00. ISBN 0804709068. LC 75-44901.
A project of the Women's Committee of the African Studies Association, this is an anthology of articles representing the results of recent field work in Africa south of the Sahara by scholars in the fields of history, economics, political science, anthropology, sociology, and women's studies. "The emphasis of the volume is on women and change in Africa—change in two senses. First, the articles discuss African women from a changed viewpoint; second, this new perspective in turn recognizes that women in Africa act as agents of change within their own societies. . . . All the articles are concerned with women's participation in activities beyond the closed circle of child care or household maintenance" (from the editors' introduction). Included are: "The *Signaries* of Saint-Louis and Gorée: Women Entrepreneurs in Eighteenth-Century Senegal" (George E. Brooks, Jr.); "The Dual-Sex Political System in Operation: Igbo Women and Community Politics in Midwestern Nigeria" (Kamene Okon Jo); " 'Aba Riots' or Igbo 'Women's War'? Ideology, Stratification, and the Invisibility of Women" (Judith Van Allen); "Luo Women and Economic Change During the Colonial Period" (Margaret Jean Hay); "Ga Women and Socioeconomic Change in Accra, Ghana" (Claire Robertson); "The Limitations of Group Action Among Entrepreneurs: The Market Women of Abidjan, Ivory Coast" (Barbara C.

Lewis); "Rebels or Status-Seekers? Women as Spirit Mediums in East Africa" (Iris Berger); "From *Lelemama* to Lobbying: Women's Associations in Mombasa, Kenya" (Margaret Strobel); "Protestant Women's Associations in Freetown, Sierra Leone" (Filomina Chioma Steady); "Women and Economic Change in Africa" (Leith Mullings); and "Less Than Second-Class: Women in Rural Settlement Schemes in Tanzania" (James L. Brain). Methodological approaches represented here are diverse, from functionalist to Marxist.

26   Hart, Charles William Merton, 1905- , and Arnold R. Pilling. **The Tiwi of North Australia.** New York: Holt, Rinehart and Winston, 1960. 118p. bibliog. $3.95. ISBN 0030057000. LC 60-7332.

"This is a case study of a system of influence and power which is based on a strange currency. The currency is woman. . . . Because men compete for prestige and influence through their control over women, women have the value of a scarce commodity. Under this system there are no illegitimate children, no unmarried females of any age, and wives are either very much older or very much younger than their husbands" ("About the Book," George and Louise Spindler, general editors of the series, Case Studies in Cultural Anthropology). Because the authors did their field work during two different periods (Hart, originally an Australian himself, in 1928-1929; Pilling, in 1953-1954), they are able to trace changes that occurred in Tiwi culture during the first half of this century. The material presented here is clearly highly relevant to recent work by feminist anthropologists, which has speculated about connections between the exchange of women by men and the development of patriarchy. Examples of this new work are Juliet Mitchell's *Psychoanalysis and Feminism* (1974; see her conclusions especially) and Gayle Rubin's "The Traffic in Women," in *Toward an Anthropology of Women* (R. Reiter, ed.; 1975).

27   Hays, Hoffman Reynolds. **The Dangerous Sex: The Myth of Feminine Evil.** New York: Pocket Books, 1972. 307p. bibliog. index. $1.25. ISBN 0671781928.

Anthropology, literature, biology, psychology and history come together in this study, which shows "that male attitudes toward women and the images of women created by men are strongly influenced by deep anxieties, which are probably universal and basic as the young male grows up in the family relationship, and also shaped by the pressures in the various cultures which man has created." Among the chapters: Of Anxiety and Ambivalence; The Double Mask of Mana; Pandora's Box; Knights without Ladies; The Female Demon; The Serpent of the Nile; and The Femme Fatale. Hays draws from a diverse number of erudite sources (e.g., Sprenger and Kramer, *Malleus Maleficarum*), and the bibliography is particularly notable for this reason. Because this book was originally published in 1964, its concerns cluster around issues brought to light by Simone deBeauvoir's *The Second Sex* and Friedan's *The Feminine Mystique*; its tone is one of grappling with the sexual crisis of the early 1960s.

28   Heuer, Berys. **Maori Women.** Wellington, New Zealand: A. H. and A. W. Reed Books; distr. Rutland, VT: Charles E. Tuttle, 1972. 66p. bibliog. index. $5.25. ISBN 058900641X. LC 72-197463.

"This book endeavors to reconstruct the role of women in traditional family
and tribal life by collating and analyzing the many references scattered throughout
the ethnographic literature. . . . The period to which the book refers extends
from 1769, when Captain James Cook rediscovered New Zealand, to approximately
1840, when New Zealand formally became a British colony" (author's note).
Major subjects covered: Cultural Attitudes towards Women; The Marriage
Contract; Women's Role in Procreation and Socialization; Women's Position
with Regard to Property; Special Roles of Women; Ritual Functions of Women;
Warfare.

29   International Congress of Anthropological and Ethnological Sciences,
      9th, Chicago, 1973. **Women Cross-Culturally: Change and Challenge.**
      Edited by Ruby Rohrlich-Leavitt. The Hague: Mouton; distr. Chicago:
      Aldine, 1976. 669p. bibliog. index. $27.50. ISBN 020201147X.
This is a collection of tremendously diverse papers written for the session on
women's status and women's movements at the IXth International Congress
of Anthropological and Ethnological Sciences. The papers are arranged in
geographical/political categories: Women in Islam and Africa; Women in Latin
America; Women in the United States; and Women in Planned Societies. In
addition, there's a section on women in anthropology. Divergent perspectives
on the problem of sexual inequality are presented. Another collection to come
out of this congress is entitled *Being Female: Reproduction, Power, and Change,*
edited by Dana Raphael (Mouton; distr. Aldine, 1975).

30   Kaberry, Phyllis Mary, 1910- . **Aboriginal Woman, Sacred and Profane.**
      London: G. Routledge, 1939; repr. New York: Gordon Press, 1973.
      294p. bibliog. index. $39.95. ISBN 0879680563.
In the forword to this classic study (originally 1939) of women of aboriginal
tribes of Australia, Kaberry writes, "the women are the focus of attention throughout this book, but I have not achieved this at the expense of limiting myself
to an account of specifically feminine pursuits. If my theme is women, it is
one that has involved a contrast and comparison of their activities with those
of the men, with due recognition of the co-operation that exists between the
sexes, the beliefs they share in common, and the laws to which they both
conform. The women have been seen in relation to their environment and to
tribal form. The women have been seen in relation to their environment and to
tribal culture in all its aspects." Chapters are included on: The Social and
Spiritual Background of the Aboriginal Child; Childhood; On the Duties of
Women in Marriage; The Laws of Marriage and the Needs of the Individual;
Rights and Duties of Women in Marriage; The Functions of Women in the
Larger Social Groups; The Spiritual Heritage of Aboriginal Woman; Women's
Ceremonies; and Women's Secret Corroborees.

31   Kaberry, Phyllis Mary, 1910- . **Women of the Grassfields: A Study of
      the Economic Position of Women in Bamenda, British Cameroons.**
      New York: Humanities Press, 1968. 220p. bibliog. index. $11.50.
The origin of this study (carried out during 1945-46 and 1947-48)—like that
of so much of the early classic anthropology—is rooted in British colonialism.
Daryll Forde of the International African Institute notes in his preface: "The

need for such research had been reported by the Cameroons Development Corporation, and shortly after a despatch was addressed by the Governor of Nigeria to the Secretary of State for the Colonies, in which he drew attention to the conditions in the Bamenda division of the Cameroons under British mandate, where, despite considerable natural resources, there was underpopulation, and social obstacles to opportunities for economic development and educational advance were apparent." Kaberry set out to study the economic position of women in the context of a broader examination of "the role of agriculture in the economy, the system of land tenure, pastoral and trade development, the introduction of new occupations, and so forth." She discovered that "women, as wives, mothers and daughters, produce most of the food and spend the greater part of the day on the farm. In this sphere of activity they enjoy considerable independence and have well defined rights; and it is in this sphere that there has been less change than in others. . . . Changes introduced in this field will affect not only the status and position of women in marriage and the family, but will radically modify the economy and the general standard of living." Ester Boserup's *Woman's Role in Economic Development* (1974), a study of the impact of development schemes on the position of women in Third World societies, would be helpful background reading for Kaberry.

32   Kingston, Maxine Hong. **The Woman Warrior: Memoirs of a Girlhood among Ghosts.** New York: Knopf; distr. New York: Random House, 1976. 209p. $7.95. ISBN 0394400674. LC 76-13674.
Kingston writes a lyrical autobiography of what it means to be a Chinese-American female. She traces her life from girlhood to womanhood in San Francisco, a life among ghosts and old legends, ritualized beliefs and old family ways. Literature, sociology, anthropology, autobiography—Kingston's book is all of these. Mainly it is a beautifully wrought chronicle of a childhood out of synch with mainstream American culture. It is a childhood hardly recalled with nostalgia—more the quality of an intricate nightmare.

33   Landes, Ruth, 1908- . **The Ojibwa Woman.** New York: Columbia University Press, 1938; repr. New York: A.M.S. Press, 1969. 247p. $17.00. ISBN 0404505813. LC 70-82362.
This ethnological field study of women in Ojibwa culture (Western Ontario) was originally published in 1938. Traditional Ojibwa culture was nomadic, with trapping constituting the primary economic activity. Scarcity of game meant that individual, autonomous households were isolated from and even hostile to one another. While economic insecurity was translated into the strictest behaviorial norms for men, women's lives were by comparison relatively unrestricted by norms and prescriptions. As a result, great variations were observable in women's behavior. Landes devotes most of her text to a discussion of the life cycle of Ojibwa women (youth, marriage, occupations, "abnormalities"). In a final chapter, she presents the life histories of three Ojibwa women.

34   Leith-Ross, Sylvia. **African Women: A Study of the Ibo of Nigeria.** London: Routledge and Kegan Paul, 1965; repr. New York: AMS Press, 1978. 367p. index. ISBN 0404121039. LC 74-15062.

Leith-Ross's study of Ibo women, originally written in the 1930s, is primarily
recommended for its status as a "classic." Like so much of the classic work
in anthropology, however, it is profoundly shaped by its British colonial origins.
The reader must wade through Leith-Ross's condescending comments on the
Ibo and must try to discern the nature of her preconceptions in order to properly
assess the accuracy of her observations. Leith-Ross contrasts four different groups
of Ibo: a "primitive" farming community with little exposure to outside influence
in Nneato; a farming-trading community in Nguru; an urban-farming community
in Owerri Town; and the urban community of Port Harcourt. In each case,
she describes women's activities, marriage, birth and religious customs, and the
effects of Western influence.

35   Little, Kenneth Lindsay. **African Women in Towns: An Aspect of
       Africa's Social Revolution.** New York: Cambridge University Press,
       1973. 242p. bibliog. index. $19.95. ISBN 052120237X. LC 73-77175.
Noting the difficulties and risks of "an investigation which seemingly takes
for its canvas virtually the whole of sub-Saharan Africa," Kenneth Little offers
as justification his desire "to open up the question of African women's position
for general discussion." The starting point for the investigation was his conviction that sexual relations in Africa are undergoing radical change, partially as
a consequence of urbanization. His most fundamental conclusion is that, "irrespective of how their traditional role is construed, African women are now on
the march." In the course of the study, Little examines African women's migrant
experience, women's roles in the urban economy and their urbanization through
voluntary associations, women's participation in the political arena, and sexual
relations, marriage and family in the urban setting. A useful study for comparison
(though not restricted to Africa) is Ester Boserup's *Woman's Role in Economic
Development* (1974), especially the sections "In the Town" and "From Village
to Town." A very recent study, which takes issue with Little's optimistic
conclusions, is Deborah Pellow's *Women in Accra: Options for Autonomy* (Reference Publications, 1977).

36*   Malinowski, Bronislaw, 1884-1942. **Sex, Culture, and Myth.** New York:
       Harcourt, Brace and World, 1962. 346p. bibliog. index. LC 62-19590.
This work is basic reading in the structure and history of the family and the
sexual division of labor imposed by family structure. Malinowski has written
the anthropological primer of marriage, parenting, kinship, and sexual patterns.
Though he does not necessarily subscribe to feminist paradigms, he does formu-
late a world view of tolerance. His analysis affirms that marriage and the family
are society's fundamental, permanent units. "But with all due deference to traditional morality I see forces in the modern world which will demand an independent
and just treatment of unmarried love and perhaps homosexual love side by side
with the standardized institutions," Malinowski writes in the persona of Anthropologist in dialogue with Man of the World. A particularly intriguing chapter
entitled "Pioneers in the Study of Sex and Marriage" reviews the work of Freud,
Edward Westermarck, Robert Briffault, Earnest Crawley, and Havelock Ellis.
In this chapter, Malinowski finds Freud's theories of *libido* and infantile sexuality
inadequate in the face of evidence from cross-cultural research, affirms Westermarck's analysis of the primacy of the marriage union, indicts Briffault's

conclusions in *The Mothers*, and praises Havelock Ellis as a mentor and a genius of "common-sense and prophetic intuition" in his theories on social ethics and human sexuality.

37   Mamdani, Mahmood, 1946- . **The Myth of Population Control: Family, Caste, and Class in an Indian Village.** New York: Monthly Review Press, 1973. 173p. bibliog. $3.95. ISBN 0853452849. LC 72-81761.
Mamdani's goal in the research he analyzes here was to explain the failure of the Khanna Study, a Harvard-based population control program conducted in the Punjab from 1954 to 1969 and jointly funded by the Rockefeller Foundation and the Indian Government. The Khanna Study proceeded on the unquestioned assumption that the people of the Punjab had (and knew they had) a "population problem" and that, therefore, they would eagerly use the contraceptives showered upon them. In fact, the villagers quickly learned to take the devices, say they were using them, and then go on living their lives as before. The Khanna Study administrators could only explain the failure of their program on the basis of the "ignorance" of the villagers and the inefficiency of techniques and administration. By analyzing the political economy of the village, in which labor power was the key source of livelihood for all but the wealthiest, Mamdani shows that the villagers were acting on the basis of conscious reproductive strategies and that birth limitation in this context could only be viewed as irrational. He further shows how a rigidly patriarchal and authoritarian family structure and the accompanying pronatalist ideology served to guarantee that large families would be in the interest of women as well as men; severe social penalties awaited the barren woman or the woman who produced few sons. Mamdani's is a pathbreaking work in the political economy and sexual politics of reproduction.

38   Matthiasson, Carolyn J., ed. **Many Sisters: Women in Cross-Cultural Perspective.** New York: Free Press, 1974. 443p. bibliog. index. $15.00. ISBN 0029203309. LC 74-2654.
Many Sisters is an anthology of articles on the anthropology of women, the general aim of which is to qualify the frequently stated belief that "women are universally oppressed" through the exploration of concrete cultural variations. Among the societies examined here are Egypt, France, Guatemala, India, Nigeria, China, Cambodia, and the Iroquois. Matthiasson provides a brief introduction and a conclusion.

39*   Mead, Margaret, 1901-1978. **From the South Seas: Studies of Adolescence and Sex in Primitive Societies.** New York: Morrow, 1939. 304, 384, 335p. bibliog. index. LC 39-17925.
"When we build a new world, what kind of world do we want to build. This is the question which is being asked of the social scientist today" (Margaret Mead, 1939). In the course of her career as an anthropologist, Mead has shown a remarkable and long-standing commitment to raising questions fundamental to her own society. If this made her unusual, her commitment to formulating answers in language accessible to a lay public made her even more so. Mead began from the premise that human life in twentieth-century America is characterized by bewildering complexity, alienation, brutality, competitiveness,

repression, and the threat of complete destruction. She looked to other societies for what they could reveal about variation in and malleability of human culture and personality, and therefore—by extension—about possibilities for change in our own society. *From the South Seas* collects in one volume her three early books—*Coming of Age in Samoa: A Psychological Study of Primitive Youth for Western Civilization* (1928); *Growing Up in New Guinea: A Comparative Study of Primitive Education* (1930); and *Sex and Temperament in Three Primitive Societies* (1935)—in each of which these same basic issues were explored. *Samoa*—a study of a rather idyllic "primitive" society, vividly contrasting with our own—posed the more specific question of whether this malleability is such that the shape of society may be altered through change in childrearing patterns or education. Manus society in New Guinea was one in which a free childhood preceded an adult world of competitiveness, puritanism, and concern with economic security. Mead was led to the qualification that the prevailing social structure does pose limits for human plasticity: "You cannot alter a society by giving its children of school age new behavior patterns to which the adult society gives no scope." While *Samoa* and *New Guinea* will be of interest to women for their exploration of socialization processes, as well as for their specific descriptions of sex-role socialization in these two societies, *Sex and Temperament* is most important for feminist studies. Here Mead's general concern with culture and personality was narrowed to the particular question of the "conditioning of the social personalities of the two sexes." She studied three different tribes, all located within a 100-mile area. "In one, both men and women act as we expect women to act—in a mild parental responsive way; in the second, both act as we expect men to act—in a fierce initiating fashion; and in the third, the men act according to our stereotype for women—are catty, wear curls and go shopping, while the women are energetic, managerial, unadorned partners." Mead was led to conclude that "until we could understand very thoroughly the way in which a society could mold all the men and women born within it to approximate an ideal of behavior which was congenial to only a few of them, or could limit to one sex an ideal of behavior which another culture succeeded in limiting to the opposite sex, we wouldn't be able to talk very intelligently about sex differences." These were important and radical conclusions to draw in 1935, and her studies remain influential today. It is unfortunate that *From the South Seas* is currently out of print. Not only do the three books form a natural sequence, but the volume also contains a preface by Mead discussing how her work evolved from 1925 to 1939. The three books are available as separate publications: *Samoa* (Morrow, 1971); *New Guinea* (Morrow, 1976); *Sex and Temperament* (Morrow, 1963). Readers will also be interested in Mead's *Male and Female* (1949; repr. Greenwood Press, 1977).

40   Mead, Margaret, 1901-1978. **Letters from the Field, 1925-1975.** New York: Harper and Row, 1978. 343p. bibliog. index. $12.95. ISBN 0060129611. LC 73-4110.

Of this collection spanning Margaret Mead's entire career as an anthropologist, the earliest letters from Samoa are most revealing of the private side of Mead. Her descriptions of the people she lived among and observed are always vivid and lively, however. Many photographs accompany the text, providing a thorough visual chronicle of Mead's astonishing professional career. Contents of this "personal record of what it has meant to be a practicing anthropologist over the last fifty years" include: Samoa, 1925-1926; Peré Village, Manus, Admiralty Islands, 1928-1929; Omaha Reservation, Summer, 1930; New Guinea—Arapesh, Mundugumor and Tchambuli, 1931-1933; Bali and Iatmul, New Guinea, 1936-1939; Return to Manus, 1953; Field Visits in a Changing World, 1964-1975.

41   Mead, Margaret, 1901-1978. **Male and Female: A Study of the Sexes in a Changing World.** New York: Morrow, 1949; repr. Westport, CT: Greenwood Press, 1977. 477p. bibliog. index. $25.00. ISBN 0837197813. LC 77-22027.

Delivered as a series of lectures in 1946 and brought together as a book in 1948, *Male and Female* represents the developments in Mead's thinking from the publication of *Sex and Temperament* in 1935 to the late forties. Her ultimate topic is the relationship between men and women in the United States in the mid-twentieth century. But she holds off her discussion of the U.S. until she has erected a backdrop of comparative patterns. First, she discusses the relation between biological sex differences and cultural conceptions of sex roles, drawing on data from the seven South Sea cultures she studied extensively. Then, she launches into a broader anthropological analysis of the ways in which different societies attempt "to develop a myth of work, to bind men to women and children, to get the children fed and reared, and to settle the problems that arise whenever individual sex impulses must be disciplined into social forms." She then finally moves into her consideration of sexual relations in the U.S.— childhood, courtship, and marriage.

42*   Medicine, Beatrice. **The Native American Woman: A Perspective.** Las Cruces, NM: ERIC/CRESS: for sale by National Educational Laboratory Publishers, Austin, TX, 1978. 107p. bibliog.

Beatrice Medicine, a Sioux Indian, is an anthropologist, a teacher, a writer, and a poet, who is currently an advanced fellow in the Anthropology Department of the University of Wisconsin, Madison. *Native American Women* was written with women's studies courses in mind.

43   Morgan, Elaine. **The Descent of Woman.** New York: Bantam Books, 1973. 280p. bibliog. $1.95. ISBN 0553111795.

In an amusing and popular style, Elaine Morgan confronts androcentric evolutionary theory head-on and spins out an alternative theory of her own. Theories positing the primacy of the male of the species, originally theological in content, are now concocted by men in the fields of biology, ethnology, and primatology. "Smack in the center [of these theories] remains the Tarzanlike figure of the prehumanoid male who came down from the trees, saw a grassland teeming with game, picked up a weapon, and became a Mighty Hunter. Almost everything about us is held to have derived from this." Morgan calls into question received answers to questions such as: why did early humans stand upright? why did they begin using weapons? why did the naked ape become naked? and why did human sex life become so complex? In her discussions of these and other questions, Morgan attempts to restore womankind to the history of evolution.

44   Murphy, Yolanda, and Robert Francis Murphy, 1924- . **Women of the Forest.** New York: Columbia University Press, 1974. 236p. bibliog. index. $11.00. ISBN 0231036825. LC 74-9912.

The authors have returned to data they collected as graduate students in their field work among the Mundurucú Indians of the Amazon Basin in Brazil, 1952-1953. Robert spent most of that year with the men, Yolanda with the women. Twenty years later, they approach the material they gathered with new questions born of the women's movement and changes in their own lives. *Women of the Forest* is an analysis of sex relations among the Mundurucú from the woman's standpoint. Mundurucú society traditionally possessed the characteristics of a classless society: production was primarily for immediate consumption, and natural resources and instruments of production were held in common. The authors agree that these features also inhibited the development of extreme male dominance. The outward shows of male power were in actuality undercut by the solidarity women enjoyed due to their collective cultivation and preparation of the principal crop, bitter manioc, and to the societal preference for matrilocality. "The men, as an organized body, are unable to dominate females as isolated individuals. . . . Rather, they confront each other as two entities, each having internal organization and cohesion and a sense of identity and common interest."

45   Newton, Esther. **Mother Camp: Female Impersonators in America.** Englewood Cliffs, NJ: Prentice-Hall, 1972. 136p. bibliog. $3.95. ISBN 0136028470. LC 76-37634.

Newton originally wrote this book as a Ph.D. dissertation in anthropology, a discipline which has until recently produced few studies of homosexuality or even of American culture. In her preface, Newton explains how she evolved intellectually and politically during and after her research. When she began, she writes, "I was prepared to find the views of deviants interesting, but never seriously considered that they could be correct." While Newton ultimately decided against a large-scale revision of the thesis for publication, despite concern about "social blindness" to sexual and class oppression in the original, the study is extremely valuable. Her careful analysis of the culture of female impersonators and drag queens in itself leads to significant new perspectives on sex-role rigidity and oppression, heterosexism, and the straight world. Trained in the participant observation methods of anthropological field work, Newton's presence is low-key; much of the text is purely descriptive and she often stands back to let her "informers" speak for themselves. Newton introduces us to a number of impersonators, interviews them about their work—how they see it, working conditions in different kinds of bars and clubs, professionalism—discusses relationships between impersonation on stage and gay street behavior, and describes two shows at length. A key theme developed throughout is the relationship between sexuality and gender and the tensions and ambiguities in this relationship.

46   Niethammer, Carolyn. **Daughters of the Earth: The Lives and Legends of American Indian Women.** New York: Collier Books, 1977. 281p. bibliog. index. $7.95. ISBN 0020961502. LC 76-56103.

This is an attempt to reconstruct the lives of American Indian women prior to the penetration of their culture and society by Europeans. Niethammer has utilized early anthropologists' writings as well as the work of contemporaries, particularly the new feminist anthropology. She discusses the culture, customs, work, and relationships of Native American women (making distinctions by tribe) throughout the life-cycle—childbirth, education, sexuality, economic role, recreation, aging. Photographs are interspersed through the book.

47   Paulme, Denise, ed. **Women of Tropical Africa.** Berkeley: University
      of California Press, 1963. 308p. bibliog. index. $12.50. ISBN 0520009894.
      LC 63-24209.
Originally published in France in 1960 as *Femmes d 'Afrique noir*, the six essays
here are by women anthropologists based on fieldwork carried out in Africa
during the 1950s. Departing from the prevailing practice in ethnographic research
of using only male informants, these investigators attempted to get beyond the
considerable obstacles typically found to impede contact with women. The
societies studied vary from those of sedentary agriculturalists to those of nomadic
pastoralists. However, certain features are shared—for example, the relative
sexual permissiveness enjoyed by women prior to marriage; a woman's enduring
attachment to her natal family though she lives with her husband's family; the
view of marriage as a means of cementing alliances and ensuring the perpetuation
of the group; and, finally, the central importance of the mother within the
family. Included here are an introduction by the editor, Denise Paulme; "Conia-
gui Women (Guinea)" by Monique Gessain; "The Position of Women in a
Pastoral Society (The Fulani WoDaaBe, Nomads of the Niger)" by Marguerite
Dupire; "The Role of Women in the Political Organization of African Societies"
by Annie M. D. Lebeuf; "Nzakara Women (Central African Republic)" by Anne
Laurentin; "Women of Burundi: A Study of Social Values" by Ethel M. Albert;
"Women of Dakar and the Surrounding Urban Area" by Solange Faladé; and
an "Analytical Bibliography" by M. Perlman and M. P. Moal.

48   Pescatello, Ann M. **Power and Pawn: The Female in Iberian Families,**
      Societies, and Cultures. Westport, CT: Greenwood Press, 1976. 281p.
      bibliog. index. $15.95. ISBN 0837185831. LC 75-35352.
Writing from the perspective of an ethnohistorian with a cross-cultural and
multi-disciplinary approach, Pescatello has written about Iberian females in
Europe, Asia, Africa, and America. She asks questions such as: how has woman
been regarded by each group and each stratum of society? what have been her
legal, civic, and political responsibilities and rights? where has she fit into the
schema of miscegenation and marriage? Other questions touch on women's
influence in social, cultural, economic and power spheres in Iberian societies.
Chapters are: The Female in the Iberian World in Historical Perspective; Iberia:
Frontiers, Fidalgos, Families, and Females; Iberia in Asia: An Experiment in
Intercultural Living; Portuguese Africa: Iberia's 'Black Mother'; Amerindia:
The Antebellum South; America in the Reconquest: Empire, Miscegenation,
and New Societies; The Nineteenth Century: Enlightenment, Independence,
and Transition; Twentieth-Century Woman: The Heritage of Hispania; The
Twentieth-Century Brasileira. A very large bibliography of English-, Spanish-,
and Portuguese-language materials.

49   Reed, Evelyn. **Woman's Evolution: From Matriarchal Clan to Patriarchal
      Family.** New York: Pathfinder Press, 1975. 491p. bibliog. index.
      $15.00. ISBN 0873484215. LC 74-26236.

At the heart of feminism (of almost any variety) is the conviction that sexual
inequality is a *man*-made and not a "natural" institution; as a *historical* development, this inequality may be presumed to be susceptible to human intervention
and change. Theories positing a matriarchal era preceding the patriarchal societies
that we know today have appealed to many feminists because, if correct, they
supply evidence for the historicity of male dominance. Matriarchal theory was
developed by the early evolutionist school of anthropology (e.g., Lewis Morgan)
and later utilized by Marxists beginning with Friedrich Engels (*Origin of the
Family, Private Property and the State*), who incorporated the theory into
a larger schema explaining the evolution of private property, class relations, and
the state. Within orthodox Marxist theory, the advent of women's oppression
as a form of property within the family was coincident with the emergence of
class. Evelyn Reed belongs to this theoretical tradition, which she elaborates
in this major work, *Woman's Evolution.* Part 1 discusses the matriarchal age
from the standpoint of the mothers, part 2 from the standpoint of the brothers.
Part 3 describes the transition from matriarchy and matrifamily to patriarchy
and father-family. Needless to say, this theory is very controversial within both
anthropology and feminist theory. Useful discussions of the controversy may
be found in Eleanor Leacock's introduction to the International Publishers
edition of Engels's *Origin*; in the R. Reiter collection, *Toward an Anthropology
of Women*; and in Z. Eisenstein's collection, *Capitalist Patriarchy and the Case
for Socialist Feminism.*

50   Reiter, Rayna R., ed. **Toward an Anthropology of Women.** New York:
      Monthly Review Press, 1975. 416p. bibliog. $15.00. ISBN 0853453721.
      LC 74-21476.

It is clear that anthropology has the potential of offering rich material to
feminists seeking an understanding of the origins and evolution of systems of
sexual oppression. However, as Reiter notes in her introduction, there is also
the potential for male bias or even double male bias in anthropological accounts—
the bias of the anthropologist and also of the society being studied if it expresses
male dominance. The seventeen essays collected here are part of the on-going
attempt by feminist anthropologists to reclaim and reinterpret cross-cultural
material. Among the topics covered are the problems of male bias in the interpretation of biological and cultural records; relations between men and women
in societies organized primarily around kinship; the matriarchy debate; the
usefulness of psychoanalytic theory for an analysis of patriarchy; Engels's *Origin
of the Family, Private Property and the State*; women in contemporary West
European peasant groups; changes in the structure of women's lives in the Third
World; and the situation of rural women in the People's Republic of China.
A collection on related topics forthcoming from Routledge and Kegan Paul
(December, 1978) is *Feminism and Materialism: Women and Modes of Production,*
edited by Annette Kuhn and Ann Marie Wolpe.

51*   Richards, Audrey Isabel, 1899- . **Chisungu: A Girls' Initiation Ceremony Among the Bemba of Northern Rhodesia.** New York: Grove Press, 1956. 224p. bibliog. index. LC 57-6537.

Richards notes in the introduction that although girls' puberty rituals have been reported in many matrilineal cultures of Central Africa, these rituals have received far less attention than have boys' initiation ceremonies. The puberty ritual offers rich material for an analysis of sexual relations, as it embodies a culture's views of sex roles, fertility, parenthood, and marriage. Girls' puberty rituals are likely to offer clues about the cultural ambivalence often associated with women's reproductive power. The ceremony observed by Richards (in 1931; she notes in 1956 that it may already be extinct) was of particular interest for what it revealed of the economic activities, social values, and social structure of the Bemba, a matrilineal people practicing matrilocal marriage. Richards first summarizes the key features of Bemba culture, then proceeds to describe and analyze the Bemba *chisungu*.

52   Rosaldo, Michelle Zimbalist, and Louise Lamphere, eds. **Woman, Culture, and Society.** Stanford, CA: Stanford University Press, 1974. 352p. bibliog. index. $12.50. ISBN 0804708509. LC 73-89861.

This is one of the very earliest anthologies by feminist anthropologists. It immediately became and has continued to be one of the basic texts for women's studies courses in anthropology. Included are both theoretical and ethnographic articles, all but two of which were first published in this volume. The geographic range is very broad, including Afro-Americans in the United States, China, Africa, Indonesia, Latin America and Europe. Several of the new and developing approaches to the anthropological study of women are represented here. Together with Rayna Reiter's *Toward an Anthropology of Women*, this collection is a good place to begin an exploration of what anthropology can say about women and the sexual structuring of society.

53   Sahlins, Marshall David, 1930- . **The Use and Abuse of Biology: An Anthropological Critique of Sociobiology.** Ann Arbor: University of Michigan Press, 1976. 120p. bibliog. $8.00. ISBN 0472087770. LC 76-24329.

Edward O. Wilson's *Sociobiology: The New Synthesis* (Harvard University Press) appeared in fall 1975 and was immediately the focus of enormous controversy within the outside academia. Sociobiology—the biological explanation of sociological phenomena, or, as Wilson has termed it, the biologicizing of the social sciences—in no way represents a "new synthesis" as Wilson claims. There is a long tradition within the history of social thought of efforts to understand society and social relations as natural and hence immalleable phenomena. As Sahlins notes, it is an intellectual tradition intimately linked to the history of capitalism—from Hobbes's depiction of the evolving market society of his day as a vicious state of nature; to the Social Darwinists, who latched onto Darwin's theory of natural selection as an explanation of the "survival of the fittest" in competitive capitalist society; to present-day Jensensists, who seek the basis of racial inequality in IQ differences. This intellectual tradition has typically appealed to the politically conservative, for if inequity could be found to have biological roots, this would seem to place it beyond the reach of human intervention. By contrast, progressive movements have gravitated to social theories positing society as historical and emergent and human nature as plastic, with change therefore inevitable and subject to human agency. Thus despite the "new" sociobiology's claims to a purely scientific status, what is at issue in the debates currently raging is a series of political questions, concerning, for example, the foundation of inequality in society and possibilities for change. Obviously, history's endless theories of woman's inferiority are a prime example of socio-biological reasoning: sexual inequality is claimed to be biologically determined. Indeed, in his most recent book, *On Human Nature* (Harvard University Press, 1978), Edward Wilson makes explicit the argument that the sexual division of labor (and power) is genetically based. Most of the debate so far has taken place in periodicals such as the *New York Review of Books* and *Science*. (See the recent anthology that documents and provides background on the debate: *The Socio-biology Debate: Readings on Ethical and Scientific Issues*, edited by Arthur L. Caplan; Harper and Row, 1978.) Sahlins writes an intelligent analysis of both the intellectual and ideological issues raised by sociobiology from the vantage point of anthropology, viewing "the ideological controversy provoked by sociobiology as an important cultural phenomenon in itself." For a discussion that explicitly addresses the implications of sociobiology for feminism, see Evelyn Reed's *Sexism and Science* (1978).

54 Schlegel, Alice, ed. **Sexual Stratification: A Cross-Cultural View.** New York: Columbia University Press, 1977. bibliog. index. $17.50. ISBN 0231042140. LC 77-2742.

A collection of original papers in the anthropology of women, with a particular focus on comparative systems of sexual stratification (i.e., social systems in which asymmetrical sexual power relations prevail). Societies examined here fall at different points along a spectrum from the more male-dominated to the more egalitarian. An important point frequently made by feminist anthropologists and reiterated here is that correct assessment of sexual power relations requires examination of informal strategies utilized by women, not just formal positions of authority.

55 Schneider, David Murray, 1918- , and Kathleen Gough, eds. **Matrilineal Kinship.** Berkeley: University of California Press, 1974. 761p. bibliog. index. $24.75. ISBN 0520025873. LC 61-7523.

Originally a 1961 publication, which grew out of a 1954 Harvard seminar, this collection of papers on the matrilineal descent problem came 100 years after the publication in 1861 of J. J. Bachofen's controversial *Das Mutterrecht (The Mothers)*. Bachofen's argument was that human society originally took the shape of what he called "primitive promiscuity," characterized by a loose form of social organization and the centrality of women to religious, political, and house-hold life. Bachofen's theory has been rejected by modern anthropology as generally unsubstantiated by available evidence. This is not to say that there is no evidence of matrilineal kinship systems, however, as this volume makes clear. "In this book three types of approach appear. . . . One interest, shared by all the authors, is in the structural analysis of particular matrilineal societies, in their mode of operation and in the generalizations that can be made about all of them. Another interest is in cultural ecology: it is concerned with the significance for the form of a kinship system of the technico-environmental features of the culture in which it is found. A third interest is evolutionary: it is concerned with typology of general levels of cultural development . . . and with the implications of the evolution of the technical, political, and economic spheres of culture for the evolution of kinship systems" (from the preface). The papers are divided into three sections: first, nine studies of matrilineal kinship systems, with papers by Elizabeth Colson, David F. Aberle, David M. Schneider, George H. Fathauer, Harry W. Basehart, and Kathleen Gough; second, seven essays by Kathleen Gough on variation in features of several matrilineal systems; and third, an essay by David F. Aberle on "Matrilineal Descent in Cross-Cultural Perspective."

56   Spradley, James P., and Brenda J. Mann, 1950- . **The Cocktail Waitress:
       Woman's Work in a Man's World.** New York: Wiley, 1974. 154p. bibliog.
       $5.00. ISBN 0471817694. LC 74-18048.
An ethnographic study of the sexual politics and sexual division of labor in a midwestern college bar, based on Mann's year of participant observation as a cocktail waitress and Spradley's contributing analysis. This is novel material for anthropology and a significant contribution to the understanding of social inequality in its sexual forms. Another ethnography unusual for its focus on sexual politics in the American context is Esther Newton's *Mother Camp: Female Impersonators in America* (1972).

57   Strathern, Marilyn. **Women in Between: Female Roles in a Male World:
       Mount Hagen, New Guinea.** New York: Academic Press, 1972. 372p.
       bibliog. index. $19.25. ISBN 0127858083.
Woman's place in Hagen society is contingent upon her marriage and marriage choices. Women link men with each other through marriage. While she can act as a go-between, the males are the "major public actors in an exchange transaction." She has no place, no status of herself. Strathern describes the structure of Hagen society, the residence and work of women with their husband's family, the household, patterns of marriage, and the material exchange and benefits of marriage. Interesting observations are made about the issues of divorce and poisoning in Hagen society. Relations between men and women in this society are aptly described as a "sex war," but it is precisely this state of affairs that "allows Hagen women a measure of genuine independence."

58   Terrell, John Upton, 1900- , and Donna M. Terrell. **Indian Women of
       the Western Morning: Their Life in Early America.** New York: Dial
       Press, 1974. 214p. bibliog. index. $8.95. ISBN 0803743513. LC
       74-10638.
"In this book we have tried to portray American Indian women as they appeared, to tell something of their spiritual beliefs and their ways of life, at the beginning of recorded history—in the western morning." This overview of Native American women in their traditional societies discusses the following topics: status, duty, food, crafts, adornment, sex, cycle, children, and health and physique. The index can help direct the reader to information about particular tribes, but the approach here is, for the most part, one seeking generalizations and commonalities.

59   Tiger, Lionel, 1937- . **Men in Groups.** New York: Random House, 1969.
      254p. bibliog. index. $2.95. ISBN 0394705882. LC 69-16459.
Men in Groups is an anthropological study that takes a sociobiological approach
to the question of sexual differentiation, hierarchy, and power relations—that
is, it seeks a foundation for social structure and social relations in human biology.
Such approaches are inevitably conservative in implication and understandably
invite the wrath of those who view human relations as plastic and who also see
inequality and hierarchy as facets of society worth changing. Tiger's thesis is
that "male bonding"—his shorthand for the exclusionary male power groupings
that characterize patriarchal society—"reflects an underlying biologically trans-
mitted 'propensity' with roots in human evolutionary history (or phylogeny)." He
follows the thread of this thesis through animal societies, politics and war,
work and play, initiations and secret societies, and human aggression. Implications
implicit throughout emerge more explicitly in his concluding remarks—for
example, that the entry of women into politics in equal numbers to men "may
constitute a revolutionary and perhaps hazardous social change with numerous
latent consequences," or that "men dominated by their wives and families
may lose a certain constructive maleness of consequence to many of their activities." He brings his far-reaching cross-cultural, cross-historical speculation home
to roost when he goes on to say, "this seems to be particularly true among
North American academic males. . . ."

60   Weiner, Annette B., 1933- . **Women of Value, Men of Renown: New
      Perspectives in Trobriand Exchange.** Austin: University of Texas Press,
      1976. 299p. bibliog. index. $14.95. ISBN 029279004X. LC 76-14847.
First immortalized in the classic work of anthropologist Bronislaw Malinowski,
the Trobriand Islanders are here revisited by Weiner, and their society reconsidered
from a feminist perspective. Weiner begins with the assumption that women's
roles in society "must be accorded equal time in any study concerned with the
basic components of social organization." In this study, Weiner explores the
relation between Trobriand women's significant and valued public participation
in economic and ceremonial activities and the matrilineal structure of Trobriand
society, finding that the latter bolsters the former. Weiner documents the
public power enjoyed by women in mortuary rituals, conception beliefs, formal
exchange of yams, and marriage rules and ethics. She suggests that though the
Trobriand Islanders have been considered "primitive" by comparison with Western
society, they have demonstrated "the value of womanness and by extension
the value of human beings and the continuity of life."

61   Witherspoon, Gary. **Navajo Kinship and Marriage.** Chicago: University
      of Chicago Press, 1975. 137p. bibliog. index. $9.50. ISBN 0226904199.
      LC 74-21340.
Witherspoon has provided the reader with the Navajo's own conception of
kinship and marriage rather than the anthropologist's interpretation of these
important cultural units. He concludes that the mother-child relationship, the
life-giving and life-sustaining relationship, is held up by Navajo culture as the
ideal relationship between and among all individuals. Kinsmen are all mothers
of a sort, and the symbols held most sacred to the Navajo are called "mother"—
earth, corn, sheep, and sacred mountain soil bundles. The book is divided into

two major parts: Navajo Kinship as a Cultural System and Navajo Kinship as a Social System.

62   Wolf, Margery. **Women and the Family in Rural Taiwan.** Stanford, CA: Standord University Press, 1972. 235p. index. $8.50. ISBN 0804708088. LC 70-183895.

Traditional Chinese society is famous as an example of sexually oppressive systems in their most extreme form. Accounts often begin with the horrors of foot-binding and female infanticide and move on from there, viewing women for the most part as victims. Wolf's book is important because she analyzes this sexually oppressive society from the inside and through women's eyes. Women thus emerge as social actors actively struggling within the existing constraints to shape the conditions of their lives and to gain what power they can within the male kinship system.

63   Wolf, Margery, and Roxane Witke, eds. **Women in Chinese Society.** Stanford, CA: Stanford University Press, 1975. 315p. bibliog. index. $12.50. ISBN 0804708746. LC 74-82782.

This collection of papers, first delivered at a June 1973 conference on women in Chinese society held in San Francisco, was written by scholars in the fields of history, literature, anthropology, and Asian studies. Both of the editors are well known for their other books on women in China: Margery Wolf for her *Women and the Family in Rural Taiwan* (1972) and Roxane Witke for her biography of the now disgraced and purged fourth wife of Mao Tse-tung, *Comrade Chiang Ch'ing* (1977). Among the essays here: "Marriage Resistance in Rural Kwangtung" by Marjorie Topley; "Women and Suicide" by Margery Wolf; "Women as Writers in the 1920's and 1930's" by Yi-Tsi Feuerwerker; "Chiang Ch'ing's Coming of Age" by Roxane Witke; "The Power and Pollution of Chinese Women" by Emily M. Ahern; "Women and Childbearing in Kwan Mun Hau Village: A Study of Social Change" by Elizabeth Johnson; and "Women in the Countryside of China" by Delia Davin. Readers may also want to look at *Women in China: Studies in Social Change and Feminism*, compiled by Marilyn Blatt Young (Center for Chinese Studies, University of Michigan, 1973).

AUTOBIOGRAPHY, BIOGRAPHY, DIARIES, MEMOIRS, LETTERS

Feminist scholars are increasingly turning to the lives of women for their texts. This chapter indicates the enormous range of materials currently available, from the political biography to the critical literary biography, from the diaries and letters of famous women to those of ordinary, little-known women. Anthologies of diaries appear here as well as anthologies of rediscovered autobiographical works. Oral histories surface, reflecting the concern of women's studies to recover the "lost" lives of minority and Third World women. Autobiography and biography have become literary forms of increased stature in the last five years with the recognition that many women have used this form with the inventiveness and vitality expected of a novelist or poet. Additional biographical sources, bibliographies, and other reference materials that point to a wealth of biographical information on women will be found in the Reference chapter. The major archival identification tool to appear is Andrea Hinding, ed., *Women's History Sources: A Guide to Archives and Manuscript Collections in the United States* (1979), which will help to uncover the lives of many American women whose contributions have been outstanding but unrecognized in major biographical sources such as James's *Notable American Women 1607-1950* (1971). Use the index to recover materials by personal name (e.g., Ellen Glasgow) or by group (e.g., painters). Material on or by artists often falls into the Fine Arts chapter.

64*   Abzug, Bella S., 1920- . **Bella! Ms. Abzug Goes to Washington.** New York: Saturday Review Press, 1972. 314p. index. ISBN 0841501548. LC 72-182486.

Abzug introduces herself: "I've been described as a tough and noisy woman, a prizefighter, a man-hater, you name it. They call me Battling Bella, Mother Courage and a Jewish mother with more complaints than Portnoy. There are those who say I'm impatient, impetuous, uppity, rude, profane, brash and overbearing. Whether I'm any of these things, or all of them, you can decide for yourself. But whatever I am—and this ought to be made very clear at the outset—I am a very serious woman." With that, Bella launches into her indictment of the military-industrial establishment and her commitment to women, minorities, and youth. Her diary from January 18, 1971, to December 28 of the same year is a brutally honest, personal account of the trivial and weighty matters on the daily agenda of the congresswoman from New York. Particularly entertaining are her trenchant observations of her fellow congressmen and their wheelings and dealings. Her style is brisk and matches the pace of the killing schedule that she chronicles.

65   Adams, Abigail (Smith), 1744-1818. **New Letters of Abigail Adams, 1788-1801.** Boston: Houghton Mifflin, 1947; repr. Westport, CT: Greenwood Press, 1973. 281p. bibliog. index. $17.25. ISBN 0837170559. LC 73-13398.

Though not as compelling as the recent work edited by Butterfield, Friedlaender, and Kline, *The Book of Abigail and John: Selected Letters of the Adams Family*

1762-1784 (Harvard University Press, 1975), the *New Letters* reprinted from volume 55 of the *Proceedings of the American Antiquarian Society* provide significant insight into the daily routines of women and social importance in American life. The "Calendar of Letters" at the beginning of the volume contains brief annotations of each letter's contents. Most of this correspondence comes from the period of John Adams's first vice-presidency and his single term as president.

66   Alexander, Shana, 1925- . **Talking Woman.** New York: Delacorte Press, 1976. 271p. $8.95. ISBN 0440085950. LC 76-25137.

Shana Alexander has written in her introduction a remarkable capsulization of a journalistic career that has endured for thirty years, beginning with her interview of Gypsy Rose Lee as a cub reporter, age sixteen. She writes with humor and clarity in conveying a career that has taken her to *Life* as a staff researcher, then writer; to *McCall's* as its first woman editor in fifty years (a disaster); to *Newsweek* as a columnist; and finally to *Sixty Minutes* as a television writer and commentator. This account is followed by a collection of some favorite pieces of her writing, many of them written with "a feminine eye" (the title of her *Life* column). Of particular interest to women's studies will be her levelheaded, thoughtful pieces on women in the public eye: Judy Garland, Bella Abzug, Cornelia Wallace, Lurleen Wallace, Patricia Hearst, Liv Ullmann, the secretaries of Watergate, Helen Gurley Brown. Other pieces deal with women-related issues such as motherhood, breast cancer, and alimony, accompanied by her running diary as a journalist.

67   Anderson, Marian, 1902- . **My Lord, What a Morning: An Autobiography.** New York: Viking Press, 1956. 312p. $5.75. ISBN 0670500119. LC 56-10402.

Autobiography of the life and struggles of the fine concert singer and first black member of the Metropolitan Opera Company, Marian Anderson. Anderson tells the story of her life from her birth in a rented room in South Philadelphia to the time of her writing, 1956. Her primary focus is on her singing, the development of her career, and her travels.

68   Anderson, Mary, 1872-1964. **Woman at Work: The Autobiography of Mary Anderson as Told to Mary N. Winslow.** Minneapolis: University of Minnesota Press, 1951; repr. Westport, CT: Greenwood Press, 1973. 266p. index. $14.00. ISBN 0837171334. LC 73-13451.

This is the autobiography of the second director of the United States Women's Bureau. Anderson was born in Sweden, emigrating to "the promised land" in 1889, at the age of seventeen, to find that what was promised was domestic or factory labor. She soon became active in the trade union movement, particularly on issues of women's working conditions. Among the topics that Anderson discusses are her experiences with the Women's Trade Union League, with Jane Addams and Hull House, and as an organizer; her work for protective legislation; her move to Washington as an employee of the Woman in Industry Service and, eventually, the Women's Bureau. She also discusses women's work during World Wars I and II and the Equal Rights Amendment.

69   Angelou, Maya, 1928- . **Gather Together in My Name**. New York: Random House, 1974. 214p. $5.95. ISBN 0394486927. LC 73-20570.
A dazzling sequel to the first volume of Angelou's autobiography, *I Know Why the Caged Bird Sings*, this chronicle of the life of a young black woman is memorable for the incredible range of life experiences that it narrates: Angelou's stints as dancer, prostitute, brothel-keeper, and cook, all in the shadow of a grim post-war economy in which blacks were particularly displaced. Her remarkable determination sounds loudly at the end of the book, when she finds herself alone with only her baby and her clothes: "I had no idea what I was going to make of my life, but I had given a promise and found my innocence. I swore I'd never lose it again." Angelou's recent collection of poetry, *And Still I Rise* (Random House, 1978), enlarges on themes developed in her autobiography.

70   Angelou, Maya, 1928- . **I Know Why the Caged Bird Sings**. New York: Random House, 1970. 281p. $8.95. ISBN 0394429869. LC 73-85598.
Angelou, who has been variously a dancer, an actress, producer, journalist, political activist and writer, has written an extraordinary, lyrical autobiography of her Arkansas childhood and her California (mainly San Francisco) adolescence. Her adventures rendered with elegant clarity have as their center the experience of growing up black and female.

71   Arling, Emanie (Nahm). **"The Terrible Siren": Victoria Woodhull**. New York: Harper and Brothers, 1928; repr. New York: Arno Press, 1972. 423p. bibliog. $20.00. ISBN 0405044747. LC 72-2587.
This is an early biography of a woman who, as the author puts it, "dared to do anything she wanted to do"—in nineteenth-century America. Feminist and socialist, suffragist, popular orator on "inflammatory" topics, advocate of free love, Woodhull emerged from a background of poverty to lead a life of courage, commitment, and flamboyant notoriety. One can get an indication of the rebelliousness of this woman from the slogan at the masthead of the *Woodhull & Claflin's Weekly*, which she and her sister, Tennessee Claflin, published in the 1870s: "PROGRESS! FREE THOUGHT! UNTRAMMELED LIVES! Breaking the Way for Future Generations." This biography was written in the 1920s by a woman who is openly admiring of Woodhull.

72   Ashbaugh, Carolyn. **Lucy Parsons: American Revolutionary**. Chicago: C. H. Kerr, 1976. 288p. bibliog. index. $10.00. ISBN 088286-143. LC 75-23909.
"Lucy Parsons was black, a woman, and working class—three reasons people are often excluded from history" (from the preface). With this biography of Lucy Parsons (1853-1942)—socialist feminist; advocate of the rights of the unemployed, workers, women, and minorities; powerful orator and organizer throughout her lifetime—Carolyn Ashbaugh has made an important contribution to the project of putting women back into history, in this case radical history. Lucy Parsons has been ignored by mainstream historians, by socialist historians (as a woman), and by feminists (as a socialist). What accounts do exist have tended to identify her only as the wife and widow of the martyred Albert Parsons, one of four radical leaders hung in the aftermath of the 1886 Chicago Haymarket

Police Riot. Ashbaugh corrects this distortion with her history of Parsons's 55 years of activity in the radical labor movement after her husband's death.

73   Austin, Anne L., 1891- . **The Woolsey Sisters of New York: A Family's Involvement in the Civil War and a New Profession (1860-1900).** Philadelphia, PA: American Philosophical Society, 1971. 189p. bibliog. index. $3.00. ISBN 0871690853. LC 78-161991.

Abby, Jane, and Georgeanna Woolsey were important during the Civil War and after for their pioneering work in social welfare programs, nursing education, and hospital nursing service—work that the author of this biography feels has not been sufficiently recognized. This book chronicles their story, set within the context of their strong family ties and the history and achievements of the whole family.

74   **The Autobiography of a Happy Woman.** New York: Moffat Yard, 1915; repr. New York: Arno Press, 1974. 373p. $23.00. ISBN 0405060734. LC 74-3926.

This autobiography was originally published in 1915, on the condition that the publishers would guarantee the anonymity of the author. It tells the life story of a woman born to relative privilege who later had to face a reversal of family fortunes. She tells of her struggle with economic deprivation and of her different jobs—teaching school, working for a newspaper, writing. The main message being conveyed is a belief in work as women's salvation, no matter what the kind of work ("whether they are scrubbing departmental store stairs, crooning over babies, clipping off dividend coupons, or cheering the despairing heart of some lover in the struggle"). The author's greatest antipathy is reserved for discontent, complaint, self-pity. As she notes in her preface, "noisy disputations, the pros and cons of feminists and anti-feminists—have no place here. Why should they? Like the feline night-prowlers, they express nothing but their own antagonisms."

75   Balabanoff, Angelica, 1878-1965. **My Life as a Rebel.** New York: Harper and Brothers, 1938; repr. New York: Greenwood Press, 1968. 324p. index. $16.00. ISBN 0837100119. LC 68-23270.

This is a stirring autobiography of a woman who was centrally involved in the revolutionary movement in Europe at the beginning of this century. In particular, it covers the International and its collapse in 1914; the Zimmerwald Movement of anti-war socialists; the socialist movement in Italy and Mussolini's betrayal; the Russian Revolution, Balabanoff's dedicated work in those difficult first years, and her ultimate expulsion from the Communist Party after Lenin's death (she was the first internationally known revolutionist to be expelled and denounced); and her continuing commitment to socialism through all this. The book is particularly interesting for the way it conveys what it was to be a *woman* in the midst of these revolutionary movements mainly led by men.

76   Barnett, Ida B. Wells [Wells, Ida B.], 1862-1931. **Crusade for Justice: The Autobiography of Ida B. Wells.** Edited by Alfreda M. Duster. Chicago: University of Chicago Press, 1972. 434p. bibliog. index. $3.95. ISBN 0226893448. LC 73-108837.

"It is . . . for the young people who have so little of our race's history recorded that I am for the first time in my life writing about myself." This is the autobiography of a courageous and inspiring black woman who was born a slave in Mississippi during the Civil War and became in adulthood a tireless crusader against racism. Best known for her fight against lynchings, she was also involved in struggles against disenfranchisement based on race, discrimination in employment, and segregation on public carriers. She was one of the founders of the NAACP, a leader in the club movement among black women, an author—as well as a committed parent. Edited by her daughter, the autobiography tells the story of both her public and her private life and how she maintained her commitment to both.

77   Barreno, Maria Isabel, 1939- , et al. **The Three Marias: New Portuguese Letters.** New York: Bantam Books, 1976. 365p. $2.25. ISBN 0553022644.
Modelled on the classic, seventeenth-century work, *Letters of a Portuguese Nun*, the *New Portuguese Letters* has as its theme "a national and personal sense of isolation and abandonment." The materials that illuminate this motif are various: poetry, essays, diary entries, and invented letters from the Marias of the world describing their passions, their enslavements, their uncertainties and frustrations stemming from their roles as wives, daughters, mothers, and lovers. "All the Marias and Marianas and Maria Anas of the book thus become a sort of universal name for woman, and these *New Portuguese Letters* a meditation on the pertinence of the original *Portuguese Letters* to the situation of women today" (Helen Lane, preface).

78   Barry, Joseph Amber, 1917- . **Infamous Woman: The Life of George Sand.** Garden City, NY: Doubleday, 1977. 436p. bibliog. index. $12.95. ISBN 0385068301. LC 76-5335.
Much of the material in this biography has been handled by the Curtis Cate biography *George Sand* (1976). A great deal of attention here is on George Sand's amorous adventures and her ability to deal with life by ignoring society's hypocritical conventions. This is a solidly documented biography, not as thorough as Cate but lively reading. Many of the citations are taken from Sand's correspondence and autobiographical writings. Renee Winegarten's recent *The Double Life of George Sand: Woman and Writer* (Banz Books, 1978) takes a psychobiographical approach to Sand that adds little or nothing to Cate and Barry.

79*   Bates, Daisy (Gatson). **The Long Shadow of Little Rock: A Memoir.** New York: McKay, 1962. 234p. index. LC 62-20233.
In September, 1957, Little Rock—known primarily as the capital of Arkansas and as a relatively liberal southern city—exploded into mass hysteria and street battles between white mobs and National Guardsmen as the attempt was made to enroll nine black students in Central High School. This struggle is the central focus of Daisy Bates's autobiography. Bates became integrally involved in the battle as a woman long active in civil rights struggles: she and her husband owned and published a newspaper, the *State Press*, whose efforts were geared toward improving the lives of southern blacks, and she was also state president of the NAACP at the time of the Little Rock confrontation. A very readable and inspiring account.

80   Beauvoir, Simone de, 1908- . **All Said and Done.** New York: Warner
      Books, 1975. $2.50. ISBN 0446811912.

Some may find the latest volume (the fifth) of de Beauvoir's autobiography
somewhat less exhilarating fare than earlier volumes. Chronicled here are reminiscences of those people whom de Beauvoir has known and loved, as well as the
external activities of her life, defenses of her later work, travels, and political
activities and events from 1962 to 1971, including her participation with Sartre
in the International Tribunal condemning American intervention in Viet Nam.
Even when de Beauvoir is delivering a travel lecture, modifying her stance on
feminism (specifically with regard to *The Second Sex*), explaining her philosophy
of life, or even rendering straight reportage, she does it with flair. The events
of which she speaks and the people who touch her life are consistently interesting
and mark her life as extraordinary by any standard. This is a translation of *Tout
compte fait.*

81   Beauvoir, Simone de, 1908- . **Force of Circumstance.** New York:
      Harper and Row, 1977. 2v. $3.95 ea. ISBN 0060905581 (v.1);
      006090559X (v.2).

The tone of this portion of the autobiography, brought out in 1964, is mellowed
by de Beauvoir's position as a preeminent literary figure, author of *The Second
Sex*, and opponent of her nation's political, social, and economic policies,
especially with regard to Algeria. In this volume, which takes the reader from
the Liberation of Paris after the war to the author's position as a celebrated
wrtier in 1963, de Beauvoir casts a cold eye on her life, her relationship with
Sartre, and her progressing years in the sense that she accepts defeats and
moments of despair with seeming equilibrium. De Beauvoir's autobiographies,
La Force des Choses included, stand as monuments to the genre because of their
piercing truth and lucidity.

82   Beauvoir, Simone de, 1908- . **Memoirs of a Dutiful Daughter.** New York:
      Harper and Row, 1974. 365p. $3.95. ISBN 0060903511.

This is the first in de Beauvoir's remarkable series of memoirs, taking the reader
from her birth in January 1908, the daughter of bourgeois Parisian parents,
through childhood and adolescence, her tragic friendship with her childhood
friend Zaza, student days at the Sorbonne, and the beginning of her friendship
with Jean Paul Sartre. De Beauvoir is at all times mistress of the autobiographical
form in this translation of *Memories d'une jeune fille rangée.*

83   Beauvoir, Simone de, 1908- . **The Prime of Life.** New York: Harper and
      Row, 1976. 479p. $4.95. ISBN 0060905492.

Taking up in September 1929, this volume of de Beauvoir's autobiography
takes the reader from her buoyant days in Paris as a young part-time teacher
and tutor, with a room of her own, enjoying the intellectual life with Sartre
and other brilliant friends, through her first permanent teaching positions in
the provinces, the Occupation, and finally to the Liberation of Paris in 1944.
Sartre and death are de Beauvoir's preoccupations in this vivid description of
her peak personal experiences in which love, war, traveling, teaching, and politics
all come together. An extraordinary chronicle of emotional and intellectual
growth, this is a translation of *La Force de L'âge.*

84   Beauvoir, Simone de, 1908- . **A Very Easy Death.** New York: Warner
      Books, 1973. 123p. $1.95. ISBN 0446894419. LC 66-15581.
De Beauvoir recounts the details of her mother's death and gives us the painful
ambivalence that characterized the relationship between the two women. Apparently de Beauvoir did not have an easy rapport with her mother over the years,
but as the painful death of the mother draws near, many of the masks that
mother and daughter have worn begin to fall away. This beautiful and moving
account of the mother/daughter relationship in middle and old age is a translation
of *Une mort très douce.*

85   Bell, Quentin. **Virginia Woolf: A Biography.** New York: Harcourt,
      Brace and Jovanovich, 1972. 2 v. in 1. 216p. bibliog. index. $12.50.
      ISBN 0151937656. LC 72-79926.
Quentin Bell is an excellent biographer, thorough and scholarly without being
pedantic or heavy-handed. This is the best biography of Woolf available and
essential reading for those who plan to study the novels in any detail. Volume
1 (from 1882-1912) records the early years of death in the family, beginnings
of nervous breakdowns, writing reviews, friendships with young Bloomsbury
figures, traveling and courtship and acceptance of Leonard Woolf. For both
volumes Bell provides complete chronologies. Volume 2, 1912 to Virginia's
suicide in 1941, chronicles her marriage, the writing of her important fiction,
the founding of the Hogarth Press with Leonard, and their life together as centers
of Bloomsbury and presiders over a world of the literary and artistic avant garde.
Bell has drawn extensively on unpublished material (as a nephew, he had access
to great quantities of materials held by relatives and friends), and his references
to this corpus are scrupulous. The excellent photographs are another bonus.
Readers interested in further biographical insight into the life of Virginia Woolf
would do well to consult Leonard Woolf's five-volume autobiography, available
from Harcourt, Brace, Jovanovich (*Growing*; *Sowing*; *Beginning Again*; *Downhill
All the Way*; and *The Journey Not the Arrival Matters*).

86   Benet, Mary Kathleen. **Writers in Love.** New York: Macmillan, 1977.
      273p. bibliog. index. $9.95. ISBN 0025089005. LC 76-25560.
The writers are Katherine Mansfield, George Eliot, and Colette; their men are
J. Middleton Murray, George Henry Lewes, and Maurice Goudeket. The point
Benet makes is that these three brilliant and creative women were emotionally
dependent on the brilliant men with whom they formed alliances to the extent
that their accomplishments might have been considerably less without this
masculine support and encouragement. Though this is a debatable literary issue,
Benet writes a critical and biographical study that demonstrates compatibility
between love and work in the lives of women artists. Perhaps more germane is
the fact that both partners in these relationships were individuals of achievement,
thus avoiding the problems inherent in relationships when one individual must
take a totally subordinate role to another.

87   Bengis, Ingrid. **Combat in the Erogenous Zone.** New York: Bantam Books,
      1973. 209p. $1.95. ISBN 0553078135.
Bengis tries to analyze love, hate, and sexuality in herself, her sex, and in men.
She says, "if you are hoping for conclusions about the possibilities for love and

hate among men and women, you will be disappointed. I have none. . . . Do I hate men or love them, hate women or love them? Do I reject sex between men and women, women and women, or celebrate and experience it as being inherently contradictory? The answer of course, is yes—to everything." Her chapters are Man-hating; Lesbianism; Love. This book is a voyage in soul-searching and the painful process of scrutinizing the ambivalences within us all, whether involved in heterosexual or gay relationships.

88   Bernhardt, Sarah, 1844-1923. **The Memoirs of Sarah Bernhardt: Early Childhood Through the First American Tour and Her Novella "In the Clouds."** New York: Peebles Press; distr. Indianapolis, IN: Bobbs-Merrill, 1977. 256p. $12.95. ISBN 0672523558. LC 77-76008.

These are the memoirs of the early years of Sarah Bernhardt—legendary actress (known for such diverse roles as Hamlet, L'Aiglon, and the Lady of the Camellias), eccentric, woman of unusual courage. In these memoirs, Bernhardt discusses her childhood, how she came to the stage, her time at the Conservatoire, at the Comédie Française and in London, and her first American tour. Also included in this volume (in English for the first time) is her novella, *In the Clouds*, which is based on her whimsical flight over Paris in a balloon, sipping champagne, in 1878. Thirty-one pages of photographs and graphics depict Bernhardt at different points in her life and in numerous roles. Readers may wish to consult Cornelia Otis Skinner's biography, *Madame Sarah* (Houghton Mifflin, 1967).

89   Blackwell, Alice Stone, 1857-1950. **Lucy Stone: Pioneer of Woman's Rights.** Boston: Little, Brown, 1930; repr. Detroit, MI: Gale Research, 1971. index. $14.50. ISBN 0810338246.

This is a biography of the American suffragist and abolitionist who was one of the founders of the National American Woman Suffrage Association and of the *Woman's Journal*. Written by her daughter, replete with anecdotes, this biography is described by Louis Filler (in *Notable American Women*) as "both a work of love and an informed study of primary importance."

90   Blackwell, Elizabeth, 1821-1910. **Pioneer Work in Opening the Medical Profession to Women: Autobiographical Sketches.** New York: Longmans, Green, 1895; repr. New York: Schocken Books, 1977. 264p. bibliog. $4.75. ISBN 0805205683. LC 76-48855.

In her introduction, Dr. Mary Roth Walsh talks of early medical education in the United States and the circumstances surrounding Blackwell's admission into medical school. Until 1870, when major universities began to accept women as well as men, a woman's best chance for medical school was to apply to one of the few female medical colleges. Even then, the woman faced significant problems in finding an internship program to accept her. Emily and Elizabeth Blackwell worked hard to open the doors of the medical profession, and by the 1890s, there were many successful medical women—a phenomenon that was shortlived, as it threatened the status of male practitioners. These sketches cover the Blackwells' early years in England, their efforts to earn money for their education, their application to schools in Philadelphia and New York, study in Europe, work in the U.S., and their continuing international work for women's health. Among other sources on the Blackwells are Elinor Rice Hays's *Those Extraordinary*

Blackwells: The Story of a Journey to a Better World (Harcourt, Brace and Jovanovich, 1967); Ishbel Ross's *Child of Destiny: The Life Story of the First Woman Doctor* (Harper and Brothers, 1949), the standard biography of Elizabeth Blackwell, though popular in approach; Dorothy Wilson's *Lone Woman: The Story of Elizabeth Blackwell: The First Woman Doctor* (Little, Brown, 1970); and Nancy Ann Sahli's *Elizabeth Blackwell, M.D. (1821-1910): A Biography* (Ph.D. dissertation, University of Pennsylvania, 1974; University Microfilms, 1974).

91   Blanchard, Paula. **Margaret Fuller: From Transcendentalism to Revolution.** New York: Delacorte Press, 1978. 364p. bibliog. index. $10.00. ISBN 0440053145. LC 78-739.

Paula Blanchard undertook this biography of Margaret Fuller (1810-1850) with the goal of developing and conveying an understanding of the woman that would go beyond the "Margaret Myth." This myth evokes the image of a harsh, opinionated, masculine spinster, a bluestocking who repudiated sensuality, love, and her identity as a woman. This perspective can only then explain her love affair and motherhood at age 38 on the basis of some mysterious "feminization" (as one of her chief biographers, Mason Wade, described it). It is Blanchard's view that the myth reveals more about the inability of our own culture to see intellectual work, sexuality, and motherhood as compatible than it does about Margaret Fuller. Blanchard is also concerned to correct the prevalent overemphasis on Fuller's Transcendentalism, bringing into focus the political and activist dimensions of her character as well. In sum, Blanchard views her book as "an attempt to view Margaret Fuller's life through the eyes of another woman, living in the 1970s with an awareness of the questions raised about women in the past decade." For a similar, though independently arrived at approach to Fuller, Blanchard recommends Bell Gale Chevigny's anthology, *The Woman and the Myth* (1976).

92   Bogan, Louise, 1897-1970. **What the Woman Lived: Selected Letters of Louise Bogan, 1920-1970.** New York: Harcourt, Brace, Jovanovich, 1973. 401p. index. $14.50. ISBN 0151958785. LC 73-9737.

Bogan, a major poet (*The Blue Estuaries: Poems 1923-1968*), received relatively little public attention until recently, though she was highly regarded by her literary peers. Trenchant, witty, impeccably critical in their literary judgments, the Bogan letters reveal a personality that sizzles with opinions and feelings about life, love, and art—mainly about poetry and writers. Many of the letters are to Edmund Wilson, with whom she maintained a life-long friendship and correspondence. There are also letters here to other literary notables such as Theodore Roethke, May Sarton, and Allen Tate. Bogan's literary likes and dislikes come across in crisp unmincing judgments. She greatly admired Swift, Yeats, and Joyce. She disliked the work of many woman writers and avoided reviewing their work because she felt that a woman critic was expected to judge her sisters favorably. She abhorred bad writing from man or woman, friend, relative, or enemy. But when she admired someone, her praise was unhesitatingly direct. In a 1934 letter about writers, she calls Ellen Glasgow "a lending-library set-up," and in the next line praises Jane Austen whom she terms "sharp as hell." Her opinions about money (she never had enough), alcohol (she drank too much), and lovers (she liked love-making "when it is really well-informed") are delivered in humorous and elegant prose. Bogan at times writes frankly about the unique situation of the woman writer, though she never comes across self-pityingly. To Edmund Wilson in 1941 she writes: "you know, as few others do, that I am a housewife, as well as a writer; I have no one to sweep floors or get meals, or get out the laundry, or, in the case of sickness, make egg-nogs and squeeze orange juice." This volume can be read profitably along with Bogan's *A Poet's Alphabet: Reflections on the Literary Art and Vocation* (1970).

93   Bradford, Sarah Elizabeth (Hopkins), b. 1818. **Harriet Tubman: The Moses of Her People.** Secaucus, NJ: Citadel Press, 1974. (Repr. of 1886 ed.). 149p. $2.45. ISBN 0806504153.
First published in 1869 under the title, *Scenes in the Life of Harriet Tubman*, the biography of Tubman (1820?-1913) was written by an abolitionist, Sarah Bradford. Tubman is probably the best known of the "conductors" on the Underground Railroad, courageous persons who guided slaves on a secret route from southern plantations to Canada and freedom, despite the threat posed by the brutal Fugitive Slave Law. Bradford tells Tubman's story from the time of her childhood to the close of the Civil War, during which she served as agent behind enemy lines, scout for Union troops, and practical nurse in Union camp hospitals. Readers with a further interest in Tubman's life should consult the later (1943) and more complete biography by Earl Conrad entitled *Harriet Tubman*.

94   Brittain, Vera Mary. **Radclyffe Hall: A Case of Obscenity?** South Brunswick, NJ: A. S. Barnes, 1969. 185p. bibliog. $5.95. ISBN 049807451X. LC 76-81684.
The publication of *The Well of Loneliness* by Radclyffe Hall (1886-1943) in 1928 marked the beginning of a heated British debate and its trial on obscenity because of its lesbian theme. Radclyffe Hall was the affluent daughter of a prominent London family. Her education was minimal and until age 34 she did nothing to indicate she would become a noted writer. This book is the only biographical study of the writer and her work aside from that of Una Troubridge, Hall's intimate friend. Much of the book gives details about the trials for obscenity, which Radclyffe fought both in London and New York. Of particular interest are the excerpts of contemporary comment about the book and the trials.

95   Brooks, Gwendolyn, 1917- . **Report From Part One.** Detroit, MI: Broadside Press, 1972. 215p. $5.95. ISBN 0910296820. LC 72-77308.
An informal autobiography pieced together to convey the sense of a poet's album, *Report From Part One* is important for both its personal and critical insights into Brooks's work. Two prefaces, by Don L. Lee and George Kent, discuss Gwendolyn Brooks's journey as a black poet, with emphasis on her increasing commitment to black writing after her 1971 trip to Africa and her movement away from Harper and Row to Broadside Press (a black press). Along with the prefaces and Brooks's statements about family, apprentice years, marriage and children, black poetry, artistic contacts, and her trip to Africa in *Report*, this volume also contains the Pulitzer Prize-winning poet's interviews with

scholars and editors (1967-1971), photographs, "African Fragment," and appendix material giving her interpretation of her work and a forecast of what she hopes to write in the future, "my newish voice."

96 Brooks, Paul. **The House of Life: Rachel Carson at Work; With Selections from Her Writings Published and Unpublished.** Greenwich, CT: Fawcett Publications, 1974. bibliog. $1.75.

This is a collection of writings by and about Rachel Carson (1907-1964), scientist and eloquent science writer, who showed definitively that technical subjects can be presented in accessible and beautiful language. Carson was author of five books—*Under the Sea-Wind* (1941), *The Sea Around Us* (1951), *The Edge of the Sea* (1955), *Silent Spring* (1962), and *The Sense of Wonder* (1965, published posthumously)—of which *Silent Spring* is best known for its prophetic indictment of the indiscriminate use of pesticides and herbicides in U.S. agriculture. Brooks has taken these selections from Carson's own writings and letters, published and unpublished, and from his own and others' reminiscences of her. Readers may also want to consult Philip Sterling's biography, *Sea and Earth: The Life of Rachel Carson* (Thomas Y. Crowell, 1970).

97 Browne, Martha (Griffith) [Griffith, Mattie], d. 1906. **Autobiography of a Female Slave.** New York: Redfield, 1857; repr. New York: Negro Universities Press, 1969. 401p. $13.00. ISBN 0837121949.

A painful and moving account of a woman born to slavery in southern Kentucky, the autobiography opens with the death of the master and the sale of the author as a young child away from her mother. It concludes when she finally is freed and resettles in the North, teaching black children in a small New England town. Yet this can hardly be seen as a happy ending, punctuating as it does a long sequence of suffering and tragedy. Mattie Griffith's account is valuable for its vivid and detailed evocation of a black woman's slave experience.

98 Browne, Rose Butler, and James W. English. **Love My Children: An Autobiography.** (2nd ed.). Elgin, IL: David C. Cook, 1974. 250p. index. $1.95. ISBN 091269243X. LC 74-80406.

In this story, Rose Browne tells both of her life and of that of her people. Mrs. Browne (Ph.D., Harvard) has taught at North Carolina State, Durham, since 1948. Her great-grandmother, a free Indian woman, worked fields to buy freedom for her husband, a Negro house slave who never adjusted to freedom. The grandmother then took three of her young children to Boston, scrubbing floors to support them. The move to Boston resulted in the family's taking advantage of the cultural opportunities abounding there, and they maintained a happy unity as well. Browne expounds her belief that blacks should maintain pride in their race, but she also recognizes that educators should seek to present a fair picture of all races.

99* Browning, Elizabeth Barrett, 1806-1861. **Diary by E.B.B.: The Unpublished Diary of Elizabeth Barrett Browning, 1831-1832.** Athens: Ohio University Press, 1969. 358p. bibliog. index. LC 68-18390.

It is a commonplace of Victorian scholarship to note that Elizabeth Barrett Browning's poor health and invalidism freed her from conventional domestic

duties and enabled her to develop as a poet. Her diaries chronicle her love of
seclusion, her interest in books and study—in short, the introspective life of a
scholar and poet. Important among the themes of the years 1831-1832 covered
in the diary are her friendship with Hugh Stuart Boyd, a local scholar, and the
loss of her beloved Hope End, the family estate in Herefordshire. The diary is
a fascinating account of the daily round of activities that English gentry enjoyed
in the nineteenth century and the interests and reading of this gifted young
woman. An interesting appendix is the text of poems that Elizabeth Barrett
Browning records writing or publishing during the keeping of this diary. The
reader also might want to look at Mary Jane Lupton's study, *Elizabeth Barrett
Browning* (Feminist Press, 1972).

100   Butscher, Edward. **Sylvia Plath: Method and Madness.** New York:
       Seabury Press, 1976. 388p. bibliog. index. $15.95. ISBN 0816492530.
       LC 75-12828.
One might reasonably question a literary biographer's motives when he repeatedly
refers to his subject as "bitch goddess," and there are significant problems in
accepting several of the judgments that Butscher imposes on Plath by assuming
motives, sometimes even facts. His focus is to arrive at a conclusion of how
Plath's fusion of method and madness resulted in her becoming a major artist.
The interview material with friends is the most illuminating aspect of Butscher's
biography.

101   Caine, Lynn. **Widow.** New York: Bantam Books, 1975. $1.95. ISBN
       0553114522.
A poignant autobiographical review of death and fear characterized in an Edna
St. Vincent Millay quotation: "Life must go on . . . I forget just why." The
author posits that our society forces most women to lose their identities when
their husbands die. She urges women to make suitable financial arrangements
with the husband as soon after the marriage as possible, concluding that she
lost lover, confidant, and counselor ("a thousand things") when her lawyer
husband died of cancer, concluding that money is power and is like a "penis
in the bank." Left with two small children, she discovered the most unpleasant
aspects of the identity, "widow," a word taken from the Sanskrit meaning
"empty." Parts of the book: The Dying; The Seasons of Grief; The Other Side
of Grief; Children Grieve, Too; and A Different Woman. This is a personal,
pragmatic approach rather than a scholarly one. Readers may also be interested
in Helena Lopata's *Widowhood in an American City* (Schenkman, distributed by
General Learning Press, 1973).

102   Canary, Martha Jane, 1852-1903. **Calamity Jane's Letters to Her
       Daughter.** San Lorenzo, CA: Shameless Hussy Press, 1976. 46p. $1.95.
       ISBN 0915288273.
Jane used her dictionary to look up words as she laboriously wrote letters for
her daughter describing her life, adventures, and hopes over the years. The
correspondence (actually only about twenty letters) from 1877-1903 is simple,
eloquent, moving. The last letter repeats a theme that Calamity Jane sounded
throughout: "there is some thing I should confess to you but I just can't. I
shall take it to my grave—forgive me & consider I was lonely." This from the

legendary western figure who counted among her professions and loves—gambler, nurse, stagecoach driver, scout, muleskinner, Wild West rider, and wife.

103   Cardozo, Nancy. **Lucky Eyes and a High Heart: The Life of Maud Gonne.** New York: Bobbs-Merrill, 1978. 468p. $15.00. ISBN 067252080X. LC 76-44665.

Maud Gonne's life was theatrical and romantic by most accounts, including this one. A leader in the Irish struggle for independence, Maud Gonne also inspired Yeats, though he is recorded as saying about the great and elusive love of his life, "I came to hate her politics."

104   Carpenter, Joseph Estlin, 1844-1927. **The Life and Work of Mary Carpenter.** (2nd ed.). London: Macmillan, 1881; repr. Montclair, NJ: Patterson Smith, 1974. 404p. bibliog. $15.00. ISBN 0875851452. LC 77-172564.

This is a biography of a nineteenth-century British social reformer of awesome energy, written by her nephew. During the course of her seventy years (1807-1877), Mary Carpenter was primarily concerned with the establishment and reform of education for poor children and children of the working class ("ragged schools"), of reformatory schools for juvenile delinquents, and with prison reform. She also carried these interests to India, which she visited four times, and to the United States and Canada. She supported the movement for higher education for women, having herself had the privilege (unusual in her day) of a good classical and scientific training under her father's tutelage (he operated a school for boys). She wrote a considerable amount on the questions of education, reformatories, poverty, and India.

105   Carrington, Dora de Houghton, 1893-1932. **Carrington: Letters and Extracts from Her Diaries.** New York: Holt, Rinehart and Winston, 1971. 514p. bibliog. index. $12.50. ISBN 0030856590. LC 79-137332.

Carrington was a member of the Bloomsbury circle because of her association with Lytton Strachey, the critic and author of *Eminent Victorians.* Carrington, an artist, devoted her life to Strachey, decorating his house in Wiltshire and entertaining guests—Bertrand Russell, Virginia Woolf, Vanessa and Clive Bell, and other Bloomsburyians. She stayed with him until his death in 1932 and killed herself out of a sense that life was not worthwhile without him. This edition of her letters, with a preface by her friend David Garnett and a comment on her early life by her brother, Noel Carrington, is more than a collection of correspondence written by an eccentric bohemian. It is a commentary on the lifestyle of distinguished intellectual pacifists of England during the first World War and the 1920s. Garnett has used as his principle of selection: "first, to choose letters that tell the story of her personal life and principal love affairs; second . . . those that illustrate her wit and charm—often revealed in the drawings in the text; third . . . those that reveal her extremely complex character . . . [including] passages from her diaries and her poems."

106   Casal, Mary. **The Stone Wall: An Autobiography.** Chicago: Eyncourt Press, 1930; repr. New York: Arno Press, 1975. 227p. $12.00. ISBN 0405074042. LC 75-12307.

Mary Casal (a pseudonym) relates in the most honest terms her life story and what it was to be a lesbian in late nineteenth/early twentieth century America. She writes at the age of 66, without prudery or euphemism, speaking of the sexual confusion and misery experienced by women—whether lesbian or hetero-sexual—brought up in ignorance and shame. She very matter-of-factly declares her belief in the naturalness of sexual desire, whether the object of that desire be male or female, and she pleads for a more human approach to sexuality by parents. Her comments on men's sexual insensitivity in marriage and women's frustration prefigure feminist analyses of the contemporary movement.

107   Cate, Curtis, 1924- . **George Sand: A Biography.** Boston: Houghton Mifflin, 1975. 812p. bibliog. index. $17.50. ISBN 0395199549. LC 75-8680.

George Sand (1804-1876) lived an incredibly rich and eventful life. Her prolific literary output is legend: Cate tells us that she wrote nearly sixty novels, 25 plays, her autobiography and volumes of essays, all the while carrying on volumi-nous correspondence to lovers, literary friends, and those who sought her advice on marital, literary, and political matters. Curtis Cate does not write from a feminist perspective, as a cursory reading of his preface will prove. Nevertheless, he is a good biographer with true sympathy for his subject and has many insights into the complexity of Sand's character. Considered a rebel by many of her con-temporaries, George Sand was a remarkably conservative woman on many moral and domestic matters. Cate is quite good in his exploration of the novels as they relate to Sand's life. Dividing his work into eight main sections, Cate examines Sand's youth; her marriage and motherhood, her love affair with Jules Sandeau and the novels *Indiana* and *Leila* from this period; her affair with Alfred de Musset; her painful and scandalous divorce from Casimir Dudevant; her years with Chopin and her major works; the revolution of 1848 and her political involvements; the years marking France's transformation from Empire to Republic; and Sand's mature years, work, and family sorrows. Notes are extensive and thorough. Cate provides us with an excellent bibliography and a useful chronological list of Sand's most significant works.

108   Chao, Pu-wei (Yang), 1889- . **Autobiography of a Chinese Woman, Buwei Yang Chao.** New York: John Day, 1947; repr. Westport, CT: Greenwood Press, 1970. 327p. $16.75. ISBN 0837137128. LC 72-100225.

The author conveys with a novelist's flair the story of her life, "written in Chinese for readers of English," and translated by her husband, Yuenren, then a faculty member at Harvard University. She calls herself a "typical Chinese woman" from a four-generation family all residing together in the same house. Having returned to China in 1924 after a first journey to America, she helped to establish a birth control clinic. She had an achievement-oriented self image, claiming that early in her life friends would "pay me the doubtful compliment of saying that I am not like a woman. . . ." Here is the tale of one who defied cultural tradition, refused to fit a stereotypical female role, and became a revo-lutionary although not in the political arena. At age 58, she looked forward to an active role upon returning to China from the States, rather than retiring to a life of serene contentment. She did not subscribe to the notion that men are people of public affairs and women are just mothers and homemakers, concluding with, "I want my father to win his point about educating his daughter just like a son."

109   Cheney, Anne, 1944- . **Millay in Greenwich Village.** University: University of Alabama Press, 1975. 160p. bibliog. index. $8.75. ISBN 0817371613. LC 74-23424.

Rejecting conventional standards, living an avant garde Greenwich Village existence to the hilt, lover and friend of many important literary figures, Millay (1892-1950) often exclaimed both privately and in her poetry that she was neither one thing nor another: "what should I be but a harlot and a nun?/ What should I be but a prophet and a liar?" Her poetry came to symbolize the spontaneity of the free woman of the pre-twenties. It is the years 1918-1925 that most occupy Cheney in this biography, years filled with poetry and lovers. Floyd Dell, Edmund Wilson, Arthur Davison Ficke, Witter Bynner, John Reed, Max Eastman, Jig Cook, John Peale Bishop, Norma Millay, Malcom Cowley, Kenneth Burke, Wallace Stevens, Theodore Dreiser, Eugene O'Neill—these were prominent literary and personal influences on Millay. The author concludes that her marriage to the wealthy, paternal Eugen Boissevain marked a decline in Millay's poetry, though it seems to have been a happy relationship. Cheney provides a good bibliography, but Karl Yost's *Bibliography of the Works of Edna St. Vincent Millay* (1936) remains most reliable. Cheney has written a psychological rather than a comprehensive biography. Students will want to be aware of Norman Brittin's *Edna St. Vincent Millay* (Twayne, 1967) and Miriam Gurko's *Restless Spirit* (Crowell, 1962).

110   Chesnut, Mary Boykin (Miller), 1823-1886. **A Diary from Dixie.** Boston: Houghton Mifflin, 1949. 572p. index. $7.50. ISBN 0395083257. LC 49-11694.

Ben Ames Williams, the editor of this important diary kept by a southern lady from 1861 to 1865, spends some time in his introduction rehearsing Mrs. Chestnut's qualifications as a diarist: her friendships with the important leaders of the Confederate army and government, her intelligence and scope of reading, her flair for writing, her ability to objectively perceive situations even when the complexities engulfed her husband and friends, her interest in recounting and chronicling current events as they unfolded, and her knowledge of all strata of the society in which she moved, including black society. "Here are men and women of flesh and blood, infinitely more human in their faults and their fancies, their flirtations and frivolities, their sins and their sorrows, their laughter and their tears than the lay figures which march solemnly through the pages of so many pages of fact or fiction dealing with the Southern scene."

111   Chevigny, Bell Gale. **The Woman and the Myth: Margaret Fuller's Life and Writings.** Old Westbury, NY: Feminist Press, 1976. bibliog. $6.50. ISBN 0912670436. LC 76-19030.

In 1883, James Freeman Clark commented to the literary man, Thomas Wentworth Higginson, of Margaret Fuller: "Margaret had so many aspects to her soul that she might furnish material for a hundred biographers, and not all could be said even then." Both a biography and critical reading of Fuller's work, this important study comments on the literary and social milieu in which Fuller moved as a friend of such luminaries as Emerson and Hawthorne, and as editor of *The Dial* and literary critic of the *New York Tribune.*

112   Chicago, Judy, 1939- . **Through the Flower. My Struggle as a Woman Artist.** Garden City, NY: Doubleday, 1975. 226p. bibliog. index. $8.95. ISBN 0385097824. LC 74-12680.

Judy Chicago articulates her life experiences and her commitment to the idea of developing a female art, of shaping a new female education and of transforming traditional cultural values. Chicago's extraordinary strength, talent, imagination, and energy suffuse every page of this autobiography, which deserves a place on reading lists for all art courses that claim to be feminist. She includes several performance pieces from feminist art groups with which she has been affiliated.

113   Chisholm, Shirley, 1924- . **The Good Fight.** New York: Harper and Row, 1973. 206p. index. $10.00. ISBN 0060107642. LC 72-10680.

In 1972, Chisholm ran for the presidency of the United States in the primary campaigns. In this book, she shares her impressions of the bewildering 1972 campaign, which saw McGovern running for President, George Wallace shot as he campaigned, and the country staggering in the aftermath of assassinations and the daily toll of the Vietnam War. Two appendices include position papers and campaign speeches by Chisholm, including a speech on the topic, "Economic Justice for Women."

114   Chisholm, Shirley, 1924- . **Unbought and Unbossed.** Boston: Houghton Mifflin, 1970. 117p. $5.95. ISBN 0395109329. LC 79-120834.

In Chisholm's autobiography (to 1970), her chapters include: Early Years in Barbados; Back to Brooklyn: Teaching, Marriage and the Political Arena; Running for Congress; How I View the Congress; Facing the Abortion Question; and Women and Their Liberation.

115   Christie, Agatha Miller, Dame, 1891-1976. **An Autobiography.** New York: Dodd, Mead, 1977. 529p. index. $15.00. ISBN 0396075169. LC 77-11689.

Agatha Christie's autobiography will, of course, fascinate the many avid readers of her detective novels, but it also can delight and amuse solely on its own merits. Christie recounts her life story from childhood to the age of 75, including tales of her travels, her friendships, her two marriages, motherhood, and, of course, her writing. She pauses frequently to make little asides on a wide range of topics, which greatly contributes to the reader's sense of this woman's vibrant and witty personality. Thirty-two photographs and paintings of Christie and the people and places important to her are interspersed throughout the autobiography.

116*   Clark, Septima (Poinsette), 1898- . **Echo in My Soul.** New York: E. P. Dutton, 1962. 243p. LC 62-14718.

Septima Clark's autobiography was highly praised when it first appeared in 1962 both for its sense of personal drama and for the history it depicts. Clark is a black woman whose life has been devoted to education of blacks and the civil rights struggle. She first taught on Johns Island off the coast of her native Charleston, South Carolina. Later she was active in the NAACP in Charleston, when it was an extremely risky involvement. She then worked at the Highlander School, a private integrated school in the Cumberland Mountains of Tennessee, until it was closed in 1961 by the state for political reasons. After that, she worked with Dr. Martin Luther King's Southern Christian Leadership Conference.

117   Cody, John, 1925- . **After Great Pain: The Inner Life of Emily Dickinson.** Cambridge, MA: Belknap Press of Harvard University Press, 1971. 538p. index. $15.00. ISBN 0674008782. LC 79-148937.

Cody attempts a psychoanalytic interpretation of Dickinson's life, carefully reading the poetry to grasp the psychological implication in her art. Careful attention is given to her use of symbols such as the sun, the bee, noon, winter, the eye—recurring again and again in the poetry and in her letters. Psychographer Cody equates these repetitions to the psychiatrist's use of the free association technique. Beginning with a review of the work of commentators on Dickinson's life, the book moves into an analysis of the poet's relationship to mother, father, and home. Other chapters deal with her years of latency in Amherst, the effect of her brother's courtship, the dynamics of her nervous breakdown, and the effect of her psychological imbalance on the creative process. Quotations from her poetry and letters are used liberally throughout. Because the preoccupation of this biography by a practicing psychiatrist is with the inner life of Dickinson, readers will want to turn to other biographers—Millicent Todd Bingham, Thomas H. Johnson, and Richard Chase, among others—for comprehensive biographical material. Jean McClure Mudge's *Emily Dickinson and the Image of Home* (University of Massachusetts Press, 1975) intensively explores the use of the house as a representation of the poet's inner reality. Because Mudge writes from the perspective of curator of the Dickinson homestead in Amherst, her knowledge of the home and its biographical relationship to the development of the poetic imagery provides a unique critical insight into Emily Dickinson's poetry.

118   Coles, Robert, and Jane Hallowell Coles. **Women of Crisis: Lives of Struggle and Hope.** New York: Delacorte Press/S. Lawrence, 1978. 291p. bibliog. $10.00. ISBN 0440095360. LC 78-5068.

As part of the Radcliffe Biographies series (which seeks "to hold a mirror up to the lives of particular women, to pay tribute to them, and so to deepen our understanding of them and ourselves"), it is significant that this volume examines the lives of women who are poor, who have struggled, but who have led interesting lives. They have been successful in attempting to impose order and meaning on their existences. Ruth James is a black migrant worker whose indomitable will turned her foreman's lust into respect for her as an individual. She achieved a modicum of personal and financial independence when he bought her a gas station to manage. Hannah Morgan is an Appalachian woman transplanted to the city, making her way in the brutal routine of factory life and helping her teen-aged daughter through the maze of sexual and drug problems in the city. The two other women are Lorna, an Alaskan Eskimo, and Helen, a white maid serving her neurotic Cambridge, Massachusetts, employers with great wariness and perceptiveness. These women present themselves and their experiences in their own eloquent voices; analysis by the Coles seems natural and unobtrusive. The link between class and sex is emphasized by the Coles and taken for granted by the women. A nice feature of this book is the essay form of the bibliography, which rambles over the territory of the literature on women from the authors' personal perspective.

119   Colette, Sidonie Gabrielle, 1873-1954. **Earthly Paradise: An Auto-biography, Drawn from Her Lifetime Writings.** New York: Farrar, Straus and Giroux, 1966. 505p. $5.95. ISBN 0374634009. LC 65-23837.

This translation of *Autobiographie tirée des oeuvres de Colette*, compiled by Robert Phelps and translated by Herma Briffault, Derek Coltman, and others, draws materials from the large corpus of Colette's autobiographical prose—portraits, memoirs, essays and *chroniques*. The personality of the novelist of *Gigi*, *Chéri*, and *Claudine* glows penetratingly through the accounts of love and work and observation that are gathered here. The editor provides a detailed chronology by which the reader can fix the dates of details, marriages, major literary accomplishments, and literary friendships in a life that must be considered extraordinary by any standard. This is a book of exquisite prose remarkable for its observations of people and nature. Readers may also be interested in a biography of Colette recently reprinted: Maurice Gondeket's *Close to Colette: An Intimate Portrait of a Woman of Genius* (originally 1957; reprint by Greenwood Press).

120*   Colson, Elizabeth, 1917- , ed. **Autobiographies of Three Pomo Women.** Berkeley: Archeological Research Facility, Dept. of Anthropology, University of California, 1974. 235p.

Reprinted here are the life-histories of three Pomo women, collected in the early 1940s, when the women were in their late fifties or sixties. The Pomo are Native Americans originally from northern California, whose culture was disrupted by whites about the end of the first half of the nineteenth century. Born in the 1870s and 1880s, these three women were raised by Pomo relatives, had little or no schooling, and spoke and thought in Pomo. In short, the dominant influences in their lives were Pomo. The life histories were prepared for publication in 1945 and published in 1956 in volume 1 of *Primary Records in Culture and Personality*, as a microcard publication. The original manuscript has been reprinted here without revisions or additions, including the outdated bibliography. However, an annotated bibliography of autobiographical statements by other Native Americans of California (eight of the sixteen are by women) appears at the end of the preface. The life histories are preceded by Colson's introductory essay on the Pomo.

121   Conrad, Earl. **Harriet Tubman.** New York: P. S. Eriksson, 1969. 248p. bibliog, index. $4.95. ISBN 083973025X.

First published in 1943 (apparently with difficulty; Conrad informs us it was rejected by white publishers), this is a very thorough biography of Harriet Tubman (1820?-1913), the famous "conductor" on the Underground Railroad. Tubman guided scores of slaves on secret routes from southern plantations to safety in Canada, despite the threat of the brutal Fugitive Slave Law. In his research for this book, Conrad began by verifying the much briefer nineteenth-century biography by Sarah Bradford, then went on to do extensive investigations in numerous libraries and government record archives, as well as interviews with Tubman's living relatives. Conrad's biography carries the reader through Tubman's death in 1913, whereas Bradford's (1869) leaves off at the close of the Civil War. Ann Petry has written fine biography for young people entitled *Harriet Tubman: Conductor on the Underground Railroad* (Crowell, 1955).

122   Cornish, Nellie Centennial, 1876-1956. **Miss Aunt Nellie: The Auto-biography of Nellie C. Cornish.** Seattle: University of Washington Press, 1964. 283p. index. $8.95. ISBN 0295738480. LC 64-25730.

The autobiography of Nellie Centennial (born in the year of the Philadelphia Centennial) Cornish, the energetic and innovative woman who in 1914 founded the Cornish School in Seattle. The Cornish School provided comprehensive training in the arts, including music, painting, dance, sculture, and drama; and it eventually attracted students from around the world. Cornish describes her family and childhood but devotes most of the account to the years of her involvement with the School, 1914 to 1939.

123   Craigin, Elisabeth. **Either Is Love.** New York: Harcourt, Brace, 1937; repr. New York: Arno Press, 1975. 155p. $9.00. ISBN 0405073798. LC 75-12311.

A middle-aged woman reminisces about her late, loved husband and the history of their relationship, begun late in their thirties. Both came to the relationship from previous, passionate attachments: his wife was recently and tragically killed in a car accident; the nature of her former love was for some time left a mystery. The story of this early love affair eventually unfolds in the form of her confessional letters to her husband and what comes forth is a passionate and moving account of deep love between two women.

124   Cressy, Earl Herbert. **Daughters of Changing Japan.** New York: Farrar, Straus, and Cudahy, 1955; repr. Westport, CT: Greenwood Press, 1975. 305p. $15.25. ISBN 0837180236. LC 75-390.

Cressy explains that his book rests on the narratives of ten Japanese young women who wrote in 1953 the stories of their lives and families for Cressy's use. Most of the accounts detail the restlessness of Japanese young women "striving for the basic freedoms that have been taken for granted. . . ." The final portrait, that of Aiko, sketches a conservative young woman who accepts the conventional mores of Japanese middle-class society in the 1950s. From the author's experience in meeting Aiko, he concludes: "not a specialist, nothing spectacular, nothing extraordinary. Prudent, honest, faithful. Perhaps here is the basic essence of Japanese womanhood." Much good material on the perceptions of young women (of the '50s) on marriage, love, parent-child relationships, and clothing.

125   Cromwell, Otelia. **Lucretia Mott.** Cambridge, MA: Harvard University Press; repr. New York: Russell and Russell, 1971. 241p. bibliog. index. $14.00. ISBN 0846215799. LC 79-139913.

Lucretia Mott (1793-1880) is an important figure in the history of nineteenth-century reform movements in the United States. Born and raised a Quaker—and even serving briefly as a Quaker minister—it was out of Mott's sense of frustration with the constriction of religious narrowness that her other reform commitments grew. She became involved early in the century with the anti-slavery movement and remained active in its radical wing throughout her lifetime. It was her exclusion from recognition as a woman delegate to the 1840 World's Anti-Slavery Convention in London that moved her to translate her feminist beliefs into political activism around women's rights. Eight years later in Seneca Falls, New York, Mott and Elizabeth Cady Stanton (whom she had met at the 1840 London convention) organized the first woman's rights convention and issued the demand for woman suffrage. Thenceforth, Mott maintained an active commitment to the movements for religious liberalization, for abolition and (after the Civil War) black equality, and for women's rights. The Cromwell biography is described as the "most complete and scholarly" by Frederick B. Tolles in *Notable American Women*. Its bibliography of manuscript and print primary sources is particularly valuable. A key primary source recommended by Cromwell is *James and Lucretia Mott: Life and Letters*, edited by their granddaughter, Anna Davis Hallowell (Houghton Mifflin, 1896).

126   Crosland, Margaret, 1920- . **Colette—The Difficulty of Loving: A Biography.** Indianapolis, IN: Bobbs-Merrill, 1973. 284p. bibliog. index. $8.95. ISBN 0672517604. LC 73-1741.
This biography of Colette (1873-1954), the celebrated French author of 73 books, is a well-researched, readable account of Colette's varied life and includes careful analyses of Colette's literary work, too. Readers interested in a more scholarly approach to Colette will do well to consult Elaine Marks's *Colette* (1960). Crosland's thesis seems to be that Colette's life, peopled as it was with lovers, husbands and friends, was essentially a solitary existence. "Unconsciously, perhaps, she knew that paradise and solitude were strangely, sadly, inescapably identical." Crosland has written further of Colette in a collection on French women writers, *Women of Iron and Velvet: French Women Writers After George Sand* (Taplinger, 1976). This readable study, generously illustrated, also looks at Marguerite Andoux, Natalie Clifford Barney, Marie Bashkirtseff, Simone de Beauvoir, Princess Marthe Bibesco, Marie-Claire Blais, Minou Drouet, Marguerite Duras, Violette Leduc, Francoise Mallet-Joris, Francoise Sagan, Nathalie Sarraute, Renée Vivien, Monique Wittig, and Marguerite Yourcenar, among others. The conclusion at which Crosland arrives: "as far as attitudes to male-dominated society are concerned, the writers will go on being *guérilleres* for some time to come."

127   Darroch, Sandra Jobson. **Ottoline: The Life of Lady Ottoline Morrell.** New York: Coward, McCann and Geoghegan, 1975. 317p. bibliog. index. $12.50. ISBN 0698106342. LC 74-16641.
Lady Ottoline Morrell (1873-1938) was born into the English tradition of wealth and privilege, a fact that made it possible for her to achieve legendary status as Bloomsbury's most sensational hostess. Intimate of literary figures (Lytton Strachey, Virginia Woolf, and T. S. Eliot), depicted in celebrated fiction (Lawrence's *Women in Love*), lover of Bertrand Russell, Ottoline is important as a literary influence though not as a creative figure in her own right. This volume is based on thousands of pieces of unpublished correspondence and provides an interesting insight into the special world that she inhabited.

128   D'Arusmont, Frances Wright [Wright, Frances], 1795-1852. **Life, Letters, and Lectures, 1834/1844.** New York: Arno Press, 1972. 220, 47, 47p. $16.00. ISBN 0405044542. LC 72-2598.

"In 1818, Frances Wright D'Arusmont (1795-1852), distant ward of LaFayette and friend of Jefferson, came from England to tour the United States. Her impressions, recorded in personal correspondence, were published in 1821 and immediately acclaimed. But a return trip in 1824 led to a journey on the Mississippi River which modified her initial enthusiasms about the New World and focused her interest on the evils of slavery. She founded a Black Utopian settlement in Nashoba, near Memphis. It failed, among rumors that it had encouraged free love. In lectures, pamphlets and in the *Free Enquirer*, which she edited with Robert Dale Owen, she advocated liberation of blacks, equality for women, liberalized divorce laws, birth control, political action, workingmen's parties, and revolution—earning from the self-righteous the title of 'great red harlot of infidelity' " ("A Note about This Volume," Annette Baxter and Leon Stein, editors). This reprint volume includes: 1) Course of Popular Lectures (with an analytical table of contents); 2) Supplement Course of Lectures; and 3) Biography, Notes, and Political Letters. These writings look to be fairly demanding; the reader might benefit by reading the autobiographical sections first to put the balance of the material in perspective. Other biographical sources on Wright are Alice J. G. Perkins and Theresa Wolfson's *Frances Wright, Free Enquirer* (orig. 1939; repr. Porcupine Press, 1972) and Richard Stiller's *Commune on the Frontier* (Thomas Y. Crowell, 1972).

129   Davidson, Sara. **Loose Change: Three Women of the Sixties.** Garden City, NY: Doubleday, 1977. 367p. $9.50. ISBN 0385036302. LC 76-2766.

An autobiographical and somewhat anecdotal work picturing the awakening of the writer and two sorority sisters as they arrived at Berkeley in 1967, before it became a symbol of unrest, and then experienced both evolutionary and, at times, shocking change in succeeding years of the decade. Neither Sara nor her suite-mates "Susie Hersh" and "Natasha Taylor" (both pseudonyms) had any premonition of the turmoil they would be involved in or of the changes they would help engineer. From their interests in the traditional campus concerns of a disappearing era, the young women became part of the movement to destroy the establishment and to turn American society around by force and by altering value systems that they deemed failures. One theme of the book is that change for its own sake, irrespective of rhetoric, and without carefully designed goals, can be an empty and unnecessarily destructive process. The author points out that the children of the 1960s were often hurt and usually disappointed because their personal expectations were exceedingly unrealistic. In the last sentences of the book, Davidson relates how her life continues to evolve, without despair and with an optimism tempered by realism.

130   Davies, Margaret Llewelyn, 1861- , ed. **Life As We Have Known It.** London: The Hogarth Press, 1931; repr. New York: Norton, 1975. 141p. $2.95. ISBN 0393007723. LC 75-14138.

This is a collection of writings by working-class women in the English Women's Co-operative Guild early in this century, which should be of interest to those looking to women's own writings as the basis for a new and less phallocentric social history. The women are of diverse backgrounds, but all write about their loves—work, marriage, childbirth and childraising, and conflict among these, especially under conditions of poverty. The collection also includes a letter from Virginia Woolf to the editor, Margaret Llewelyn Davies (who had asked her to write a preface to the book). The letter is interesting both for what it conveys of Virginia Woolf's political sentiments and as a general statement on the ambiguity of potential solidarity between women of different classes.

131   Davis, Allen Freeman, 1931- . **American Heroine: The Life and Legend of Jane Addams.** New York: Oxford University Press, 1975. 339p. bibliog. index. $3.95. ISBN 0195018974. LC 73-82664.

Davis, whose interest in Jane Addams (1860-1935) grew out of his work on the settlement movement, has two purposes in this book on Addams: first, to put together a careful account of the life, motivations, and work of this famous social reformer, feminist, and pacifist of turn-of-the-century America, in a way that goes beyond the myths and legend of the woman as precocious child or saintly woman; and second, to examine the legends themselves for what they can tell us about U.S. society from 1889 to 1935. Davis spends much time on the period leading to the founding of Hull House and the early years at Hull House, but also discusses Addam's involvement in other social movements including woman suffrage, the Progressive movement, and pacifism. He is both admiring and critical of Addams, attentive to her contradictions and limitations. The standard biography of Addams is James Weber Linn's *Jane Addams: A Biography* (Appleton-Century, 1935; repr. Greenwood Press, 1968). A nephew of Addams, Linn was the recipient of all of Addams's manuscripts (published and unpublished), letters, records, and clippings. His work is based on this voluminous collection, as well as on his personal relationship with Addams over the course of almost sixty years. In addition, Addams was able prior to her death to approve much of the manuscript.

132   Davis, Almond H. **The Female Preacher; Or, Memoir of Salome Lincoln.** New York: Arno Press, 1972. (Repr. of 1843 ed.). 162p. $9.50. ISBN 0405044895. LC 72-2599.

"Little is known about Salome Lincoln Mowry (1804-1841) before May, 1829 when, with her co-workers, she joined in a strike against a wage cut at the New England mill where they were employed. But when the others, no longer able to endure, returned to work, Salome Lincoln parted company with them and journeyed from town to town throughout New England, spreading the word that in the eyes of the Lord all were equal, and that women as well as men had the right to speak forth" ("A Note about This Volume," A. K. Baxter and L. Stein, eds.).

133   Davis, Angela Yvonne, 1944- . **Angela Davis: An Autobiography.** New York: Random House, 1974. 400p. $8.95. ISBN 0394489780. LC 73-20580.

Political repression is the theme of this moving autobiographical account of Davis's experiences up to and including her trial and acquittal for the Marin County Courthouse murder of a California judge in August 1970. A fascinating and inspiring writer, Davis is always in control of her story even when describing the sometimes inhuman treatment she received from her jailers and the insane interpretation of justice regularly meted out to blacks in the American judicial system. Intensely personal as well as political, Angela Davis describes her modest family background, her experiences in Birmingham as a child, her student days at Brandeis and in Europe when Herbert Marcuse was her mentor, and her radical political activities in California with a thoughtfulness and grace that illustrate her sense of presence even in the face of incredible odds. She is particularly fine when she is describing the oppression of jails and the personalities of jailers and the jailed—all products of the repressive system Davis has fought as a socialist. The plight of the political prisoner is especially on Davis's mind. Though Davis talks of this at some length in her autobiography, readers will want to be aware of a collection of essays edited by Davis, *If They Come in the Morning* (The Third Press, 1971), which describes her own experience as a political prisoner and the larger experience of blacks and political repression.

134   Decossart, Michael. **The Food of Love: Princesse Edmond de Polignac (1865-1943) and Her Salon.** London: H. Hamilton, 1978. 243p. bibliog. index. ISBN 0241897858.

A well-reviewed biography of the Singer Sewing Machine fortune heiress, *Food of Love* describes the international reputation that the Duchesse de Polignac maintained as a patron of the arts and a friend of celebrities. A lesbian, she carried on her affairs with great, almost grim, discretion. The Duchesse de Polignac was her title by marriage.

135   Deiss, Joseph Jay. **The Roman Years of Margaret Fuller: A Biography.** New York: Crowell, 1969. 338p. bibliog. index. $4.95. ISBN 0690010176. LC 70-81941.

Diess notes that most biographies of Margaret Fuller (e.g., *Woman in the Nineteenth Century*) have emphasized her American experience to the neglect of "the dramatic Roman climax of her life" in the late 1840s. This period is controversial for a number of reasons. First, her task of reporting on the turbulent events in Italy, 1847-1850, brought into focus her deepening political radicalism. Second, it was during this time that Fuller, characterized as a spinster and a bluestocking in the States, took an Italian lover and bore his child (whether/when they married is still a matter for debate). Deiss writes the story of this period in Fuller's life, making extensive use of manuscript and archival material as well as Fuller's works and secondary sources, quoting frequently from Fuller herself. Readers will also want to be aware of a new, feminist biography of Fuller: Paula Blanchard's *Margaret Fuller: From Transcendentalism to Revolution* (1978).

136   Demeter, Anna. **Legal Kidnapping: What Happens to a Family When the Father Kidnaps Two Children.** Boston: Beacon Press, 1977. 148p. bibliog. $8.95. ISBN 0807027421. LC 76-48502.

On the surface, this true story of the kidnapping of a woman's two children by her estranged husband may seem bizarre and unreal; the issues raised by Anna Demeter (pseudonym of the woman physician who is the mother of the kidnapped children) are, however, shockingly commonplace. When Anna Demeter stands firm in her intention of seeking a divorce from her tyrannical husband (also a physician), he retaliates by kidnapping two of the couple's four children, ages two and six. Demeter's narrative of her fearful marriage, which she knew she must dissolve though she was in terror of her husband's uncontrollable temper, is as much the point of this tale as the kidnapping and custody issue. Many women who have contemplated divorce will find familiar Anna Demeter's psychological fears of her husband. In the eloquent foreword, Adrienne Rich writes of this story: "its meaning—and the only purpose in its telling—lies in that commonality. Everyone—whether woman, man, or child—is diminished by the conventions that allow or encourage men to exercise rights of property ownership over their wives and children." There is another lesson here: namely, that women, no matter their professional status, may be perceived as aberrant or at fault in domestic struggles if the issue is a woman's independence of body and spirit.

137   De Mille, Agnes. **Where the Wings Grow.** Garden City, NY: Doubleday,
        1978. 286p. $8.95. ISBN 0385121067. LC 76-18339.
In this particularly fine and sensitively remembered memoir, Agnes de Mille offers a lyrical recollection of girlhood, young womanhood, and womanhood as an experience of wholeness and continuity. De Mille is a dancer, choreographer, and writer.

138   Dennis, Peggy. **The Autobiography of an American Communist: A
        Personal View of a Political Life, 1925-1975.** Westport, CT: L. Hill,
        1977. 302p. index. $12.95. ISBN 0882080814. LC 77-23607.
Peggy Dennis's autobiography is written with sensitivity, honesty, and perhaps too much modesty in the recounting of her own considerable achievements. Born into a Russian immigrant communist family, Peggy Dennis's has indeed been "a political life," including a fifty-year commitment to the Communist Party, U.S.A., which she only terminated (with pain and reluctance) in 1976. There is a great deal to interest contemporary feminists in this woman's rich lifetime of experience with political struggle and political thought and in her clearsighted assessments, as a socialist and a feminist, of political movements. At the center of her story is her 33-year relationship with Gene Dennis, who died of cancer sixteen years before this book was written. With characteristic candor, she describes the ambivalence of a tie that offered deep intimacy of a rare sort, but demanded great sacrifices from her, as she struggled to hold her own in relation to a very dynamic, driven, and internationally prominent man, while carrying disproportionate responsibility for child care and household demands. In her treatment of both political and personal history, Dennis demonstrates a willingness to admit and accept complexity and contradiction. Interested readers might also want to look at Vivian Gornick's sensitive portraits of American communists in *The Romance of American Communism* (1977), and the excellent review of both Gornick and Dennis in *Chrysalis*, no. 5, 1977. The *Chrysalis* piece discusses another personal account of the American Communist Party experience that may be of interest: *A Fine Old Conflict*, by Jessica Mitford (Knopf, 1977).

139   Deutsch, Helene, 1884- . **Confrontations With Myself: An Epilogue.**
        New York: Norton, 1973. 217p. bibliog. $6.95. ISBN 0393074722.
        LC 73-4380.

This autobiography is of interest for at least two reasons. First, Deutsch was an important early disciple of Freud, and in *Confrontations* she relates the story of her growing up, her work, her marriage, and motherhood. Second, Deutsch's major work, *The Psychology of Women,* has aroused considerable feminist wrath in recent years for its Freudian orthodoxy, and this memoir provides a way of putting the theories developed in that book into perspective. She begins her preface to *Confrontations* by saying, "only after completing this autobiography did I realize that it forms a supplement to the autobiography hidden in my general work *The Psychology of Woman.* That is why I have decided to call this book an epilogue."

140   Devlin, Bernadette, 1947- . **The Price of My Soul.** New York: Vintage
       Books, 1970. 224p. $1.95. ISBN 0394708431. LC 71-44605.
Delvin writes with candor and anger of her radicalism as leader of the Catholic protest movement (1968-1969), during which Northern Ireland monopolized world headlines. Growing up in a poor Catholic Republican family, she explains, made her a socialist and civil rights advocate. Her winning a seat in Parliament at age 21 was due to a constellation of social, economic, and political problems out of which she emerged a candidate by the process of elimination. Her contempt for many members of Parliament and the press that sought to exploit her is expressed forcefully: "they have discovered that their little child of Parliament is a monster who doesn't care about their Parliament, or their parliamentary system, or their parliamentary formalities, or their parliamentary parties." Throughout she asserts her conviction that hers is not a quarrel between the ideologies of Catholicism and Protestantism, but rather a struggle against the oppression of the Unionist Party government.

141   Dickinson, Emily, 1830-1886. **The Letters of Emily Dickinson.** Edited
       by Thomas H. Johnson and Theodora Ward. Cambridge, MA: Belknap
       Press of Harvard University Press, 1958. 3v. index. $30.00. ISBN
       0674526252. LC 58-5594.
Johnson is the editor of the complete Dickinson corpus—poetry and prose. The letters are a meticulously gathered and ordered collection culled from libraries and private collections throughout the United States, chiefly from the American Antiquarian Society, Amherst College, Harvard College, the New York Public Library, and Yale University Library. Letters are arranged in clusters that parallel biographical segments of her life in Amherst, a life lived exclusively at home after her thirtieth year. Many of the letters were written in draft and recopied. Johnson has dated much of the correspondence, since Emily rarely dated her letters after 1850. The editor of Dickinson's works remarks of the correspondence: "The noteworthy characteristic of the Dickinson letters, like that of the poems, is acute sensitivity. Indeed, early in the 1860s, when Emily Dickinson seems to have first gained assurance of her destiny as a poet, the letters both in style and rhythm begin to take on qualities that are so nearly the quality of her poems as on occasion to leave the reader in doubt where the letter leaves off and the poem begins." Volume 1 contains letters from 1842-1854; volume 2, 1855-1879; volume 3, 1880-1886. Volume 3 also contains appendices, including biographical sketches of recipients of the letters and individuals mentioned in them. An index and index of poems are in volume 3.

142   Dickinson, Emily, 1830-1886. **Selected Letters.** Edited by Thomas
         H. Johnson. Cambridge, MA: Belknap Press of Harvard University
         Press, 1971. 364p. bibliog. $15.00. ISBN 0674250605. LC 78-129120.
This comprises selections from the three-volume collection, *The Letters of
Emily Dickinson*, annotated above.

143   Douglas, Emily Taft, 1899- . **Margaret Sanger: Pioneer of the Future.**
         Garrett Park, MD: Garrett Park Press, 1975. 298p. bibliog. index.
         $8.50. ISBN 0912048751. LC 75-19862.
A biography of the woman who devoted her life to the effort to make birth
control knowledge and technology available to women in a legal context that
identified birth control with obscenity. First published in 1970, Douglas's
study gives an account of Sanger's life from her birth in 1879 to her death in
1966. For readers with further interest in Sanger's life and crusade, *Woman's
Body, Woman's Right*, by Linda Gordon, provides a history of Sanger's work
set within the context of a social history of birth control in the United States.
Readers may also want to consult Margaret Sanger's autobiography or the following biographies: *Birth Control in America*, by David M. Kennedy (1970);
Margaret Sanger: Woman Rebel, by Vivian L. Werner (Hawthorn Books, 1970);
and *The Margaret Sanger Story and the Fight for Birth Control* (orig. 1955);
repr. Greenwood Press, 1975).

144   Dreier, Mary E. **Margaret Dreier Robins: Her Life, Letters, and Work.**
         New York: Island Press Cooperative, 1950; repr. Washington: Zenger,
         1975. 278p. index. $11.95. ISBN 0892010169. LC 75-34239.
This biography is "the best published source" on Margaret Dreier Robins (1868-
1945), according to Allen F. Davis in *Notable American Women*. Robins was
active and highly influential in the Women's Trade Union League (WTUL)
during its years of greatest efficacy (1904 to World War I). The League was an
organization largely drawn from the middle and upper class that sought to
organize working women into unions and to improve their working conditions
through labor legislation. As such, it has been seen as an important example of
women's cross-class organizing during a period when the suffrage cause was
increasingly attracting conservative women with narrow aims. Much of Robins's
work centered in Chicago, where she was in contact with Jane Addams and the
settlement movement. She was also very involved in the garment workers' strikes
of 1909-1911 in Chicago, New York, and Philadelphia and worked several years
as editor of the WTUL's *Life and Labor*. Readers interested in the work of the
WTUL should also be aware of Alice Henry's two books, *The Trade Union
Woman* (orig. 1915; repr. B. Franklin, 1973) and *Women and the Labor Movement*
(orig. 1923; repr. Arno Press, 1971). Originally from Australia, Henry emigrated
to the United States in 1906 and was soon working with the WTUL as office
secretary of its Chicago branch. Later she helped found and edited *Life and
Labor*. Her two books discuss the history of unionism among women, the
WTUL, women's working conditions, and labor legislation.

145   Drinnon, Richard. **Rebel in Paradise: A Biography of Emma Goldman.**
         New York: Harper and Row, 1976. 349p. bibliog. index. $4.45. ISBN
         0060904690.

A biography—first published in 1961 and based on the author's thesis—of one
of the most inspiring and beloved heroines of the contemporary women's movement, Emma Goldman (1869-1940). Immigrant to the United States from Russia,
Goldman was an anarchist and feminist, an eloquent orator and writer, one of
the earliest birth control activists (whose historical contribution to this movement
is often neglected), a critic of communism who nonetheless sought eagerly to
make a contribution to the fledgling Soviet Union, a passionate supporter of
the Catalonian revolutionaries during the Spanish Civil War—and, what is particularly meaningful for women in the current movement, she was a woman who
fought courageously to integrate her anarchist and feminist politics into her
personal life and relationships, in a much less tolerant era than our own. A lengthy
bibliographical essay on Goldman's life and works is appended. Readers may
also wish to explore Goldman's autobiography *Living My Life*, and Alix Kates
Shulman's book, *To the Barricades: The Anarchist Life of Emma Goldman*
(1971).

146   Du Maurier, Daphne, Dame, 1907- . **Myself When Young: The Shaping
      of a Writer.** Garden City, NY: Doubleday, 1977. 204p. index. $7.95.
      ISBN 0385130163. LC 76-56283.
Du Maurier's background was a brilliant one: daughter of Gerald du Maurier,
the famous actor and manager. Cornwall, England, played a significant part in
her childhood, in her married life, and in her novels.

147*   Dunham, Katherine. **A Touch of Innocence.** New York: Harcourt,
       Brace and World, 1959. 312p. LC 59-10256.
Katherine Dunham—a celebrated black dancer and choreographer with her own
dance company—prefaces this book with the following: "this book is not an
autobiography. It is a story of a world that has vanished, as it was for one child
who grew up in it—the Middle West through the boom years after the First
World War, and in the early years of the Depression. . . ." Dunham then goes
on to recount the moving story of her first nineteen years, speaking of herself
in the third person. *A Touch of Innocence* was widely and very favorably reviewed
when it appeared in 1959, primarily for its vividness as a family chronicle and
for its depiction of a young black woman's growing up. There is little in the
account about dance, as it concludes when Dunham breaks free of her family
at the age of nineteen, after she had passed the civil service examination to become
a librarian.

148   Earhart, Amelia, 1898-1937. **The Fun of It: Random Records of My
      Own Flying and of Women in Aviation.** Detroit, MI: Gale Research,
      1975. (Repr. of 1932 ed.). 218p. $14.00. ISBN 081034078X. LC
      71-159945.
In this breezy autobiographical account of growing up and becoming interested
in flying, Amelia Earhart applies the light touch for which she became so famous
and leaves out details of family difficulties in her youth. Her account of the
fame that came to her from flying is modest and understated. Flying and
anything to do with flying emerge as the joys of her life, again understated.
An excellent biographical sketch of Earhart is Katherine A. Brick's article in
Notable American Women. Muriel Earhart Morrissey has written an authoritative

full-length biography, *Courage Is the Price* (1963). Publisher George Putnam's biographical account is *Soaring Wings* (1939). Earhart's own books include *20 Hrs. 40 Min.* (1929) and the posthumously published *Last Flight* (1937). Earhart is very supportive of other women pilots' achievements in *The Fun of It*. She provides background of early efforts and includes several illustrations and photographs of pioneers.

149   Ellis, Anne, 1875-1938. **The Life of an Ordinary Woman.** Boston: Houghton Mifflin, 1929; repr. New York: Arno Press, 1974. 300p. $20.00. ISBN 0405060920. LC 74-3946.

A volume in the Arno reprint series, Women in America, this is the personal history of Anne Ellis and her pioneer family, who crossed the plains by ox team and came to settle in the mining camps of Colorado. Life in Colorado as Ellis describes it during the late nineteenth century was a colorful affair, though rough and brutal in many respects. The author did stints as a domestic, a baker, laundress, boarding house proprietress, and nurse, and she coped variously with poverty, her mother's early death, the care of siblings, and later her own family, always striving for beauty and culture in the midst of the very difficult and grimly realistic business of life in the Colorado mining camps. Ellis wrote two other books, the autobiographical *Plain Anne Ellis* (1931) and the narrative of her asthma experiences, *Sunshine Preferred* (1934).

150   Engel, Barbara Alpern, and Clifford N. Rosenthal, comps. **Five Sisters: Women Against the Tsar.** New York: Knopf, 1975; repr. New York: Schocken Books, 1977. 254p. bibliog. index. $6.95. ISBN 0805205616. LC 76-48814.

Engel and Rosenthal have edited and translated the memoirs (previously unavailable in English) of five revolutionary Russian women, politicized in the first wave of revolution in Russia (1860 onward): Vera Figner (1852-1943); Vera Zasulich (1849-1919); Praskovia Iranovskia (b. 1853); Olga Liubatovich (1854-1917); and Elizaveta Kovalskaia (1849?-1933). They differed in social and geographic background, but they were all affected by the populist and feminist ideas circulating at the time and were all ultimately motivated by revolutionary aims grounded in the pursuit of personal and political liberation. " . . . on the one hand, these women were pioneers, rebelling against the patriarchal relationships that oppressed all women; and on the other, . . . they soon perceived that fundamental social changes were necessary to produce significant improvement in women's position." The revolutionary involvements of these women ranged from propaganda work among the peasantry to the direct confrontation of the state that culminated in the assassination of Tsar Alexander II (1881).

151   Evans, Mary Augusta Tappage, 1888- . **The Days of Augusta.** Seattle, WA: Madrona, 1977. 79p. $5.95. ISBN 0914842048.

Edited by Jean E. Speare, with photography by Robert Keziere, this is a photographic essay of Augusta Tappage, born at Soda Creek, Cariboo County, British Columbia, in 1888. The stunning black and white photographs document Augusta's life as an old woman. Augusta's mother was Soda Creek Indian, her father, French. The text appears to be poetry in Augusta's own words relating her experiences: mission school, marriage and giving birth, death and disease she has experienced, her parents and family, life in Canada and the traditions and crafts she has known. An important and beautiful source in the area of native American women.

152   Fauset, Arthur Huff, 1899- . **Sojourner Truth: God's Faithful Pilgrim.** New York: Russell and Russell, 1971. (Repr. of 1938 ed.). 187p. bibliog. index. $16.00. ISBN 0846213788. LC 75-139920.

Originally published in 1938, this is a biography of the black woman born to slave parents in New York around 1797, immortalized for her inspiring, spontaneous speech at a woman's rights convention in Akron, Ohio, in 1852 ("Dat man ober dar say dat women needs to be helped into carriages, and lifted ober ditches, and to have de best places everywhere. . . . Nobody eber helped *me* into carriages, or ober mud puddles, or give *me* any best place! And ain't I a woman?" . . .). Truth was born Isabella Van Wagener and claimed to have been reborn when she was over forty, after which she became known as Sojourner Truth and devoted her life to the abolitionist struggle. Fauset writes in a popular style, with much dialogue and reconstruction of events. The other major biography of Sojourner Truth is Hertha Pauli's *Her Name Was Sojourner Truth* (orig. 1962; Avon Books, 1976). Also of historical interest is the *Narrative of Sojourner Truth* (orig. 1878; repr. Arno Press, 1968), written for Truth by Olive Gilbert in 1850 and sold by Truth to maintain herself during her speaking tours.

153   Federal Writers' Project. **Lay My Burden Down: A Folk History of Slavery.** Edited by B. A. Botkin. Chicago: University of Chicago Press, 1945. 185p. index. $10.00. ISBN 0226067211. LC 45-5576.

"In 1934 Lawrence D. Reddick proposed to Harry L. Hopkins, director of the Federal Emergency Relief Administration, a Negro project 'to study the needs and collect the testimony of ex-slaves' in the Ohio River Valley and the lower South. In 1936 the work thus begun was continued and extended under the Works Progress Administration by white and Negro workers of the Federal Writers' Project in the states of Alabama, Arkansas, Florida, Georgia, Indiana, Kansas, Kentucky, Louisiana, Maryland, Mississippi, Missouri, North Carolina, Ohio, Oklahoma, South Carolina, Tennessee, Texas, and Virginia" (from the introduction). *Lay My Burden Down* is a selection of excerpts and complete narratives from the Slave Narrative Collection, a selection that involved reducing the bulk of the collection from over 10,000 to some 500 or 600 manuscript pages. Excerpts and narratives are arranged topically. The importance of this book for women's studies comes both from its general depiction of the experience of slavery in the U.S. through oral history and from the high percentage of women among the ex-slaves interviewed. A series of very arresting photographs is included, and a list of informants and interviewers is appended.

154   Fetherling, Dale, 1941- . **Mother Jones, The Miners' Angel: A Portrait.** Carbondale: Southern Illinois University Press, 1974. 263p. bibliog. index. $11.85. ISBN 0809306433. LC 73-12444.

Mary Harris "Mother" Jones (1830-1930) was an extraordinary woman whose fifty years of tireless activity as a labor organizer began only in the second half of her lifetime, preceded by what most would assess as a full (and tragic) life of fifty years (as dressmaker, teacher, wife and mother, and—prematurely—

widow, all of whose children died). Relatively little has been written about Mother Jones. This biography by Dale Fetherling has been called the "most complete account yet" by Fred Thompson in his introduction to Jones's autobiography. Readers will also want to look at the autobiography, written when Mother Jones was 94. Another biographical source, now out of print, is Irving Werstein's *Labor's Defiant Lady: The Story of Mother Jones* (Crowell, 1969).

155   Fischer, Christiane, 1947- , ed. **Let Them Speak for Themselves: Women in the American West, 1849-1900.** Hamden, CT: Archon Books, 1977. 346p. bibliog. index. $15.00. ISBN 0208016457. LC 77-5094.

Fischer has assembled a collection of personal narratives by women living in California, Arizona, Nevada, and Colorado in the second half of the nineteenth century. These women were originally for the most part from many different states in the U.S.; three came from Europe and one was an Indian of the Paiute tribe. Fischer observes that very few of them had participated in the decision to travel West, which meant an abrupt uprooting of their family and community lives. There are 25 accounts in the collection, representing experiences Fischer divides into seven categories: Life in Mining Camps and Mining Towns; Life on Farms and Ranches; Army Wives; Working Women; Life in the Growing Cities; Childhood and Adolescence in the West; and Life in the West as Seen through the Eyes of Travellers. Many of these narratives offer rich detail about the most mundane aspects of the women's lives ("Thursday 21st. Swept and dusted house prior to beginning the great domestic dread of the household: washing. Made bread and washed, back ached. . . ."). Fischer provides a general introduction, commentaries on each selection, a list of times and places described in the excerpts, and a list of references and suggestions for further readings on women and conditions in the West, 1849-1900.

156*   Fitzgerald-Richards, Dell. **The Rape Journal.** Oakland, CA: Women's Press Collective, 1974. 16p.

This is one woman's excruciating chronicle of rape and its legacy of terror, rendered in poetry and prose.

157   Fleming, Alice (Mulcahey), 1928- . **The Senator from Maine: Margaret Chase Smith.** New York: Dell, 1976. 142p. index. $1.25. ISBN 0440982235.

As the only woman ever to be elected to four full terms in the Senate and to serve in both houses of Congress, Margaret Chase Smith is a figure of considerable biographical significance on the American political women's scene. In this simple biography, with no bibliography, Fleming has written of Smith from her girlhood in Skowkegan, Maine, through her career as a businesswoman and her life as a political figure. Smith came to politics through the familiar pattern—her husband was a congressman who died in office. Unlike most women who have come to Congress via this route, Smith had the confidence, initiative, and backing to make a distinguished career of her own in Congress. In 1964, Smith became the first woman ever to try for the presidential nomination from a major party.

158   Flexner, Eleanor, 1908- . **Mary Wollstonecraft: A Biography.** New
       York: Coward, McCann, and Geoghegan, 1972. 307p. bibliog. index.
       $8.95. ISBN 0698104471. LC 72-76664.
Eleanor Flexner, best known for her seminal history of the Woman Suffrage
Movement, *Century of Struggle*, writes a biography of Mary Wollstonecraft—
"the woman who first effectively challenged the age-old image of her sex as
lesser and subservient human beings" and author of *A Vindication of the Rights
of Woman* (1792). Flexner focuses on the question, "how it came about that
this particular woman, virtually alone among her contemporaries, demanded
that the 'rights of man' be extended to women and that women be allowed to
enter their full human heritage." Wollstonecraft's story is inspiring, intriguing,
and tragic: the story of an early feminist, her attempts to actualize her political
beliefs in her personal life, and the tremendous price she paid for those attempts.
Readers may wish to compare Flexner's biography with Claire Tomalin's *The
Life and Death of Mary Wollstonecraft* (1975) and Margaret George's *One
Woman's "Situation": A Study of Mary Wollstonecraft* (1970). A probing
dissection of Mary's affair with Gilbert Imlay with its serious consequences,
and of her marriage occurs in Margaret Tims's *Mary Wollstonecraft, A Social
Pioneer* (Millington, 1976).

159   Flynn, Elizabeth Gurley, 1890-1964. **The Rebel Girl: An Autobiography,
       My First Life (1906-1926).** New York: International Publishers, 1973.
       351p. index. $12.50. ISBN 0717803678. LC 72-94154.
Elizabeth Gurley Flynn writes of the break-up of her marriage on the eve of
her son's birth, "his [her husband's] attitude was undoubtedly a normal one,
but I would have none of it. I did not want 'to settle down' at nineteen. A
domestic life and possibly a large family had no attractions for me. . . . I wanted
to speak and write, to travel, to meet people, to see places, to organize for the
IWW. I knew by now I could make more of a contribution to the labor movement
than he could. I would not give up." Flynn was an important labor organizer
and orator who became a socialist at age sixteen and immediately was able to
attract large audiences each evening speaking in New York City. Her planned
second autobiographical volume was never completed. This volume tells of her
childhood, her becoming a socialist, her activities as an agitator of the International
Workers of the World (IWW) and strike leader up to 1918 (including some stories
of the Lawrence Textile Strike in 1912 and the Patterson Silk Strike of 1913),
and her work in defense of civil liberties and labor rights during World War I
and its aftermath, the Palmer Raids (including the story of her work to free
Sacco and Vanzetti). The volume ends with 1927, the year during which Flynn
became so exhausted and ill that it was ten years before she could resume public
life. Flynn's views as a feminist are everywhere apparent in this stirring account.

160   Forten, Charlotte L., 1837-1914. **The Journal of Charlotte Forten:
       A Free Negro in the Slave Era.** New York: Collier Books, 1961. 286p.
       bibliog. index. $2.45.
Ray Allen Billington introduces Forten's journal: "Charlotte L. Forten was a
delicate young woman of sixteen when in 1854 she left her native Philadelphia
to launch the educational and teaching career described in the following *Journal*.
Her interests were those of other intelligent girls reared in that calm Quaker

city during its antebellum days; she read widely and with a catholic taste that embraced everything from the classics to sentimental poetry, attended lectures avidly, listened rapturously to the musical recitals of wandering artists, gazed worshipfully on the steel engravings that passed for art among unsophisticated Americans, and took mild pleasure in the ailments that were the stock in trade of all well-bred females during the Victorian era. Yet one thing distinguished Charlotte Forten from other Philadelphia belles. She was a Negro, destined to endure the constant insults that were the lot of persons of color in pre-Civil-War America." This is a fine introduction to this remarkable journal.

161   Frank, Anne, 1929-1945. **The Diary of a Young Girl.** Garden City, NY: Doubleday, 1967. 308p. $7.95. ISBN 0385040199. LC 67-66285.
Anne Frank's *Diary* is so well-known and so acclaimed that it hardly needs introduction or recommendation. In it, historical record and personal narrative are skillfully intertwined, producing a painfully moving account of two years in the adolescence of a young Jewish woman, forced with her family to live in hiding in Nazi-occupied Amsterdam during World War II. This edition includes an afterword, taken from Earnest Schnabel's *Anne Frank: A Portrait in Courage*, which provides historical background to the diary and fills in what is known of Anne Frank's life and of her ultimate death in the Nazi concentration camp at Belsen.

162   Frederics, Diana, pseud. **Diana: A Strange Autobiography.** New York: Dial Press, 1939; repr. New York: Arno Press, 1975. 284p. $15.00. ISBN 0405073593. LC 75-12315.
In what is perhaps not such a strange autobiography after all, "Diana" tells of her background, familial and social, and her attempts to fit into the "normal" construct of life around her—marriage, heterosexuality. She finally makes a break from accepted norms of behavior and finds a relationship with "Leslie." There is much pain in this autobiography and much thoughtful probing with regard to the guilt and family imbroglios that lesbians confront almost daily. Since this is a reprint of the 1939 edition (in the Arno Series on Homosexuality), perhaps Dr. Victor Robinson's introductory remarks can be understood as enlightened for the '30s: "that charming women should be lesbians is not a crime, it is simply a pity. It is not a question of ethics, but of endocrines."

163   Friedman, Myra. **Buried Alive: The Biography of Janice Joplin.** New York: Morrow, 1973. 333p. $7.95. ISBN 0688001602. LC 78-189274.
Janis Joplin's passion, rage, and despair spoke in direct and vital ways to both men and women; it would therefore be a distortion of her personality to identify her uniquely as a feminist heroine. Nonetheless, there is much in her life and all she expressed in her music that evokes the particular pain of a strong, passionate woman in search of mutuality in intimacy. Friedman's biography seems to be the most adequate of those that have appeared. She met Janis in 1968 and spent much time with her—traveling, drinking, talking—in the two years before Janis's death in 1970. Here she tells Janis's story from its beginning in conservative Port Arthur, Texas, to its conclusion in rock star fame. Among other sources on Joplin are Deborah Landau's *Janis Joplin' Her Life and Times* (Paperback Library, 1971), now out of print; David Dalton's *Janis* (Simon and

Schuster, 1971), an impressionistic collage of interviews, travelogues, photographs, *Rolling Stone* articles, and music and lyrics; and Peggy Caserta's sensationalist *Going Down With Janis* (Lyle Stuart, 1973).

164   Fromm, Gloria G., 1931- . **Dorothy Richardson: A Biography.** Urbana: University of Illinois Press, 1977. 451p. bibliog. index. $15.00. ISBN 0252006313. LC 77-8455.

Dorothy Richardson (1873-1957) occupies a strange niche in contemporary history. Compared to Joyce and Proust because of her experimental narratives, she never achieved their stature. Fromm concludes that Richardson was an important innovator who failed to achieve greatness because she was unable "to choose between art and life, to give herself up with her whole heart to the creative imagination." Her most notable masterpiece was *Pilgrimage*, a triumph of autobiographical fiction, that recorded among other involvements her affair with H. G. Wells. This is probably the definitive biography of Richardson, using the material from the Beinecke Library at Yale and augmenting that material through interviews with Richardson's friends and family. Richardson is especially important to Women's Studies as a forgotten genius and a pioneer in literary form.

165   Gandhi, Indira Nehru, 1917- . **Indira Gandhi: Speeches and Writings.** New York: Harper and Row, 1975. 221p. index. $10.00. ISBN 006011407X. LC 75-4268.

This is divided into nine major sections: Reminiscences; Gandhi and Nehru; Family Life; Speeches, 1966-1970; The Congress Party; Foreign Policy and the United Nations; Indo-Pakistan War: Birth of Bangla Desh, 1971; Speeches, 1971-71; Twenty-five Years of Independence, 1947-1972. The reader cannot help but come away from Gandhi noting the remarkable quality of her life, always a political one. Her reminiscences of Mahatma Gandhi and Nehru are particularly striking, and always we are reminded of the complexity of the Indian political climate with its fierce nationalistic segmentation, illiteracy, exponentially increasing population, and high mortality rate. The theme of the speeches is sounded again and again; she champions the building of a new social order. Though one may question Ghandi's methods, there can be no doubt that she has held one of the most difficult positions of world power, one bound to be criticized within India on issues of family planning, caste, political parties, and economic growth because of the diversity of special interests. Readers may be interested in Anand Mohan's *Indira Gandhi: A Personal and Political Biography* (Meredith Press, 1967; repr. Hawthorn Books, 1970).

166   Gaskell, Elizabeth Gleghorn Stevenson, 1810-1865. **The Life of Charlotte Brontë.** New York: Oxford University Press, 1975. 476p. $8.50. ISBN 019250214X. LC 20-26881.

Gaskell's biography of Brontë is very important, for she knew Charlotte Brontë, interviewed Brontë's father and husband as the biographer, and had extensive conversations with the novelist's lifelong friend, Ellen Nussey. The biography was written at the request of Charlotte's father, and because of this, Gaskell came up against some formidable biographical problems—how much could she reveal about the father, the husband, and Charlotte herself while the two clergymen were alive and observing her efforts? Mrs. Gaskell has been faulted for many of the details of Charlotte's life and of the Brontë family that she has omitted. But the marvel may be that she included so much with several of the principals alive when it was published in 1857. Margot Peters has written the definitive modern biography of Brontë, *Unquiet Soul* (Doubleday, 1975).

167   Gehm, Katherine. **Sarah Winnemucca: Most Extraordinary Woman of the Paiute Nation.** Phoenix, AZ: O'Sullivan Woodside, 1975. 196p. bibliog. $8.95. ISBN 0890190305. LC 75-12660.
Gehm writes a biography of Sarah Winnemucca (1844?-1891), a princess of the Paiute Nation who devoted her life to the struggle to improve the lives of Native Americans in the United States. Her life and actions have not surprisingly proved controversial, not least because of her efforts to publicize the corruption of the Indian Bureau. The biography is written for a general audience, and events in Winnemucca's life are frequently dramatized. A bibliography for further research on the Nevada Paiutes, the Bannock War of 1878, and early Nevada is appended. Readers may also want to consult Sarah Winnemucca's own book, *Life Among the Piutes—Their Wrongs and Claims* (1883).

168   George, Margaret. **One Woman's "Situation": A Study of Mary Wollstonecraft.** Urbana: University of Illinois Press, 1970. 174p. bibliog. $6.50. ISBN 0252000900. LC 70-100381.
In one of the best of the studies on Wollstonecraft, the preface discusses the critical heritage of Wollstonecraft's writings. George interweaves critical commentary of Mary the writer with biographical details of Wollstonecraft the woman and feminist. Critical documentation is excellent.

169   Gilbert, Julie Goldsmith. **Ferber: A Biography.** Garden City, NY: Doubleday, 1978. 445p. index. $10.50. ISBN 0385039603. LC 76-57512.
This biography of Ferber (1887-1968), written by Ferber's great-niece, is culled from Ferber's two autobiographical works, her diaries, notebooks and recollections of family and friends. It is the only biography of this novelist, playwright, journalist, short-story writer, and feminist of the Midwest who lived to the age of 81. A colorful and splendidly written biography, this contains many interesting photographs of Ferber and her friends.

170   Gilman, Charlotte (Perkins) Stetson, 1860-1935. **The Living of Charlotte Perkins Gilman: An Autobiography.** New York: Appleton-Century, 1935; repr. New York: Arno Press, 1972. 341p. index. $18.00. ISBN 0405044593. LC 72-2604.
According to Carl Degler (in *Notable American Women*), this autobiography is the primary source on Charlotte Perkins Gilman's life in the absence of any available papers. Gilman was a leading intellectual of the women's movement in turn-of-the-century America and her best-known book, *Women and Economics*, is one of the key theoretical works of nineteenth-century feminism. As is so often the case with critical thinkers and social activists, Gilman's acute perception regarding existing social conditions was matched by a painful estrangement from those conditions. Her first marriage and her pregnancy were

accompanied by extreme bouts of depression culminating after her daughter's birth in a complete breakdown and, ultimately, separation and divorce. Similar struggles with depression were to plague her periodically throughout her life. From 1888 to 1900, Gilman remained single, supporting herself through her writing and lectures, traveling across the United States and to Europe. She was involved in the feminist movement in California, spent some time at Jane Addam's Hull House in Chicago, and pursued her growing interest in socialism through contacts with Fabians Beatrice and Sidney Webb and G. B. Shaw in London. In 1900, she remarried, a marriage that endured until her husband's death in 1934 but which seems to have been very much on her terms. She committed suicide in 1935, suffering from breast cancer. Gilman writes at length of her feelings and her depressions, quoting often from her journal, as well as of her travels, lectures and writing.

171   Giovanni, Nikki. **Gemini: An Extended Autobiographical Statement on My First Twenty-Five Years of Being a Black Poet.** Indianapolis, IN: Bobbs-Merrill, 1972. 149p. $5.95. ISBN 0672514222. LC 75-161244.
Although Nikki Giovanni does not directly address the subject of poetry or of being a black woman poet, in a sense this very personal stream of thought—lacking in plan, bounding between extremes of playfulness and anger—is an eloquent statement about Nikki Giovanni, the poet. Her verse is militant, lacking in control, startling in its polemic, always opinionated. So is this unusual autobiography.

172   Giovanni, Nikki. **A Poetic Equation: Conversations Between Nikki Giovanni and Margaret Walker.** Washington: Howard University Press, 1974. 135p. $6.95. ISBN 0882580035. LC 73-85494.
Margaret Walker, novelist (*Jubilee*), and Nikki Giovanni, poet, talk about issues of concern to black women artists. Conversation between these women of two generations ranges from the rearing of children to the writing of poetry, from Ralph Ellison to Angela Davis, from the Poor People's Movement to the Black Panthers. Predictably, Walker strikes a moderate chord, Giovanni, a militant one.

173   Gippius, Zinaida Nikolaevna [Hippius, Zinaida], 1869-1945. **Between Paris and St. Petersburg: Selected Diaries of Zinaida Hippius.** Urbana: University of Illinois Press, 1975. 329p. bibliog. index. $12.50. ISBN 0252003071. LC 75-4857.
Many consider Hippius's diaries more impressive than her poems, short stories, and essays. In the preface to the diaries, her translator and editor of this volume, Temira Pachmuss, writes, "Hippius's diaries are works of art. Her skill as an artist is inevitably reflected in her diaries, even though they were not written for subsequent publication. They reveal aspects of her personality not expressed in her poetry or published prose works. They further illuminate her views on literature, religion, politics, freedom, ethics, love, marriage, life, death, God, the Holy Trinity—in fact, the entire evolution of her *Weltanschauung* may be reconstructed from her diaries. In them she defined her attitude toward other people, her concept of creative work, her criteria for imaginative literary criticism, and above all, her credo as a poet. Hippius's diaries, written in her minute and

graceful script, are a valuable, highly artistic personal confession. Their intrinsic value is justification for their publication in English in the present volume."

174   Giroud, Françoise, 1916- . **I Give You My Word.** Boston: Houghton-
       Mifflin, 1974. 275p. $8.95. ISBN 0395172195. LC 74-8791.
Françoise Giroud is the powerful editor of the French weekly news magazine, *L'Express.* This book was culled from about thirty hours of taped interviews, which she then shaped into an informal autobiography. As an influential media woman in France, her insights are political and historical. Her career has been spectacular: film assistant to Jean Renoir, editor of *Elle*, friend of French leaders and literati, and international journalist.

175*   Glasgow, Ellen Anderson Gholson, 1873-1945. **Letters of Ellen Glasgow.**
       Edited by Blair Rouse. New York: Harcourt, Brace, 1958. 384p. index.
       LC 58-5473.
It is revealing to look at *Letters* for information about Glasgow and her personal style. The letters (from 1897 to 1945) reveal a craftswoman much involved with the publication of her writing, family matters in Richmond and elsewhere, and health concerns. Famous names appear among her correspondents—for example, Van Wyck Brooks, Maxwell Perkins, Carl Van Vechten. But one looks in vain for wit, for humor, for feeling in these letters. By contrast, Glasgow's autobiography, *The Woman Within*, is extraordinary for its quality of letting go.

176*   Glasgow, Ellen Anderson Gholson, 1873-1945. **The Woman Within.**
       New York: Harcourt, Brace, 1954. 307p. LC 54-11329.
Some critics have argued that *The Woman Within*, Ellen Glasgow's autobiography (which appeared ten years after her death), is the finest thing she ever wrote. Glasgow's place as an American novelist ranks with those of Edith Wharton and Willa Cather. Her life in Richmond, Virginia, was marked on one level by peace and order, in that she lived and wrote in the same house in which she grew up throughout her life. On the other hand, in her private life, she experienced a good measure of personal tragedy—suicide, death, and nervous breakdowns of the closest family members; the death of her lover at an early age; and a scarcely concealed hatred of her miserly father, whom she appears to hold responsible for a good part of the family's tragedies. "My father had little compassion for the inarticulate, and his Calvinistic faith taught him, the soulless; and because of this and for many other reasons, including this iron vein of Presbyterianism, he was one of the last men on earth [my mother] should have married. Though he admired her, he never in his life, not for so much as a single minute, under-stood her. Even her beauty, since he was without a sense of beauty, eluded him." Glasgow writes with considerable candor here, and one begins to under-stand how this writer coped with tragedies over which she had no control. She poured all her energies into writing and the perfection of her craft; she gave her affection to her dogs (her father was cruel to animals), speechless creatures who returned her affection without making complex emotional demands.

177   Glendinning, Victoria. **Elizabeth Bowen.** New York: Knopf; distr.
       New York: Random House, 1978. 331p. bibliog. index. $12.50. ISBN
       0394405331. LC 77-10604.

Elizabeth Bowen (1899-1973) was a major writer of novels and of short stories.
Her best works—*The Death of the Heart* (1938), *The Heat of the Day* (1949),
and *The House in Paris* (1935)—are masterpieces of emotional intensity and humor.
Her biographer points out that she is the last of the great Anglo-Irish writers.
Much attention is given in this biography to the novelist's family home in Ireland,
Bowen's Court. Glendinning concentrates on the personal biographical material,
without much attention to the literary material except as Elizabeth Bowen
perceived her own effort. Consult Edwin Kenney's *Elizabeth Bowen* (1975)
for a more scholarly consideration of Bowen's literary significance. Especially
interesting in Glendinning's work may be the description of the writer's unique
relationship with her husband, a relationship that tolerated other deep friendships and loves. The book contains a useful bibliography of secondary sources
and of Bowen's works.

178   Godbold, E. Stanly. **Ellen Glasgow and The Woman Within**. Baton Rouge:
      Louisiana State University Press, 1972. 322p. bibliog. index. $12.50.
      ISBN 0807100404. LC 71-165068.
A major critical biography of Ellen Glasgow (1873-1945), the prolific novelist
of Richmond, Virginia. Born and raised in Virginia, she was intimately familiar
with the polar differences in Virginia society from her own background. Her
mother was a member of Virginia aristocracy, her father came from a wealthy
industrial family. Godbold critically examines the life of a woman who experienced immense personal success as an author and at the same time led an extremely
isolated life. Her most consuming interest, aside from writing, was in her dogs
and the SPCA. Her autobiography, *The Woman Within*, and the novels *Barren
Ground* (1925) and *Vein of Iron* (1935) demonstrate Glasgow's commitment
to individual strength. Godbold traces the life skillfully and provides an extremely
helpful bibliography of works by Glasgow and manuscripts and material about
Glasgow. Those who would rather miss the details of her fussy old age might
better concentrate on *The Woman Within*.

179   Goldman, Emma, 1869-1940. **Living My Life**. Gloucester, MA: Peter
      Smith, n.d. 2v. $16.00. ISBN 0844606480.
Born in 1869 to a Jewish ghetto family in Kovno, Russia, Goldman commonly
asserted that her "real" life began in 1889 when she moved to New York City,
met her lifetime lover and comrade, Alexander Berkman, and became involved
in the American anarchist movement. Her father's disappointment that she was
not a son, her factory work in Russia and the U.S., her exposure to nihilist and
populist circles and literature in Russia, the gap between the myth and the
reality of life in the U.S.—all of these were among the elements in Goldman's
experience that laid the basis for her lifelong commitment to anarchist and
feminist politics. Goldman became well-known as a magnetic speaker in her
lecture tours across the U.S., addressing audiences on a variety of topics including
anarchism, the new drama (Ibsen, Strindberg, Shaw), feminism, and current
political issues. Several times she was imprisoned for the views she advocated,
and she became a dauntless fighter for the right of free speech. She considered
the suffrage demand naive and narrow, but she was a staunch advocate of legal
birth control. In 1919, Goldman and Berkman were deported to Russia. Goldman's initial support for the Soviet regime collapsed in disillusionment after

two years and she left for Europe. Her autobiography, published in 1931, lacks only an account of her work later in the thirties in solidarity with the revolutionaries fighting in Spain. Goldman is remarkable as a revolutionary who throughout her life attempted to live her political beliefs, anarchist and feminist. She stands out among her feminist contemporaries for the profundity of her analysis of sexual oppression and for her affirmation of independence *and* sexual expression for women. Candor about her personal as well as her public life is one of the chief features of *Living My Life*.

180   Goldsmith, Margaret Leland, 1894- . **Christina of Sweden.** Philadelphia,
       PA: R. West, 1977. (Repr. of 1935 ed.). $17.50. ISBN 0849210410.
Christina of Sweden (1627-1689) "has puzzled historians because, despite her unusual talents, her inherited opportunity of becoming one of the great statesmen of her age, she accomplished nothing at all. And the writers of history, many of whom think in terms of power and of conquests, have wondered for three centuries why she gave away her throne, and why, turning her back even more emphatically on Protestant Sweden, she became a Roman Catholic." Christina's childhood was one of spectacular flux: her father died when she was a child; her mother, a neurotic, demonstrated startling mood swings. Her sexual "peculiarities" and her intellectual acumen were legend on the European continent even as a young woman. In 1650, she underwent the official coronation as queen; by 1651, she had decided to abdicate since she did not wish to marry and to produce an heir. Much to the shock of her countrymen, she toured Europe after her abdication, converting to Catholicism and engaging in love affairs with women. She spent her life surrounding herself with luminaries of science, the arts, and literature, constantly anxious over her financial situation as she travelled around Europe and dabbled in European politics. A well-written biography of a woman who lived the bohemian life despite her station by birth.

181   Gridley, Marion Eleanor, 1906- . **American Indian Women.** New York:
       Hawthorn Books, 1974. 178p. bibliog. index. $5.95. ISBN 0801502349.
       LC 73-362.
Contents of this biographical treatment of Native American women are: Wetamoo–Squaw Sachem of Pocasset; Pocahontas–The Savior of Jamestown; Mary Musgrove Matthews Bosomworth–Indian Empress; Nancy Ward–Beloved Woman of the Cherokees; Sacajawea–The Girl Guide; Sarah Winnemucca–Army Scout; Winema–The Peacemaker; E. Pauline Johnson–Canada's Famous Poet; Susan La Flesche Picotte–The First Indian Woman Physician; Gertrude Simmons Bonnin–A Modern Progressive; Roberta Campbell Lawson–Leader of Three Million Women; Pablita Velarde–Artist of the Pueblos; Maria Montoya Martinez–Master Artisan; Annie Dodge Wauneka–A Modern Crusader; Esther Burnett Horne–Sacajawea's Great-Great Granddaughter; The Tallchief Sisters–Prima Ballerinas; Wilma L. Victor–Educator in Government; Elaine Abraham Ramos–College Vice-President. Though this book could be used effectively in school libraries, it also deserves a place in undergraduate collections because of the dearth of material on American Indian women. The bibliography provides an excellent starting point for biographical material on Native American women.

182   Grier, Barbara [Damon, Gene], 1933- , and Coletta Reid, 1943- , eds.
       Lesbian Lives: Biographies of Women from the Ladder. Baltimore, MD:
       Diana Press, 1976. 433p. bibliog. index. $5.75. ISBN 0884470121.
       LC 76-53806.

Absolutely essential for understanding the development of lesbian thought and
consciousness, these selections were taken from *The Ladder*, which from 1956
to 1972 was the only journal providing a forum for lesbian thought and life.
Among the biographical subjects in this volume are: Amelia Earhart, Colette,
Octave Thanet, Willa Cather, Mary Casal, Radclyffe Hall, H. D., Charlotte
Cushman, Dame Ethel Smyth, Rosa Bonheur, Madame de Staël, Juliette Recamier,
Dorothy Thompson, Margaret Fuller, Edith Hamilton, and Carey Thomas.
The editors have divided the biographical materials (sketches, book reviews
and bibliographies on the "variant" women) into sections: Famous Couples,
Adventurers, Novelists, Queens and Their Consorts, Poets, Artists, Writers and
Pathbreakers. Though this book cannot be comprehensive, it is the best source
for consistently well-written, well-researched articles on lesbian women. Lesbian-
ism is stressed as a *positive* element of the women's lives. In addition to portraits
of specific women, the editors have included articles on groups—"Poetry of
Lesbiana: Lesbian Poets"; "Guiding Lights: Ladies Bountiful"; "Women Composers"; "And the Ladies Gathered: Martha McWhirter's Female Communal
Society." The introduction by Grier is an important commentary on lesbian
culture and the role of *The Ladder* in the dissemination of lesbiana in the
United States. The picture and bibliography, which complement almost every
article, are further indicators of the usefulness of this volume.

183   Guffy, Ossie, 1931- . **Ossie: The Autobiography of a Black Woman.**
       New York: Norton, 1971. 224p. $6.50. ISBN 0393074587. LC
       74-141940.

"I'm going to try to tell it like it was, hoping it will throw a little light on the
millions of us that ain't been rightly seen before." The millions whose lives
Ossie Guffy is trying to reveal through her autobiography are the poor of the
United States, especially blacks, and, more particularly, black women—the
many women, mothers, and workers "trying to do the work of mother and
father and sometimes needing a little help to keep from going under." Guffy
has much to say about the struggles of black men and women and how the
love between them so often leaves the black woman alone to somehow provide
for their children. (" 'There, there,' my grandma soothed, 'You got to be strong.
The Lord gives us the strength to face what we gotta face.' My mother stopped
crying. 'If that's true, Mama,' she said accusingly, 'how come he only gives it
to women?' ") But Guffy also presents a picture of male/female struggle radically
different from more familiar white middle-class images. The women in this
moving account always know at some level—no matter how deep their anger—
that what they are confronting in black men is more a product of racist oppression
than of sexual power and privilege. Guffy's visions of a better life point to the
possibility of economic security, the self-discovery and revitalization of impoverished black communities, and the flowering of love and mutual respect between
black men and women.

184   Hahn, Emily, 1905- . **Mabel: A Biography of Mabel Dodge Luhan.**
       Boston: Houghton Mifflin, 1977. 288p. bibliog. index. $10.00. ISBN
       0395253497. LC 76-58905.
In many ways, Mabel Dodge Luhan might be considered a silly unstable woman:
rich, much married and divorced, an international socialite. Her salon included
many of the famous names of turn-of-the-century aristocracy and literati,
e.g., D. H. Lawrence. This is an interesting study of how a compelling and ambitious woman of the early twentieth century found an outlet for her sexual and
cultural energies. It has a useful index.

185   Hall, Nancy Lee. **A True Story of a Drunken Mother.** Plainfield, VT:
       Daughters, 1974. 151p. $3.00. ISBN 0913780057. LC 74-79918.
Described as a "fictionalized autobiography," this is a nightmarish account of
uncontrollable drinking habits, marital infidelity, domestic violence, and child
neglect. It is told in the spare style of a woman who recounts the events of a
very difficult life without analysis of what these events mean or how they fit
together. And perhaps this accounts for the power of her futile struggle to cope
with six children, a drinking problem and an incompatible husband during the
World War II period. Displacement, alienation, anonymity, and hopelessness
are the themes of Hall's chronicle.

186   Hall, Ruth, 1933- . **Passionate Crusader: The Life of Marie Stopes.**
       New York: Harcourt, Brace, Jovanovich, 1977. 351p. bibliog. index.
       $14.95. ISBN 0151712883. LC 77-73054.
As egomaniacal and self-centered as Stopes undoubtedly was, no one denies
that her life (1880-1958) was extraordinary by any standard. Her most memorable
accomplishment was the founding of Great Britain's first birth control clinic.
Stopes's visibility as a flamboyant spokeswoman for birth control and for a
clearer public understanding of sexuality during the 1920s and 1930s over-
shadows her contributions as a noted paleobotanist. On a lesser scale, she dabbled
in the arts. Hall, a journalist, has written a biography that explores the contribution of Stopes as social pioneer but takes note of her many eccentricities as
a private woman. Like many early birth control advocates, Stopes was elitist
in her approach to the question, believing that the lower classes were unfit to
breed more of their own. Her central belief was that the human race could be
greatly improved by the eugenic application of birth control. Ironically, this
fascist approach was considered very liberal in Marie Stopes's day. Along with
her outrageous pronouncements she had many good ideas that have had great
impact in Britain—for example, that the state accept the responsibility to provide
free birth control services, which has been a fact in Britain since 1975. Hall has
done a commendable job in sifting the huge corpus of documentation on this
contradictory personality.

187   Hamilton, Alice, 1869- . **Exploring the Dangerous Trades: The Autobiog-
       raphy of Alice Hamilton, M.D.** Boston: Little, Brown, 1943; repr.
       New York: A. M. Kelley, n.d. 433p. index. $15.00. ISBN 0678011044.
This is the autobiographical account of a woman physician who was at the fore-
front of the early development of the field of industrial disease treatment in
the United States, facing the indifference of the American Medical Association

and the resistance of industrialists who refused (as they refuse today) responsibility for disease engendered in their plants. Also important in Hamilton's account are her experiences living at Jane Addams's Hull House, with the peace movement, the war industries, and her perceptions of the tumultuous history she lived through.

188   Harper, Ida Husted, 1851-1931. **Life and Work of Susan B. Anthony.** New York: Arno Press, 1969. (Repr. of 1898-1908 ed.). 3v. $55.00. ISBN 0405001029. LC 70-79184.

Susan B. Anthony (1820-1906) is generally credited with being the prime mover—in collaboration with Elizabeth Cady Stanton—of the nineteenth-century suffrage struggle. Their partnership was an exceptionally fortuitous one, reflecting Anthony's exceptional political and organizational sense and Stanton's writing and speaking talents. Devoting over fifty years to the struggle for woman suffrage, Anthony died in 1906 without seeing her goal realized. Publisher of the feminist journal, *Revolution*, founder and vice-president of the National Woman Suffrage Association (1869-1890), tireless campaigner for both a federal suffrage amendment and state-by-state action, president of the National American Woman Suffrage Association (1892-1900): this is but a skeletal account of the life-work of a woman whose political commitments were not limited to feminism alone, but extended into abolitionism, temperance, and the labor movement as well. As the end of the nineteenth century approached and a new generation of women took over the suffrage struggle, Anthony was persuaded to prepare her memoirs with the aid of Ida Husted Harper (co-author of the monumental *History of Woman Suffrage*). The resulting three-volume *Life and Work of Susan B. Anthony* is, along with the *History of Woman Suffrage*, the key primary source on Anthony. Based on Anthony's own recollections, over 20,000 letters, her diaries of fifty years, her scrapbooks, the files of the Garrison *Liberator*, women's rights papers and records, and more, it not only covers her entire life and career in great detail but is also a document of suffrage history. Volume 1 covers the period 1820-1880; volume 2, 1880-1897; and volume 3, 1898-1907; many photographs illustrate the text. Three later biographies deserve note: Rheta Louise Dorr's *Susan B. Anthony: The Woman Who Changed the Mind of a Nation* (orig. 1928; repr. A.M.S. Press, 1970), Katherine Susan Anthony's *Susan B. Anthony: Her Personal History and Her Era* (orig. 1954; repr. Russell and Russell, 1975), and Alma Lutz's *Susan B. Anthony: Rebel, Crusader, Humanitarian* (orig. 1959; repr. Zenger, 1975). The Lutz biography has an extensive bibliography covering manuscript collections and published material.

189*   Hedgeman, Annà (Arnold). **The Trumpet Sounds: A Memoir of Negro Leadership.** New York: Holt, Rinehart and Winston, 1964. 202p. LC 64-21938.

Anna Arnold Hedgeman grew up in the only black family residing in Anoka, Minnesota. Her real awakening as a black woman in racist America took place following her move in 1922 to Holly Springs, Mississippi, to teach at the all-black Rust College. She soon left teaching and embarked on what was to be a lifelong commitment to the struggle for civil rights. Her story, which covers four decades of civil rights activity from 1922 through the 1963 Freedom March on Washington, is history as much as autobiography, and was praised as such

when it originally appeared. During the course of her career, Hedgeman served
in such positions as executive director of a black YWCA branch, assistant to
the mayor of New York, and assistant to the administrator of the Federal
Security Agency.

190   Hellman, Lillian, 1905- . **Pentimento.** Boston: Little, Brown, 1973.
       297p. $8.95. ISBN 0316355208. LC 73-7747.
"Pentimento" is an artistic term that refers to a reworked painting. As the
painting ages, the paint becomes transparent, and one can see the original lines.
This is the metaphor for Hellman's reminiscences of people who have been close
to her in childhood and during her successful writing career. Because of the
recent film "Julia" (1973), many will be familiar with Hellman's unique relationship with a childhood friend who died working actively in the Nazi Resistance
movement. Others who appear in the beautifully recalled memoir are eccentric
relatives and her lover, Dashiell Hammett. The essence of their unique and enduring
love relationship is distilled in the chapter "Turtle," which deals with their life
together on their farm.

191   Hellman, Lillian, 1905- . **An Unfinished Woman: A Memoir.** Boston:
       Little, Brown, 1969. 280p. $8.95. ISBN 0316355186. LC 76-75019.
Hellman has a crisp way with sentences. This conversational memoir describes
her childhood shuttling back and forth between New York and New Orleans
as well as her stint as a journalist during the Spanish Civil War and in Russia
during the Second World War. It describes her success as a playwright (*The
Children's Hour, The Little Foxes, Toys in the Attic,* etc.) and the brilliant
writers and artists she knew over the years—in New York, in Hollywood, in
Europe. The photographs are good ones of Hellman and the special people in
her life, among them, Dorothy Parker and Dashiell Hammett. It is in her recounting of her thirty-year affair with Hammett that her writing is best, and it is good
to read of an extraordinary relationship that endured the years through successes
and bad times, too.

192   Hemenway, Robert E., 1941- . **Zora Neale Hurston: A Literary Biography.**
       Urbana: University of Illinois Press, 1977. 432p. bibliog. index. $15.00.
       ISBN 0252006526. LC 77-9605.
With a foreword by Alice Walker, this is a major biographical and critical work
about a woman of many gifts: folklorist, novelist, and student of Franz Boas.
An important figure during the Harlem Renaissance, Hurston published more
during her life than any other Afro-American woman; yet her fortunes flagged,
her personality was a tortured one, her life one of instability and bickering with
other famous black culturati. She died on welfare in Florida, a comparatively
early death (1901-1960), championing until the end the cause of a separate
and aesthetically worthy black culture. Another study of Hurston, now out of
print, is Marian Murray's *Jump at the Sun: The Story of Zora Neale Hurston*
(Third Press, 1975).

193   Hemingway, Mary Welsh, 1908- . **How It Was.** New York: Knopf;
       distr. New York: Random House, 1976. 537p. index. $12.50. ISBN
       0394491093. LC 76-13672.

At times trivial, at times more a housewifely list than an autobiography, this makes an important statement about what it must be to be "attached" in the full sense of the word to a genius. Though Mary was a rather good journalist in her own right, once she married Ernest, her life became the shadow of his. Her reporting confined itself to monitoring the expressions on her famous husband's face: his interests became hers, his dark moods became hers to assuage. Most of the material is based on her diaries and his letters to her. Though Ernest had his compelling moments, Mary's descriptions of such domestic scenes as Ernest throwing wine in her face when guests came to dinner, shattering ashtrays in anger, and reviling her ("you slut") on occasion suggest that Mary's role was a distinctly subordinate one.

194   Holden, Edith, 1871-1920. **The Country Diary of an Edwardian Lady, 1906: A Facsimile Reproduction of a Naturalist's Diary.** New York: Holt, Rinehart and Winston, 1977. 176p. $14.95. ISBN 0030210267. LC 77-71198.

A most unusual form of diary, this recently discovered and very beautiful work is a record of an Englishwoman's observations of birds, animals, and plants during 1906. Very little is known of this talented illustrator and diarist of flora and fauna except that she moved from Warwickshire to London when she married a sculptor in 1911. Apparently she did not make much of her diary and never sought its publication. She died rather strangely—drowned in the Thames while gathering chestnut buds.

195   Holiday, Billie, 1915-1959. **Lady Sings the Blues.** New York: Avon Books, 1976. 192p. $1.50. ISBN 0380004917.

A working woman at six, raped at ten (*she* was taken to the police station bleeding and crying, only to be locked in a cell after this experience), Billie Holiday's "childhood" in Baltimore and New York prepared her for prostitution by age fourteen. She found this life to be easier and financially more rewarding than the back-breaking labors of life as a maid, though she ended up serving time in prison as "a wayward woman" because of this work. She started singing in Harlem during the '20s in one of the many night spots where musicians came to jam; soon she was meeting musicians who would dramatically shape her career—Benny Goodman, Harry James, Roy Eldridge, Charlie Shavers, Lester Young, Benny Webster, Cab Calloway. When she joined Count Basie's band, she began a grueling life on the road that gave her a chance to see the country and develop her skills as a singer with some of the greatest talents in jazz history. She also learned about bigotry as the only woman traveling with a white, male band led by Artie Shaw. Her career was marked by hospitalization and, finally, imprisonment for drugs. In 1947, she was sentenced to one year at the Federal Woman's Reformatory at Alderson, West Virginia. Though she made an incredible comeback at Carnegie Hall only ten days after her release, New York state's denial of her request for a cabaret card virtually crippled Billie Holiday's career. Her autobiographical account ends with details of her successful European tour, her relationship with Louis McKay, narcotics arrest and hospitalization (a cycle she was to repeat until her death in 1959). This is the unpretentious and honest autobiography of a talented and troubled woman. The appended discography lists all known recordings by Billie Holiday,

both commercial and private transcriptions. A recent source on Holiday is
Hettie Jones's *Big Star Fallin' Mama: Five Women in Black Music* (Viking
Press, 1974), which also discusses Ma Rainey, Bessie Smith, Mahalia Jackson,
and Aretha Franklin.

196*   Holt, Rackham. **Mary McLeod Bethune: A Biography.** Garden City, NY:
        Doubleday, 1964. 306p. LC 64-11040.

Mary McLeod Bethune (1875-1955) was born a woman, a black, and one of
seventeen children. She managed, despite these three initial counts against her,
to gain an education, which enabled her to embark on a teaching career in the
South. More and more committed to the task of increasing educational opportunities for blacks, Bethune began to dream of starting her own school. This
she managed to do in 1904, when she opened the Daytona (Florida) Education
and Industrial Training School for Negro Girls (later renamed Bethune-Cookman
College). In 1933, she was appointed director of the Division of Negro Affairs
in the National Youth Administration. She was also a founder of National
Council of Negro Women. Holt's biography is recommended by Gerda Lerner
in her *Black Women in White America* (1972). Other sources on Bethune are
Catherine Owens Peare's *Mary McLeod Bethune* (Vanguard Press, 1951) and
Emma Sterne's work of the same title (Knopf, 1957).

197   Hourwich, Andria Taylor, and Gladys Louise Palmer, eds. **I Am a
        Woman Worker.** New York: Affiliated Schools for Workers, 1936;
        repr. New York: Arno Press, 1974. 152p. $12.00. ISBN 0405061021.
        LC 74-3954.

During the period of radical union organizing in the 1930s, a network of education
programs for workers flourished that were known as the Affiliated Schools
for Workers. Best known were the Bryn Mawr Summer School for Working
Women, the School for Workers in Industry at the University of Wisconsin,
and the Vineyard Shore Workers School on the Hudson in New York State.
Workers were recruited for summer sessions and weekend institutes where they
were taught history and political economy and encouraged to make connections
between what they learned and their own experiences. *I Am a Woman Worker*,
first published in 1936, is one of a series of "scrapbooks" of writings by workers
to come out of this period of radical worker education. Collected here are
selected, very brief stories written by women who attended various workers'
schools. The stories are grouped into five topics—Getting a Job, Life in the
Factory, Open Shops and Company Unions, Trade Unions and Organized Shops,
and On Strike!

198   Howe, Julia (Ward), 1819-1910. **Margaret Fuller (Marchesa Ossoli).**
        Westport, CT: Greenwood Press, 1970. (Repr. of 1883 ed.). 298p.
        $11.25. ISBN 0837140897. LC 69-13936.

Julia Howe, a friend of Margaret Fuller's, wrote the introduction to *Love Letters
of Margaret Fuller* (orig. 1903). Howe's portrait is too loving to be critical,
although it does contain manuscript letters and journal sections that stand on
their own. As a view by a contemporary of Fuller's sympathetic to her as a woman,
this bears looking at. However, the Chevigny biography, *The Woman and the
Myth* (1976), contains a fuller, more objective and critical view than Howe attempts.

199   Hsieh, Ping-Ying, 1906- . **Girl Rebel: The Autobiography of Hsieh Pingying, with Extracts from her New War Diaries.** New York: John Day, 1940; repr. New York: Da Capo Press, 1975. 270p. $18.00. ISBN 0306706911. LC 74-34583.

Lin Yutang, whose daughters, Adet and Anor Lin, translated *Girl Rebel*, wrote in his 1940 introduction to the volume: "Miss Hsieh's story is the story of Young China in the convulsions of an age of social upheaval. No one has so exciting an account to give of an indomitable struggle with poverty and persecution, and no one quite so typifies the spirit of rebellion in youth as Miss Hsieh in her personal struggle with her own family. From bound feet to army puttees, from childhood engagement to free marriage and divorce, is a far cry, but in this book Miss Hsieh travels the entire road of that social change.... Although she tells of her experiences as a girl soldier, both in the Revolution of 1927 and in the present war [1940], the larger significance of the book lies in its reflection of a great social change through a personal story."

200   Hurston, Zora Neale, 1902-1960. **Dust Tracks on a Road.** New York: Arno Press, 1969. (Repr. of 1942 ed.). 294p. $12.00. ISBN 0405019270. LC 70-94133.

Hurston's accomplishments as anthropologist, folklorist, novelist, and song writer are no less than dazzling. However, the acclaim she received during her lifetime was minimal, and she died a pauper in 1960. She tells the story here of the extraordinary patchwork of people and experiences that were her work with the same down-to-earth quality that characterizes her novels. She concludes her autobiography in a flash of Hurston wit: "Consider that with tolerance and patience, we godly demons may breed a noble world in a few hundred generations or so. Maybe all of us who do not have the good fortune to meet, or meet again, in this world, will meet at a barbecue."

201*   Jackson, Mahalia, 1911-1972. **Movin' On Up.** New York: Hawthorn Books, 1966. 212p. LC 66-22315.

This is the autobiography of the inspiring black gospel singer, Mahalia Jackson—from her birth in a poor district of New Orleans in 1911 through the civil rights struggles of the early '60s. Jackson collaborated with a writer, Evan McLeod Wylie, in producing the account, which is written in a personal style and laced with vivid anecdotes. Some examples of Jackson's faith and outlook: "my aunt Duke always worried about me getting mixed up with show business, but I finally convinced her that I am a church woman"; "when I cry when I'm singing, I'm not sad like some people think. I look back where I came from and I rejoice"; "it can be hard singing for records and television, with their orchestras and their time limits. But I keep at it because I think my music can do some good for people." The book includes a selected discography, which unfortunately is probably quite dated. A recent source on Mahalia Jackson (and others) is Hettie Jones's *Big Star Fallin' Mama: Five Women in Black Music* (Viking Press, 1974).

202*   Jacobi, Mary (Putnam), 1842-1906. **Life and Letters of Mary Putnam Jacobi.** Edited by Ruth Putnam. New York: Putnam's Sons, 1925. 381p. LC 25-5667.

Mary Putnam Jacobi was one of the first women in the United States to break through the barriers excluding women from the practice of medicine. Determined, persevering, and convinced of the supreme importance of satisfying work in a person's life, Jacobi never questioned her right to a medical education and battled her way into being accepted—over the objections of the faculty—as the first woman student at the École de Médecine in France. Returning to the U.S. in 1871, she embarked on a distinguished career that combined private practice, prolific medical writing, and hospital, educational, and professional responsibilities—as well as marriage and motherhood. She was a pioneer in her concern for the increasingly important issue of environmental contributions to illness. This volume combines autobiographical accounts with letters to family and friends. Together with a companion volume, *Mary Putnam Jacobi, M.D.: A Pathfinder in Medicine* (Putnam's Sons, 1925), it gives a good account of her life. The second volume includes selections from Jacobi's medical writings and a complete bibliography. Particularly remarkable is her detached, scientific description of the course of the illness that eventually resulted in her death.

203   Jacobs, Harriet (Brent) [Brent, Linda], 1818-1896. **Incidents in the Life of a Slave Girl.** New York: Harcourt, Brace and Jovanovich, 1973. 210p. $3.45. ISBN 0156443503. LC 72-90506.
First published in 1861, *Incidents* is one of very few slave narratives written by women, and it speaks directly to the specific oppression experienced by women under slavery. Brent tells her reader: "slavery is terrible for men, but it is far more terrible for women." Brent gives an account of her growing up in slavery (1818-1845), how she fled at age 27 to escape sexual exploitation by her master, her seven brutal years in hiding, and her eventual success in reaching free territory. Her autobiography was written with editorial help from Lydia Maria Frances Child, a Massachusetts writer and abolitionist (*Appeal in Favor of That Class of Americans Called Africans*, published in 1833, was an important antislavery treatise written by Child).

204   Johnson, Diane. **The True History of the First Mrs. Meredith and Other Lesser Lives.** New York: Knopf; distr. New York: Random House, 1972. 232p. bibliog. $7.95. ISBN 0394480341. LC 72-2227.
A primary aim of the new women's scholarship is to examine the hidden lives of women, both ordinary and extraordinary. Johnson's biography of Mary Ellen Peacock Meredith, daughter of one eminent nineteenth-century novelist and wife of another, is an example of the best of this research. In the process of learning a great deal about Mary Ellen Meredith and female Victorian rebellion, we cull much about "the lesser lives" of all Victorian women. Diane Johnson clarifies her intent in writing revisionist literary history in the preface: "the life of Mary Ellen is always treated, in a paragraph or a page, as an episode in the lives of Peacock or Meredith. It was treated with a certain reserve in early biographies because it involves adultery and recrimination, and makes all the parties look ugly. More recent biographies of Meredith repeat the received version of the story with a certain brisk determination, a kind of feigned acceptance. . . . Mrs. Meredith's life can be looked upon, of course, as an episode in the lives of Meredith or Peacock, but it cannot have seemed that way to her." The book is beautifully written.

205   Jones, Mary (Harris), 1830-1930. **The Autobiography of Mother Jones.**
       New York: Arno Press, 1969. (Repr. of 1925 ed.). 242p. $14.00.
       ISBN 0405021305. LC 71-89741.
Mary Harris "Mother" Jones: born in Cork, Ireland, in 1830, daughter of poor
Irish rebels; immigrant to the United States as a child; dressmaker and teacher;
wife and mother of four, who lost her husband and all her children to a yellow
fever epidemic in Memphis in 1867; dressmaker once again in Chicago, until
the great Chicago fire of 1871 wiped out her business. This is already the material
of a lifetime; yet the courageous commitment and service to the labor movement for which Mother Jones is known only began in 1880, when she was
already fifty years old. Mother Jones lived to be 100 (this autobiography was
written when she was 94) and continued her labor organizing throughout the
second fifty years of her lifetime. Her most passionate commitment was to the
miners' struggles, but her autobiography yields a broader picture of U.S. labor
history in the late nineteenth and early twentieth centuries. Readers may also
wish to consult a recent and more complete biography of Mother Jones, Dale
Fetherling's *Mother Jones, the Miners' Angel* (1974).

206   Josephson, Hannah Geffen. **Jeannette Rankin: First Lady in Congress:**
       A Biography. Indianapolis, IN: Bobbs-Merrill, 1974. 227p. bibliog.
       index. $8.95. ISBN 0672519216. LC 74-3887.
A straight-forward account of the Montana suffragist and the first woman to
serve in the United States Congress, this biography traces Rankin's roots and
education, her pacifist stance in both World Wars (a role that was politically
disastrous for her), and her career as feminist, political reformer, and public
person. Rankin (1880-1973) served only two terms in Congress, though her
taste for politics was lifelong: "I never left Congress. I was there with Wayne
Morse and Ernest Gruening voting against the Tonkin Bay Resolution," she
said at age ninety.

207   Kahn, Kathy. **Hillbilly Women.** Garden City, NY: Doubleday, 1973.
       230p. bibliog. $7.95. ISBN 0385014112. LC 72-96246.
Though the women's movement presumes to speak for and represent all women,
it has naturally tended to reflect the demands and visions of those with most
access to the media—white, middle-class women. *Hillbilly Women* presents the
personal histories, told in their own words, of nineteen poor and working-
class women from southern Appalachia. The portraits that emerge are of very
strong women whose experiences and needs demand a conception of sexual
liberation intimately linked with class liberation. Economic security, health,
safety on the job, education—these are among the visions that the idea of control
over one's life would bring to the minds of these women, and children and
family are an integral part of their visions. Among the women represented here
are miners' wives, cotton mill workers, union organizers, and those who migrated
from Appalachia to the Cincinnati slums. Kathy Kahn has written sensitive
introductions to the volume and to each selection, setting the personal histories
within the context of Appalachian history. Harriette Arnow's powerful novel
about an Appalachian woman, *The Dollmaker*, would make good reading in
conjunction with *Hillbilly Women.*

208   Kapp, Yvonne Mayer, 1903- . **Eleanor Marx.** New York: Pantheon
       Books, 1977. 2v. bibliog. index. v.1: $10.00. ISBN 0394421434.
       v.2: $17.95. ISBN 0394421515. LC 77-77538.

In addition to being the youngest of Karl Marx's three daughters, Eleanor Marx
was herself a political writer, translator of authors such as Flaubert and Ibsen,
editor of some of her father's works, indefatigable political organizer and
speaker popular in the working-class movement, and a woman who risked
living openly with a married man within the suffocating atmosphere of bourgeois
Victorian England. Kapp's recent biography does not go beyond the earlier *Life
of Eleanor Marx, 1855-1898* (by Chushichi Tsuzuki, 1967) in its use of sources.
Its value lies rather in its meticulous and sensitive rendering of the life of this
extraordinary woman. The book lays the basis for a recognition of Eleanor
Marx's historical importance in her own right, particularly within the struggle
between dogmatic and critical tendencies in Marxism and Marxist movements.

209   Kearns, Martha. **Käthe Kollwitz: Woman and Artist.** Old Westbury,
       NY: Feminist Press, 1976. 237p. bibliog. $5.50. ISBN 0912670150.
       LC 76-6764.

Kearns dedicates her biography of Käthe Kollwitz (1867-1945) "to women and
their revolutionary potential to create a new world." Drawing heavily on *The
Diary and Letters of Kaethe Kollwitz* (Regnery, 1955) and writing from an
explicitly feminist perspective, Kearns recreates the life story of this extraordinary woman, artist, and socialist. Kollwitz is best known as a printmaker whose
some 270 woodcuts, etchings, and lithographs convey powerful images of
protective mothers and the strength and beauty of working-class women. Kearns's
account is accompanied by 32 prints and photographs, some well-known and
some rather rare. Other Kollwitz collections are: *Prints and Drawings of Käthe
Kollwitz*, selected and introduced by Carl Zigrosser (Dover Publications, 1969),
which offers 83 illustrations in a large format (approximately 12x10 inches);
and Mina and Arthur Klein's *Käthe Kollwitz: Life in Art* (orig. 1972; repr.
Schocken Books, 1975).

210   Kennedy, David M. **Birth Control in America: The Career of Margaret
       Sanger.** New Haven, CT: Yale University Press, 1970. 320p. bibliog.
       index. $18.50. ISBN 0300012020. LC 79-99827.

Because this is more fully a history of the Birth Control Movement than a comprehensive biography of Margaret Sanger, Kennedy's emphasis is properly on
the intellectual, familial, and social influences that brought Sanger to a position
of leadership in birth control from 1914-1942 (e.g., her Catholic girlhood and
her awakening to the ideas of Havelock Ellis and Freud on sexuality). Though
Sanger began as a radical, Kennedy points out the conservative support that
Sanger's birth control reform movement attracted: eugenicists, in their campaings
to control immigrant population increase; Protestant churches, in their endorse-
ments of family stability; and the federal government, in the self-serving interests
of social control during the Depression and wartime. Kennedy sees Margaret
Sanger as an emotional leader rather than an intelligent strategist, as one who
never really understood the sexual ignorance of the masses. Though he credits
her with dynamism, he depicts her as absorbed with her own heroinism. The
excellent bibliographical essay together with the selected bibliography will

well serve the researcher on Sanger and the Birth Control Movement. For a complete though less scholarly biography of Sanger's life, see Emily Taft Douglas, *Margaret Sanger: Pioneer of the Future* (Holt, Rinehart and Winston, 1970).

211   Kennedy, Florynce, 1916- . **Color Me Flo: My Hard Life and Good Times.** Englewood Cliffs, NJ: Prentice-Hall, 1976. 168p. $7.95. ISBN 0131524716. LC 76-17893.

The format of this book—many pictures, newspaper clippings, captions and inserts interspersed with text—fits Flo Kennedy: lawyer; black woman with hat, buttons, and caustic speaking style; journalist; and feminist activist. She has been an organizer and a protestor at major rallies and confrontations to support oppressed people—blacks, lesbians, prostitutes, political radicals. Her speeches are considered offensive by some, to which Kennedy responds, "honey, if they pay me $1000 to speak, they must want to hear what's on my mind. And if they pay me nothing, they are certainly going to hear exactly what is on my mind." She has supported ERA and abortion since her early affiliation with NOW and is the author of *Abortion Rap*.

212   King, Coretta Scott, 1927- . **My Life With Martin Luther King, Jr.** New York: Avon Books, 1970. 351p. index. $1.50.

As the title would lead one to expect, Coretta King tells her story very much in terms of her career as Martin Luther King's wife. Nonetheless, much of her own strength and vision come through. Inevitably, Martin Luther King's commitment to the Civil Rights Movement swept up and involved all members of his family. Coretta gives an account of their backgrounds, their relationship, the evolution of their ideas and politics, and the history of their part in the Movement (which constitutes a history of the Movement itself). As this book was written so soon after Martin's murder on April 4, 1968, we unfortunately learn little of Coretta's life in its aftermath. A selection of photographs depicting the Kings' family life and Movement activities is included.

213   Kollontai, Aleksandra Mikhailovna, 1872-1952. **The Autobiography of a Sexually Emancipated Communist Woman.** New York: Herder and Herder, 1971; repr. New York: Schocken Books, 1975. 137p. bibliog. $2.95. ISBN 0805204865. LC 74-26921.

Translated from the German (*Autobiographie einer sexuell emanzipierten Kommunistin*) by Salvator Attanasio, this is the rather restrained autobiography (originally 1926) of Alexandra Kollontai, Russian revolutionary who advanced a socialist-feminist politics within the male-dominated ranks of Communist Party leaders in the early days of the Soviet Union. Kollontai was responsible for much of the early progressive Soviet legislation concerning women's rights and sexual emancipation. She was also important for her support of the Workers' Opposition in its struggle for Communist Party democratization. These involvements created tension in Kollontai's relationship with the Party and were probably responsible for her virtual exile from the USSR in 1922 as diplomat to Norway (and later, Mexico and Sweden). Kollontai's sense of delicacy in dealing with her controversial politics and Party history undoubtedly explains her sparse treatment of these subjects in the autobiography. However we are fortunate that this new edition restores all of Kollontai's elisions and emendations, providing the reader with material originally excised and offering insight into areas of particular sensitivity. Also included in this edition is her essay, "The New Woman," a chapter from *The New Morality and the Working Class* (1920) that discusses a series of heroines from early twentieth-century Russian fiction who exemplify the new independence and individuality of working-class women in their work and their sexuality. Kollontai's major works are listed at the end of the volume.

214   Larcom, Lucy, 1824-1893. **A New England Girlhood.** Goucester, MA:
        Peter Smith, 1973. 274p. $5.50. ISBN 0844624314.
The women factory workers of the textile mills in Lowell, Massachusetts, have been a frequent focus for historical investigation for a variety of reasons. First, the history of their recruitment and integration into factory work provides a case-study in how an industrial labor force was created out of a rural popula-tion in the U.S. Second, the Lowell factories were touted as "model" work-places, featuring attractive and airy mills, decent boarding facilities, religious facilities, etc. (though the women were working twelve to fourteen hours a day). Third, the women somehow found time to produce remarkable writings for their literary magazine, the *Lowell Offering*, which attracted international acclaim. Finally, the mill workforce was more than three-fourths women, at a time when factory work for women was considered controversial. It is of course this last factor that has made the Lowell factories an important topic for the new women's history and the renewed interest has resulted in the publication of new studies on the topic as well as the reissuing of works long out of print. Lucy Larcom's *A New England Girlhood* (1889) is, along with Harriet Robinson's *Loom and Spindle* (1898, reprint Press Pacifica, 1976), a classic if somewhat over-rosy account of life in the mills by a woman who lived and worked there and wrote for the *Lowell Offering*. Despite the romantic light in which she casts the experience, a fair amount of information about living and working condi-tions at Lowell emerges haphazardly along the way. A short reminiscence by Larcom, *Loom and Spindle*, and an important article on mill magazines by Bertha M. Stearns (1930) are among the selections reprinted in a recent Arno collection, *Women of Lowell* (1974). Readers will also want to be aware of the recent publication of excerpts from the *Lowell Offering* edited by Benita Eisler (1977); Philip Foner's collection (*The Factory Girls*, 1977) of little known writings by more militant factory operatives who repudiated the *Lowell Offering* as a company organ, voicing their dissatisfaction in their own journals and periodicals; and the reprinted *The Golden Thread*, by Hannah Josephson (1949, reprint Russell and Russell, 1967).

215*   Laski, Marghanita, 1915- . **George Eliot and Her World.** New York:
        Scribners, 1973. 119p. bibliog. index. ISBN 0684155117. LC 77-83677.
Less substantial certainly than the biographical works by Gordon S. Haight and Ruby Redinger, Laski's small volume is extraordinarily rich in detail for its size and also visually rewarding, with more than 100 illustrations. Trans-atlantic in the United States and Thames and Hudson in London have produced a series of such treatments on famous authors, all of consistently high quality, with more substance than a coffee table book and less weight than a full-scale biographical treatment. Laski does offer an evaluative view of Eliot (not an

altogether flattering one) with speculations about Eliot's possible discovery of infidelity on the part of G. H. Lewes, her companion of many years. Laski also writes of the significant problems that Eliot presents as a biographical subject due to the sanctimonious biography written by her husband, John Cross, to whom she was married only eight months before her death. Cross took upon himself the mission of concealing much of what he felt Eliot might have wished him to exclude of her life. Excellent references are made to illustrations and existing secondary works on Eliot.

216   Leach, Joseph. **Bright Particular Star: The Life and Times of Charlotte Cushman.** New Haven, CT: Yale University Press, 1970. 453p. bibliog. index. $25.50. ISBN 0300012055. LC 76-99829.
A contemporary of George Eliot, George Sand, and Elizabeth Barrett Browning, Charlotte Saunders Cushman (1816-1876) was probably the most famous woman of her day; and her art as an actress was probably held in greater esteem both in England and in America than the combined literary talents of Eliot, Sand, and Browning. Her famous tragic roles were Lady Macbeth, Queen Katherine (*Henry VIII*) and Meg Merriles (*Guy Mannering*, the stage adaptation of Sir Walter Scott's novel). These roles she performed over and over for adulatory audiences in America and England. Leach writes that her reputation was as much enhanced by her pristine personal life as by her talent; she neither married nor apparently had love affairs. Renowned for her solicitous behavior toward her family, adored by a public who knew that she had risen "from genteel poverty on a Boston side street to the pinnacle of international fame," and after her death to a sort of national sainthood, neither Charlotte Cushman's close companionship with the American sculptor Emma Stebbins nor her penchant for playing male roles in the theater received much comment. An excellently documented biography of a talented woman much adored during her life but inexplicably forgotten soon after, this has many fine photographs.

217   Leduc, Violette, 1907-1972. **La Batarde.** New York: Farrar, Straus and Giroux, 1965. 488p. $12.95. ISBN 0374182329. LC 65-20104.
The sensuous prose of this autobiography of Violette Leduc (novelist of *Thérese and Isabelle, The Golden Buttons*) makes it one of the outstanding autobiographical volumes of the century. More experimental than Simone de Beauvoir, Leduc includes the reader in her self-revelation to the extent that we drink of her loneliness and the solitude that the human condition imposes on us all. Her life as an illegitimate child, her exploration of the complexity of the mother-daughter relationship, her sexual consciousness, and narcissism all reveal a complexity so compelling and a probing of self so honest that the reader becomes a part of the complexity and richness of detail. Leduc's final entry (August 22, 1963): "this August day, reader, is a rose window glowing with heat. I make you a gift of it, it is yours. One o'clock. I am going back to the village for lunch. Strong with the silence of the pines and chestnut trees. I walk without flinching through the burning cathedral of summer. My bank of wild grass is majestic and full of music. It is a fire that solitude presses against my lips." The preface by de Beauvoir provides a fine introduction to Leduc's artistic intent.

218   Lerner, Gerda, 1920- . **The Grimké Sisters from South Carolina:**
       Pioneers for Woman's Rights and Abolition. New York: Schocken
       Books, 1971. 404p. bibliog. index. $3.95. ISBN 0805203214. LC
       74-163333.

Gerda Lerner's book has become recognized as the standard biography of the
nineteenth-century feminists and abolitionists, Sarah Moore Grimké (1792-1873)
and Angelina Emily Grimké (1805-1879). Born to a Charleston, South Carolina,
family of wealth and high social standing and brought up surrounded by numerous
slaves, the Grimké sisters attained almost immediate notoriety when they began
abolitionist agitation in the North in the 1830s. Both became important writers
for the cause, and Angelina in particular was a very popular orator. Their speeches
before mixed audiences elicited censure as "unwomanly behavior," and their
ensuing advocacy of the rights of woman in addition to abolitionism marked
the early stage of the intertwining of these two movements. Among the important
published writings of the Grimké sisters are: *Appeal to the Christian Women
of the Southern States* (1836); *An Appeal to the Women of the Nominally Free
States* (1837); *Letters to Catharine E. Beecher* (1838); and *Letter From Angelina
Grimké Weld, to the Woman's Rights Convention, Held at Syracuse, September,
1852,* by Angelina Grimké; and *Letters on the Equality of the Sexes and the
Condition of Women,* by Sarah Grimké. Lerner includes the printed speeches
of Angelina Grimké as an appendix to this volume. Her bibliography is substantial, including published and unpublished Grimké writings, biographical sources,
minutes and proceedings, newspapers and journals, writings of contemporaries,
and selected secondary sources. An important early biographical source available
in reprint edition is Catherine H. Birney's *The Grimké Sisters* (orig. 1885;
repr. Greenwood Press, 1969).

219   Levertov, Denise, 1923- . **The Poet in the World.** New York: New Direc-
       tions, 1973. 275p. bibliog. index. $9.50. ISBN 0811204928. LC
       73-78785.

"The poet—when he is writing—is a priest; the poem is a temple; epiphanies
and communion take place within it. . . . Writing the poem is the poet's means
of summoning the divine; the reader's may be through reading the poem, or
through what the experience of the poem leads him to." Levertov outlines
her theory and practice of poetry. She alludes to the work of the poets she
most admires—William Carlos Williams, Wallace Stevens, Charles Olson, Robert
Creeley, Gary Snyder, and Allen Ginsberg. The material here is drawn from a
wide variety of prose writings: interviews, statements of poetics, journal entries,
a personal recollection of the poet's trip to North Vietnam, essays on teaching.
Levertov's dedication to teaching emerges very clearly; the second half of the
book contains many specific accounts of the poet's pedagogical techniques.

220   Lewis, Oscar, 1914-1970. **The Children of Sanchez: Autobiography**
       of a Mexican Family. New York: Random House, 1961. 499p. $15.00.
       ISBN 0394419227. LC 61-6270.

"This book is about a poor family in Mexico City, Jesus Sanchez, the father,
age fifty, and his four children: Manuel, age 32; Roberto, 29; Consuelo, 27;
and Marta, 25. My purpose is to give the reader an inside view of family life
and of what it means to grow up in a one-room home in a slum tenement in

the heart of a great Latin American city which is undergoing a process of rapid social and economic change" (from Oscar Lewis's introduction). *The Children of Sanchez* was preceded by Lewis's *Five Families: Mexican Case Studies in the Culture of Poverty* (1959; repr. Basic Books, 1975, with a new introduction by Margaret Mead), which "tried to give the reader some glimpses of daily life in five ordinary Mexican families, on five perfectly ordinary days."

221 Lewis, Oscar, 1914-1970, et al. **Four Women: Living the Revolution; An Oral History of Contemporary Cuba.** Urbana: University of Illinois Press, 1977. 481p. bibliog. $15.00. ISBN 0252006399. LC 76-54878.
Four Women is volume 2 of the larger work, *Living the Revolution: An Oral History of Contemporary Cuba.* It presents the personal histories of four Cuban women before and after the revolution in 1959. The histories are drawn from lengthy tape-recorded interviews collected during 1969-1970, selected from the 150 interviews with women conducted during the research. There was no original intention of publishing a separate study of women, and the focus in the interviews was not on women's liberation as such. However, topics such as marriage, children, daughters' futures, women's work in the labor force, etc., did come up naturally in the course of the interviews. The four women selected for inclusion in this volume represent divergent backgrounds: a domestic servant, a former counter-revolutionary turned religious, a psychologist, and a former prostitute. The period when this research was conducted preceded the recent acceleration in Cuba's efforts to promote women's liberation (exemplified by the new Family Code of 1975). Authors Oscar Lewis, Ruth M. Lewis, and Susan M. Rigdon provide a lengthy introduction chronicling the history of the women's movement in Cuba through the mid-1970s. Readers will want to be aware of Margaret Randall's *Cuban Women Now: Interviews with Cuban Women* (1974). Randall presents portions of interviews conducted with fourteen women, in which the question of women's liberation was directly addressed.

222 Lewis, Richard Warrington Baldwin. **Edith Wharton: A Biography.** New York: Harper and Row, 1975. 592p. bibliog. index. $15.00. ISBN 0060126035. LC 74-1833.
This highly acclaimed biography of Wharton (Pulitzer Prize, among others) portrays Wharton's strength of character, her enormous literary creativity and dedication, her personal energy for philanthropic and literary causes, and her total dedication to living in a style closely resembling high art. Lewis never loses sight of his role as literary biographer: that of interpreting the relationship between the artist's work and life. Careful analysis of the process of writing the novels is given along with colorful accounts of Wharton's dazzling international life and her associations with the most gifted writers and critics of the day—Henry James and Bernard Berenson, for example. An important appendix is the "Beatrice Palmato" fragment, an unpublished, somewhat pornographic piece of fiction on an incestuous theme. For a more informal, consistently appreciative account of Wharton's life written by a friend, see Percy Lubbock's *Portrait of Edith Wharton* (1947, reprint 1969). Lubbock, an important critical voice, felt that criticism would be out of place in his "likeness of Wharton as her friends knew her and as she lives in their memory." Louis Auchincloss, another Wharton biographer and critic, has written *Edith Wharton: A Woman*

in Her Time (Viking, 1971), an entertaining biography with excellent photographs. Wharton's autobiography, *A Backward Glance* (1934), is purposefully circumspect about "uncongenial" material but a graceful and beautifully written memoir.

223   Lindbergh, Anne (Morrow), 1906- . **Gift from the Sea.** New York:
         Vintage Books, 1978. 140p. $1.95. ISBN 0394724550. LC 77-14351.
This jewel-like autobiographical meditation on Lindbergh's life as wife, mother, writer, woman appeared in 1955 when she was thinking about the middle-age responsibilities of running a large and complicated household (Lindbergh had five children). The setting of her meditation was a simple seaside retreat where she went alone to think about the evaluate her hectic life and to work toward evolving "another rhythm with more creative pauses in it. . . ." Anne Morrow Lindbergh is a careful thinker and she writes with simple grace. Her revelations about love, life, and the relentless pace of daily living are not so startling as they are reasonable and intelligent. Her diaries and letters have this same thoughtful, careful quality. See *Bring Me a Unicorn: Diaries and Letters of Anne Morrow Lindbergh, 1922-1928* (Harcourt Brace Jovanovich, 1972)—dealing with her college years at Smith and her meeting Charles Lindbergh; *Hour of Gold, Hour of Lead, 1929-1932* (Harcourt Brace Jovanovich, 1973)—chronicling engagement and marriage to the famous Lindbergh, a public life, and the tragic kidnapping and murder of their first son; *Rooms and Open Doors: Diaries and Letters of Anne Morrow Lindbergh, 1933-1935* (Harcourt Brace Jovanovich, 1974)—detailing their public lives and the aftermath of their private tragedy; *The Flower and the Nettle: Diaries and Letters 1936-1939* (Harcourt Brace Jovanovich, 1976)—recounting the Lindberghs' busy life with a growing family and Ann Lindbergh's increasing self-confidence as a woman and writer.

224   Lindborg, Kristina, and Carlos Julio Ovando. **Five Mexican-American
         Women in Transition: A Case Study of Migrants in the Midwest.**
         San Francisco, CA: R. and E. Research Associates, 1977. 111p. bibliog.
         $8.00. ISBN 0882474448. LC 76-56558.
"In this study, Mexican-American migrant women's attitudes and experiences regarding such aspects of life as courtship, love, marriage, motherhood, women's rights and education are explored. The study is not an analysis of Mexican-American culture and society as a whole from the point of view of the migrant woman, but rather a consideration of certain domains of Mexican-American life considered of significance by the women themselves. It focuses on four Mexican-Americans from migrant farm-worker backgrounds and one Mexican recently immigrated from Mexico" (from the introduction). The authors set these oral histories in context through an examination of the portrayal of Mexican and Mexican-American women in literature and a concluding theoretical analysis. However, the bulk of the text is devoted to the five very revealing self-portraits.

225   Lutz, Alma. **Emma Willard: Daughter of Democracy.** Boston: Houghton
         Mifflin, 1929; repr. Washington: Zenger, 1975. 291p. bibliog. index.
         $12.50. ISBN 0892010185. LC 75-37635.
Frederick Rudolph has called Lutz's study of Emma Willard (1787-1870) "a definitive biography" (*Notable American Women*). Willard was largely a

self-taught pioneer advocate of improved women's education. Somewhat quaintly calling her schools "female seminaries," Willard was in fact committed to instituting a classical and scientific curriculum to match or even go beyond those available in boys' colleges. At the same time, however, she opposed identical education for the sexes, and her program had something of the "finishing school" about it, as Willard strove to prepare her upper-class women students for marriage and motherhood. Willard's best known school, situated in Troy, New York, survives today as the Emma Willard School. Lutz includes a substantial bibliography listing Willard's own writings (both textbooks and treatises on education) and works on Willard and the history of women's education.

226   Lynd, Alice, and Staughton Lynd, eds. **Rank and File: Personal Histories by Working-class Organizers.** Boston: Beacon Press, 1973. 296p. $3.95. ISBN 0807005096. LC 73-6247.

A collection of inspiring personal histories of labor organizers—some primarily active in the 1930s, some active since World War II. Though of the twenty rank and filers represented here only three are women, the vividness of their accounts and the general dearth of such materials make this book valuable for feminist labor history. The women are: Christine Ellis—immigrant from Yugoslavia, Communist Party organizer of the unemployed during the 1930s, and outspoken opponent of the Korean War (which nearly resulted in her deportation and finally earned her ten months in jail); Stella Nowicki—ten years an organizer in the meatpacking industry on Chicago's southwest side beginning in the early 1930s, organizer with a number of others of the Back of the Yards Youth Council (which preceded the organization for which Saul Alinsky is best known, The Back of the Yards Council), and, recently, member of a women's liberation group; and Sylvia Woods—black woman who took part as a child in the movement led by Marcus Garvey, who helped to create a democratic local branch of the United Auto Workers during World War II, who believes that black working people can only move forward through an alliance with white workers, and who worked actively in the national campaign to free Angela Davis.

227   Lytton, Constance Georgina, Lady, 1869-1923. **Prisons and Prisoners: Experiences of a Suffragette.** Boston: Charles River Books, 1977. (Repr. of 1914 ed.). 337p. $25.00. ISBN 0715811541.

The 1914 edition appeared under the title: *Prisons and Prisoners: Some Personal Experiences.* Lady Lytton's recollections of her initiation into the British Suffrage movement began in 1908, when she met Mrs. Pethick-Lawrence and Annie Kennedy at the Esperance Club for working women. Previous to that time, she had lived the existence of a well-bred single woman at home, an invalid chiefly interacting with family and close friends. Lady Lytton recalls her conversion to the Women's Social and Political Union, her friendship with the Pankhursts, and her commitment to radicalism in support of suffrage, which resulted in her four imprisonments and ensuing illness as a result of prison conditions. She documents the inequity of treatment given to the wealthy and the poor that she observed in prison and graphically reports the routines of prison life. Her description of the torture of forcible feeding meted out to the hunger strikers aroused shock in the minds of the British public who read her account in 1914.

228   McCarthy, Mary Therese, 1912- . **Memories of a Catholic Girlhood.**
       New York: Harcourt, Brace and Jovanovich, 1957. 245p. $4.75.
       ISBN 0151588597. LC 57-8842.

Mary McCarthy's brilliant eight-part memoir series reads like her fiction—
vital, absorbing writing. Yet McCarthy's childhood and young womanhood,
strange as they were, actually happened. Her parents died in the 1918 influenza
epidemic when she was six. Her childhood was passed shuttling between the
homes of wealthy, eccentric, self-absorbed grandparents. From the Minneapolis,
Catholic, McCarthy grandparents, she learned "a sour, baleful doctrine (of
Catholicism) in which old hates and rancors had been stewing for generations,
with ignorance proudly stirring the pot." From her Protestant-Jewish grandparents, she absorbed the tedium of an unchanging routine that included a
daily diet of shopping, dressing up, and playing cards. Both backgrounds were
intellectually mediocre; McCarthy seems to have been saved by Vassar. Throughout these exceptional portraits of growing up, there are numerous glints of wit
and humor and a constant self-analysis probing for the "truth" amid this stock-
pile of childhood memories and associations. Her observations of the grand-
mothers, their foibles, and their aging are particularly vivid.

229   McLeod, Enid. **The Order of the Rose: The Life and Ideas of Christine
       de Pizan.** Totowa, NJ: Rowman and Littlefield, 1976. 185p. bibliog.
       index. $13.50. ISBN 0874718104. LC 76-360987.

Perhaps because Simone de Beauvoir identified Christine de Pizan (c1363-c1429)
as "the first woman to take up pen in defense of her sex," she is receiving some
attention by contemporary feminists as a champion of women's rights during
the waning of the Middle Ages. Christine is interesting for her views on equal
educational opportunity for women, and especially intriguing for the position
she held at court enabling her to argue and discuss her views with the leading
intellectuals of the day. Her own literary output, mainly in the genre of the
courtly lyric, is more notable for the fact that she was able to write and gain
recognition for it than for its literary merit. Her work has been largely ignored
since her death. McCleod writes that Christine de Pizan's feminism was moderate,
calling for men to treat women as human beings rather than as either objects
to worship or to debase, the two poles of medieval thought on women. A strict
moralist, one of Christine's most noted prose works was an assult on Jean de
Meun's *Roman de la Rose* for its views of sensuality and its attack on marriage.
Another useful but brief summary of her life can be found in Alice Kemp-Welch's
Six Mediaevel Women (1913).

230   Madsen, Axel. **Hearts and Minds: The Common Journey of Simone de
       Beauvoir and Jean-Paul Sartre.** New York: Morrow, 1977. 320p.
       bibliog. index. $10.95. ISBN 0688032060. LC 77-2896.

Since Sartre and de Beauvoir have said much about their private and public
lives and said it so eloquently, Madsen has pursued a wise course in relying
extensively on Sartre's *Les Mots* and de Beauvoir's autobiographical volumes in
giving an account of their years together. Clearly Sartre and de Beauvoir needed
to be treated together in a biography; their intellectual and political commitments
have been undertaken as a couple. De Beauvoir's fiction deals repeatedly with
the autobiographical details of her relationship with Sartre. Perhaps because

the analysis of the relationship has been a consistent preoccupation of thie celebrated couple, Madsen chose to tell their story in terms of factual achievements and chronological details from the summer of 1929 to the spring of 1977, and to refrain from an analytic approach to the complex intertwining of their lives. Along with many excellent photographs, Madsen has included a complete French and English bibliography of their books.

231   Marshall, Dorothy. **Fanny Kemble.** New York: St. Martin's Press,
       1978. 280p. bibliog. index. $8.95. ISBN 0312281625. LC 77-3854.
Seven biographies of Fanny Kemble (1809-1893) have been published between 1931 and 1972. Of these, the best documented has been *Fanny Kemble and the Lovely Land* (1973), by Constance Wright. Readers looking for a good bibliography on Kemble should turn to Wright first, for Marshall provides only a bibliographical note on the books. However, for a readable general approach to Fanny Kemble's youth, her early acting career, her life with her plantation-owner husband in America, and her triumphant return to the stage in 1848, this becomes a good choice. Packed as it is with the daily details of houses and lifestyle, Marshall's study does not analyze Kemble's turbulent life and complex personal relationships, though these images are familiar from earlier biographies.

232   Martin, George Whitney. **Madam Secretary: Frances Perkins.** Boston:
       Houghton Mifflin, 1976. 589p. bibliog. index. $16.95. ISBN
       0395242932. LC 75-38637.
This is a biography of Frances Perkins (1882-1965), first woman to be appointed to the United States Cabinet—Perkins served as Secretary of Labor under President Roosevelt, 1933-1945. Martin describes her childhood, her early work with the settlement movement and the Consumer's League, her marriage, her appointment to the New York State Labor Department, and, finally, her work as Secretary of Labor.

233*   Matthiessen, Francis Otto, 1902-1950. **Sarah Orne Jewett.** Boston:
       Houghton Mifflin, 1929. 160p. index. LC 29-9532.
While there are more current biographies of Jewett—John E. Frost's *Sarah Orne Jewett* (1960) and Richard Cary's *Sarah Orne Jewett* (1962)—as well as the *Letters*, edited by Richard Cary (1967), Matthiessen's biography has long been the standard one. His description of Jewett's Maine upbringing and her ordered life in Boston with Annie Adams Fields is written in simple, unadorned prose. In documenting Jewett's life, Matthiessen has relied heavily on Jewett's letters and on incidents drawn from her sketches of Maine; he also used materials and perceptions of friends and relations close to the prominent New England writer. This noted American critic regards Sarah Orne Jewett's work as fiction of the first rank, applauding her as "the daughter of Hawthorne's style." Of her achievement, Matthiessen writes, "in the whole group of proud Brahmins whom Miss Jewett knew, and revered as far wiser and stronger than herself, there is not one with her severity of form and subtle elimination. Their words are heavy and diffuse, lacking balance, lacking concentration. And so they are sinking slowly, while hers go lightly forward, and she takes her place next to Emily Dickinson—the two principal women writers America has had."

234   May, Antoinette. **Different Drummers: They Did What They Wanted.**
       Millbrae, CA: Les Femmes, 1976. 156p. bibliog. index. $4.95. ISBN
       0890879079. LC 76-11373.
The biographees here are dancer Isadora Duncan, aviator Amerlia Earhart,
opera star Madame Schumann-Heink, theosophist Helena Blavatsky, actress
Sarah Bernhardt, and presidential candidate Victoria Woodhull. The purpose
of these short biographies is to describe women of creativity and singleminded-
ness who pursued careers in politics, spiritualism, dancing, acting, and flying.
Each was a revolutionary woman of her day. The language is straightforward
and the bibliography, manageable. It could serve as a source of supplemental
reading on these six women for undergraduates, and as a particularly good source
for a browsing area in high school or undergraduate libraries.

235   Mead, Margaret, 1901-1978. **Blackberry Winter: My Earlier Years.**
       New York: Morrow, 1972. 305p. $11.95. ISBN 0688000517.
Mead lived a life of remarkable diversity, and this personal chronicle records
the variety of experiences that brought Mead to her position as acclaimed
anthropologist—but more, as American household word. Remembered here
are Pennsylvania school days, DePauw and Barnard college experiences, friends
and mentors Ruth Benedict and Franz Boas. She writes lovingly and candidly
about her family, especially her sociologist mother. Somehow she brings off
the accounts of her three marriages—Luther Cressman (m. 1923—minister);
Reo Fortune (m.1928—psychologist); Gregory Bateson (m.1936—anthropologist)—
with humor and candor. Family relationships, despite the divorces, are dear
to Mead, and her description of rearing her only daughter, Catherine, is particularly good. The early field trips (Samoa, New Guinea, Bali) get attention here
along with accounts of difficulties she overcame in pursuing her unusual career.

236   Mead, Margaret, 1901-1978. **Ruth Benedict.** New York: Columbia
       University Press, 1974. 180p. bibliog. $10.00. ISBN 0231035195.
       LC 74-6400.
The first part of the book is a biographical tribute to Benedict as "one of the
first women to attain major stature as a social scientist." It was not until 1921,
at the age of 34, that Benedict began to study anthropology under Franz Boas.
She served as a role model to a generation of women anthropologists including
Mead. Among the beautifully written selected papers of Benedict that Mead
gives us here are: Configurations of Culture in North America; Magic; An
Introduction to Zuni Mythology; Primitive Freedom; Self-Discipline in Japanese
Culture; The Study of Cultural Patterns in European Nations; Anthropology
and the Humanities.

237   Mellow, James R. **Charmed Circle: Gertrude Stein and Company.**
       New York: Praeger, 1974. 528p. bibliog. index. $12.95. ISBN
       0275504301. LC 73-7473.
Probably the most complete biography of Gertrude Stein to date, *Charmed
Circle* deals with the special and enduring forty-year relationship between
Stein and Alice Toklas. The texture of Stein's artistic life—peopled by cultural
luminaries such as Picasso, Matisse, and Hemingway—is culled from memoirs,
recollections, and letters. There is much about the daily life of the writer in

the midst of her circle in Paris and at the country house at Bilingin, and the process of creation that took place in these residences. Quite moving is the portrait of Alice Toklas alone, in financial straits but alert in the years following Stein's death (Stein died in 1946, while Toklas lived until 1967). The book suffers from lack of a chronology but the bibliography is exceptionally complete. Much of the research has been done at the Collection of American Literature, the Beinecke Rare Book and Manuscript Library, Yale University. Richard Bridgman's *Gertrude Stein in Pieces* (New York: Oxford University Press, 1970) is useful to read along with Mellow. Mellow states that he is more interested in capturing the life-style of Stein than the legend; he has accomplished this end. Other recent, related sources are Linda Simon's *Biography of Alice B. Toklas* (Doubleday, 1977); and *Dear Sammy: Letters From Gertrude Stein and Alice B. Toklas* (Houghton Mifflin, 1977). This last is a collection of Stein's and Toklas's letters to Samuel M. Steward, an American professor of English who conducted a correspondence with the two women from 1932 to 1967. The letters illuminate the Stein/Toklas relationship and are filled with details of their lives together.

238   Merriam, Eve, 1916- , comp. **Growing Up Female in America: Ten Lives.** Garden City, NY: Doubleday, 1971. 308p. bibliog. $7.95. ISBN 0385060831. LC 79-157611.
"No ten women, however diversified their life styles, could possibly represent what it was like growing up female in America. These specimen lives, portrayed first hand through autobiographies, diaries, journals, and letters, are intended as a beginning attempt only. . . ." Included here are: Eliza Southgate (1783-1809), schoolgirl; Elizabeth Cady Stanton (1815-1902), founder of the Woman Suffrage Movement; Maria Mitchell (1818-1889), astronomer; Mary Ann Webster Loughborough (1836-1887), wife of a Confederate officer; Arvazine Angeline Cooper (1845-1929), pioneer; Dr. Anna Howard Shaw (1847-1919), minister and doctor; Susie King Taylor (1848-1912), born a slave; "Mother" Mary Jones (1830-1930), labor organizer; Elizabeth Gertrude Stern (1890-1954), in the Jewish ghetto; Mountain Wolf Woman (1884-1960), Winnebago Indian; and a section of miscellany. Eve Merriam has written an introduction to the collection and a brief introduction to each woman's life history.

239   Mikhail, E. H., ed. **Lady Gregory: Interviews and Recollections.** Totowa, NJ: Rowman and Littlefield, 1977. bibliog. index. $12.50. ISBN 0874719615. LC 77-1322.
Lady Gregory was one of those women frequently labeled an inspiration to genius. This is how she is remembered most often in her relationship to W. B. Yeats. As one of the principal figures of the Irish Renaissance, however, she transcended the roles of friend, inspiration, and hostess. She was a dramatist in her own right and co-founder and director of the Abbey Theater. She believed strongly in an Anglo-Irish prose idiom for literary use and set about perfecting this idiom. Lady Gregory was Ireland's preeminent collector of folklore, and Yeats learned much from her about the Irish folk tradition. Mikhail's is an informal collection of interviews and impressions recorded by Lady Gregory's contemporaries, among them George Moore, Yeats, Sean O'Casey, and Hallie Flanagan. The volume is useful especially in the absence of a definitive biography.

240   Milford, Nancy. **Zelda: A Biography.** New York: Harper and Row,
       1970. 424p. bibliog. index. $12.50. ISBN 0060129913. LC 66-20742.
Zelda Fitzgerald (1900-1948), wife of F. Scott Fitzgerald and a novelist in her
own right (*Save Me the Waltz*, 1932), was an extraordinary woman involved in a
complex, intense, and finally insanity-provoking love affair and marriage with
an acknowledged genius. The problem was that Zelda was a genius, too, desperately
trying to surface as an artist while living with an egomaniacal artist. In this
absorbing, feminist biography of Zelda, Milford carefully documents the bind
between love and art in which Zelda was caught. Zelda's story—girlhood as a
Southern belle in Montgomery, Alabama, symbol of "the lost generation,"
and the center of the international literary society of the '20s as F. Scott
Fitzgerald's wife, flapper extraordinaire, finally victim of mental breakdowns
due to her frustration in dealing with Scott and realizing her own artistic capacity—
is an incredible narrative of a woman's struggle for self-knowledge. When Zelda
tried to assert her talents, she was silenced by her husband and developed
severe feelings of inferiority and failure. Scott borrowed heavily from her letters
and diaries for his own work and certainly used her character in the best of his
work. Diagnosed as schizophrenic, Zelda was a patient in many hospitals over
the years before her death in a hospital fire six years after her husband's death.
There is no question that Zelda and Scott were both victims of their relationship—at once a creative and destructive union. Milford does an admirable job
in analyzing Zelda's fiction and her flight into insanity.

241   Millay, Edna St. Vincent, 1892-1950. **Letters of Edna St. Vincent**
       Millay. Westport, CT: Greenwood Press, 1972. (Repr. of 1952 ed.).
       384p. index. $21.00. ISBN 0837164826. LC 72-6177.
Edited by Allan Ross Macdougall, these letters illustrate the poet's admirable
skill with prose. The collection is revelatory of the private and the public
woman, as it includes letters about Millay's poetry, to and about her family,
and to editors, critics, and fellow poets. Steepletop was the home she shared
with her husband and many of the letters were written there; in later years,
she relied much upon her husband, Eugen Boissevain, and the conveniences
of telephone and telegraph to handle correspondence. The divisions of the correspondence run: I. Childhood and Youth in Maine (1900-1912); II. College Years,
Barnard and Vassar (1913-1917); III. Post-College Years (June, 1917 to end of
1920); IV. European Trip (1921-22); V. New York—The Orient—Steepletop
(1923-1925); VI. Steepletop (1926-1930); VII. Steepletop—Paris—Florida
(1931-1935); VIII. Florida—New York—Steepletop (1936-1945); IX. Steepletop—
Ragged Island (1946-October, 1950).

242   Millett, Kate. **Flying.** New York: Knopf; distr. New York: Random
       House, 1974. 545p. $8.95. ISBN 0394489853. LC 73-20766.
In this book, altogether different from *Sexual Politics*, the most remarkable
feature is its length. As difficult as it is to read straight through because of its
sheer mass, it is a fascinating book in small doses. Main preoccupations of Millett
here are coping with being a celebrity after *Sexual Politics* and dealing with her
bisexuality. Some may find her inner conflicts concerning lesbianism excruciat-
ingly drawn out; overall however, Millett writes in great detail and writes well,
relentlessly exposing her own complex sexual life. Most interesting is Millett's

personal voice here as opposed to her academic voice in *Sexual Politics*. Millett's latest novel is *Sita* (Farrar, Straus and Giroux, 1977).

243   Millett, Kate. **The Prostitution Papers.** New York: Ballantine Books, 1976. 149p. $1.75. ISBN 0345254341.

Millett subtitled this slim volume "A Quartet for Female Voice"; the four women's accounts that comprise the papers originally appeared as a quartet score in four columns across two pages (in *Woman in Sexist Society*, edited by Vivian Gornick and Barbara Moran, 1971). Millett decided, back in the summer of 1970, that instead of "inventing something" herself through book-study on the subject of prostitution, she would find women who could teach her what it was actually like. Four-way conversations were held and taped between Kate, Lix Schneider (her collaborator), "J" (a white call girl), and "M" (a black heroin addict). These conversations were then edited by Millett into four separate accounts, of which M's and J's are far and away the more compelling. Millett says in her 1976 introduction that she now views *The Prostitution Papers* as a bridge between the academic scholarship of *Sexual Politics* and "the record of life put down in real speech" of *Flying*.

244   Millett, Kate. **Sita.** New York: Farrar, Straus and Giroux, 1977. 321p. $10.00. ISBN 0374265461. LC 77-2267.

Millett's autobiographical account of her painful love relationship with Sita has as its primary characteristic a wrenching honesty. The eroticism and essence of Sita haunt and compel Millett through this chronicle of an affair on the verge of collapse after a duration of several years. Millett spares few details of the agony that a relationship as intense as hers with Sita can impose. Millett is the rejected and tormented lover. More than a dissection of a lesbian love affair, *Sita* captures an alternative lifestyle lived in San Francisco and New York, which included not only Sita and her complex nuclear and extended family but Millett's former husband and New York literary friends. This is perhaps the most romantic personal account in print about intense personal friendships between women.

245*   Mitchell, Hannah Maria Webster, 1871-1956. **The Hard Way Up: The Autobiography of Hannah Mitchell, Suffragette and Rebel.** London: Faber, 1968; repr. London: Virago, 1977. 260p. index. $4.35. ISBN 0860680029.

This is an extraordinary autobiography by a working-class English woman who was both socialist and feminist. Mitchell tells of her growing up on a farm in Derbyshire, England, and of the antagonism that flared between her and her mother over Hannah's hatred of household tasks. Hannah fled her home and family as soon as she could, moving to Bolton, where she supported herself through exploitative jobs, became involved in the socialist movement, and soon married a comrade. Her latent feminism blossomed with the marriage and her discovery of the limits of her male socialist comrades' commitment to women's freedom. She writes, "I soon realized that married life, as men understand it, calls for a degree of self-abnegation which was impossible for me . . . and that a lot of the Socialist talk about freedom was only talk and these Socialist young men expected Sunday dinners and huge teas with home-made cakes, potted meat and pies, exactly like their reactionary fellows." Mitchell writes with a certain bitterness, but does not become cynical or lose her political commitment. Her perceptions about the conflicts of socialist feminism speak directly to the concerns of women facing the same struggles today: "No cause can be won between dinner and tea, and most of us who were married had to work with one hand tied behind us, so to speak. Public disapproval can be faced and borne, but domestic unhappiness, the price many of us paid for our opinions and activities, was a very bitter thing." The Virago edition has a preface by Sheila Rowbotham.

246   Moffat, Mary Jane, and Charlotte Painter, comps. **Revelations: Diaries of Women.** New York: Random House, 1974. 411p. bibliog. $2.95. ISBN 0394711513.

The diary is a literary form that has traditionally been an important outlet for women "partly because it is an analogue to their lives: emotional, fragmentary, interrupted, modest, not to be taken seriously, private, restricted, daily, trivial, formless, concerned with self, as endless as their tasks." The editors have assembled an impressive array of samples here from 32 women, from diaries of the early nineteenth century to those of recent date, reflecting the secret and spontaneous feelings of very young girls, of older women, of famous and anonymous women. Among examples from published and unpublished diaries are Anaïs Nin, Ruth Benedict, Anna Dostoevsky, Mary Boykin Chestnut, Käthe Kollwitz, and Virginia Woolf. The listing of other published diaries at the end of the volume will give direction to further study in this area. Another important bibliographic source is Jane Dupree Bego's *Annotated Bibliography of Published Women's Diaries*, published by the author (Pound Ridge, NY, 1977).

247   Moody, Anne, 1940- . **Coming of Age in Mississippi: An Autobiography.** New York: Dell, 1970. 348p. $1.50.

When published in 1969, Anne Moody's autobiography was hailed as one of the best accounts of growing up black in the rural South. Written when she was only 28, *Coming of Age* covers Moody's life up to her graduation from college and the Canton (Mississippi) Freedom Day march in 1964. Particularly vivid and moving is the first section of the work, "Childhood," which tells of the writer's early years in Wilkinson County in Mississippi's black belt, daughter of a sharecropping family. Anne was the only child in her family to go on to college and an involvement in the Civil Rights Movement in the South. Her autobiography becomes history in the depiction of the era of the sit-ins and voter registration drives.

248   Moore, Carman. **Somebody's Angel Child: The Story of Bessie Smith.** New York: Thomas Y. Crowell, 1969. 121p. bibliog. index. $6.95. ISBN 0690750099. LC 77-94797.

Elisabeth "Bessie" Smith was born in 1898 in Chattanooga, Tennessee, and orphaned as a child. Moore emphasizes throughout the biography that Bessie Smith's preeminent place in blues history is the result of her considerable vocal talent and her experiences of personal tragedy and poverty from childhood. She dealt with the blues in her life by singing in public. As a child, she sang on the street and in the local theaters. Later she toured with Ma Rainey, a major blues stylist. Throughout her career, which was most successful in the 1920s, she drank heavily. "The Empress of the Blues" hit financial and personal disaster by 1930. In October of 1937, she was killed in an automobile crash on Route 61 outside of Clarksdale, Mississippi. She was 39, had made more than a million dollars, and sold over ten million records. Moore includes a selected discography and a short bibliography. Readers may also want to look at Hettie Jones' *Big Star Fallin' Mama: Five Women in Black Music* (Viking Press, 1974), which discusses Bessie Smith, Billie Holiday, Ma Rainey, Mahalia Jackson, and Aretha Franklin.

249   Morris, Jan, 1926- . **Conundrum.** New York: Harcourt Brace Jovanovich, 1974. 174p. $6.95. ISBN 015122563X. LC 74-525.
"I was three or perhaps four years old when I realized that I had been born into the wrong body, and should really be a girl. I remember the moment well, and it is the earliest memory of my life." In *Conundrum*, Jan Morris (formerly James Humphry Morris)—writer, father of five children—describes the long and painful process of self-discovery that eventually led him to undergo surgery and hormonal treatment to become the woman he felt himself to be. Written in very personal terms, this autobiography brings into sharp relief questions about the relationship of biological sex, psychological gender identity, and cultural sex roles.

250   Mountain Wolf Woman, 1884-1960. **Mountain Wolf Woman, Sister of Crashing Thunder: The Autobiography of a Winnebago Indian.** Edited by Nancy Oestreich Lurie. Ann Arbor: University of Michigan Press, 1961. 142p. $5.00. ISBN 0472091093. LC 61-5019.
In the foreword to this eloquent autobiographical statement by Mountain Wolf Woman, whose brother's story was published in the '20s (Paul Radin, *Crashing Thunder*, New York, 1926), Ruth Underhill writes of research on American Indian women up to 1961: "even yet, we are inclined to judge the Indian woman's life by these modern standards. If we are to see her as living a full life in her own sphere, studies in depth are needed and will be for some time. Michelson (1933) gave the curt account which was all an Arapaho woman felt inclined to tell. Gladys Reichard, in Dezba, painted a sympathetic picture of a Navajo matriarch, from a white woman's point of view. In the same year, I collected the disjointed statements of an ancient Papago woman, too old to organize and tell a connected story. In 1959, Carmen Lee Smithson published a detailed account of life among Havasupai women, though not in their own words. Nancy Lurie's tape recording of the year-by-year experiences of a Winnebago woman thus far stands almost alone as source material for a woodland Indian woman's activities and attitudes." Mountain Wolf Woman relates in detail her earliest recollections in Black River Falls, Wisconsin, of growing up, of marriage, and of the ritual use of peyote. Children and grandchildren play important roles in this autobiography in which Mountain Wolf Woman counterpoints details of traditional life against technological realities. Lurie's description of the process of carrying out this oral history project is fascinating.

251   Murray, Pauli, 1910- . **Proud Shoes: The Story of an American Family.** Spartanburg, SC: Reprint, 1973 (Repr. of 1956 ed.). 276p. $15.00. ISBN 0871521369. LC 73-2566.

Pauli Murray evokes a childhood in North Carolina and the strong omnipresent personalities of Grandfather and Grandmother. She records Grandmother's tirades at the neighbors, and Grandmother and Grandfather's constant but loving bickering between each other, with a keen ear for tone and tempo. Though the simplicity of Murray's story is achieved by filtering the story of the family through her perceptions as a child, the consciousness of inequities and perpetual prejudice are no less the poignant for it. In the last chapter, she summarizes the indignities suffered during her black childhood in the South despite the presence of strong family: "our seedy run-down school told us that if we had any place at all in the scheme of things it was a separate place, marked off, proscribed and unwanted by the white people. We were bottled up and labeled and set aside—sent to the Jim Crow car, the back of the bus, the side door of the theater, the side window of the restaurant. We came to understand that no matter how neat and clean, how law abiding, submissive and polite, how studious in school, how churchgoing and moral, how scrupulous in paying our bills and taxes we were, it made no essential difference in our place."

252   Nash, Mary, 1925- . **The Provoked Wife: The Life and Times of Susannah Cibber.** Boston: Little, Brown, 1977. 369p. bibliog. index. $12.50. ISBN 0316598313. LC 76-30336.
Cibber's story illuminates the position of woman and actress in the eighteenth-century. Dominated by her father, tyrannized by her husband, Theophilus Cibber, Susannah Cibber was a gifted actress and singer of the 1700s. Chosen by David Garrick to act in his productions, and by Handel to sing his works, Susannah was one of the most popular actresses of her day. Her husband enjoyed the financial success of his wife until her affair with William Sloper. Out of greed and vengeance, Theophilus took Sloper to court, where the relationship between Susannah and her lover was made into a public scandal, the subject of bawdy cartoons and lewd songs. Though Susannah made a brilliant comeback despite the machinations of her insensitive slandering husband, her position in society was permanently damaged. She and Garrick were the most popular stage couple of the period. Her life is an example of great strength despite the brutal marital property laws of the day and the constrictions of eighteenth-century morality. Nash writes of her achievement: "her life was a sustained and eloquent supplication for acceptance in the British establishment. Yet she lies, not like Garrick or Congreve or Dryden or Mrs. Oldenfield, theater's royalty, within the Abbey itself, but in an anteroom of fame, within the sound of ceremony, neither remembered nor utterly forgotten, not really a private person nor quite a public figure."

253   Nestor, Agnes, 1880-1948. **Woman's Labor Leader: An Autobiography of Agnes Nestor.** Rockford, IL: Bellevue Books, 1954; repr. Washington: Zenger, 1975. 307p. index. $15.00. ISBN 0892010207. LC 75-37823.
For this autobiography of an important woman labor organizer, Nestor's experience as a glove worker in Chicago in the late 1890s gave her a first-hand understanding of the exploitation of workers. Her success in leading her fellow women workers out on a victorious strike in 1898 convinced her to devote her life to organizing women workers. This she went on to do, primarily through the International Glove Workers Union, but also in work with the Women's Trade

Union League. Nestor is noted for her contribution to the achievement of protective legislation for women and children and to the achievement of the eight-hour day.

254   Nies, Judith. **Seven Women: Portraits from the American Radical Tradition.** New York: Viking Press, 1977. 236p. bibliog. index. $8.95. ISBN 0670635995. LC 76-49942.

Nies maintains that because American social history imprisons women in a context of conservatism, there is seldom recognition of the pivotal roles that they have played in radical political and social change. The seven women chosen for inclusion—Sarah Moore Grimké (1792-1873); Harriet Tubman (1820-1913); Elizabeth Cady Stanton (1815-1902); Mother Jones (1830-1930); Charlotte Perkins Gilman (1860-1935); Anna Louise Strong (1885-1970); and Dorothy Day (1897-)—each represent a different point on the spectrum of American radicalism and each defy conventional notions of radicalism. Very helpful is the section listing further readings and individual biographies for each of these radical women.

255   Nin, Anaïs, 1903-1977. **The Diary of Anaïs Nin.** New York: Harcourt, Brace and Jovanovich, 1966-1976. 6v. v.1-4, $9.50ea. v.5, $7.95. v.6, $12.95. LC 66-12917.

(The coverage in the volumes is as follows: v.1. 1931-1934; v.2. 1934-1939; v.3. 1939-1944; v.4. 1944-1947; v.5. 1947-1955; v.6. 1955-1966.) Perhaps more than any single writer, Anaïs Nin has made the diary form a respected genre of literature. Her novels, stories, and other artistic work grow out of the diary, and she wrote, "I have a natural flow in the diary, what I produce outside is a distillation, the myth, the poem." Though the diaries are chiefly chronicles of thoughts and dreams, Nin does talk of people and places. Volume 1 begins when Nin is about to publish her first book, a critical appreciation of D. H. Lawrence, and ends in the winter of 1934 when she travels to New York for a brief visit. Included here are her friendships with Otto Rank, Henry Miller and Artaud, among other important figures. Volume 2 takes up in New York, where Nin is working as Rank's assistant in 1934. These are years of intense personal friendships with Lawrence Durrell and Gonzalo More, her Paris houseboat days, her continuing association with Henry Miller. Volume 3 chronicles her acting in Provincetown; friendships with Frances Field, Robert Duncan, Caresse Crosby, Jean Varda, and the beginning of her handpress in her Macdougal Street studio. In volume 4, Nin moves into the bohemian celebrity world and begins gaining notoriety for her writing, also starring in movies. Her role as mentor to Gore Vidal is prominent. Volumes 5 and 6 recall her increasing reputation, her traveling and speaking, and the constant thread of her friendship with Miller.

256   Nin, Anaïs, 1903-1977. **Linotte: The Early Diary of Anaïs Nin, 1914-1920.** New York: Harcourt, Brace, Jovanovich, 1978. 518p. index. $14.95. ISBN 0151524882. LC 77-20314.

Anaïs Nin began this diary when she moved with her family from Barcelona to New York in 1914. This marks the beginning of an extraordinary diary that was to last a lifetime and has made Anaïs Nin one of the most celebrated diarists of all time. Though this earliest diary does not have the power and beauty of the maturer diaries (indeed, it is the most artless, and the only diary to be published as it was written with spare editing), it contains charming accounts of adolescence and young womanhood and brims with love for family and with lyrical wonder at the world. She recounts, with a keen eye for detail and with the characteristic Nin flair for optimism, the life of the immigrant family in New York City. Early photographs, sketches, and fascimile pages of the diary accompany the text. "Linotte," or linnet (little bird), is the signature that Nin used in letters to her father; and mainly the diary is an extended letter to her father, the Spanish composer and pianist, Joaquin Nin.

257   Nin, Anaïs, 1903-1977. **A Woman Speaks: The Lectures, Seminars, and Interviews of Anaïs Nin.** Edited by Evelyn J. Hinz. Chicago: Swallow Press, 1975. 270p. index. $12.50. ISBN 0804006938. LC 75-15111.
"The issues which Nin treats in her lectures are characteristically contemporary ones—the status of women, racial injustice, space-age technology and its relation to art, trends in art and psychology, alienation—in some ways issues with which she does not deal in the *Diary* or at least not directly," we are told in the introduction to this collection. Much of the material is derived from the question/answer sessions following her lectures.

258   Ning, Lao T'ai-t'ai, 1867- . **A Daughter of Han: The Autobiography of a Chinese Working Woman.** By Ida Pruitt, from the story told her by Ning Lao T'ai-t'ai. Stanford, CA: Stanford University Press, 1967. 254p. $10.00. ISBN 0804706050. LC 68-10633.
Lao T'ai-t'ai begins her story at her birth in 1867 and leaves off with the invasion of the Japanese in 1937 and 1938. Ida Pruitt, who published the narrative in 1945, left Peiping in 1938 and did not hear of Lao T'ai-t'ai again. Lao T'ai-t'ai's life story is one of essentially unrelieved suffering as a member of the impoverished classes and as a woman. Included in her narrative are chilling tales of foot binding, arranged marriage, abandonment, and her efforts to keep herself and her children from starvation. A valuable first-hand account of a woman's life in pre-revolutionary China, this autobiography can provide rich comparisons with accounts of the changes that have taken place in Chinese women's lives since the 1950s.

259   O'Connor, Ellen M. **Myrtilla Miner: A Memoir.** By Ellen M. O'Connor. **The School for Colored Girls.** An address by Myrtilla Miner. New York: Arno Press, 1969. (Repr. of 1885 and 1854 eds.). 129, 12p. $7.50. ISBN 0405019335. LC 73-92235.
"Myrtilla Miner has been one of the forgotten heroines in the fight for Negro education. Yet she eminently deserves the tribute of later generations as a pioneer of education which was a wilderness in her time. Myrtilla Miner, a white woman from upstate New York, established a Normal School for Free Negro Girls in Washington, D.C. in 1851 with but one hundred dollars—raised with difficulty—in her possession. She invaded Washington, D.C., a stronghold of pro-slavery and anti-Negro sentiment with the aim of preparing Negro girls to become teachers of their race" (from Florence Freedman's introduction). O'Connor

wrote her memoir of Myrtilla Miner in 1885 as secretary of the Institution for the Education of Colored Youth. Appended to it is Miner's 1854 address, "The School for Colored Girls," which was actually a report about the progress of the school and its precarious financial situation in the form of an appeal for funds.

260   Osen, Lynne M. **Women in Mathematics.** Cambridge, MA: MIT Press, 1974. 185p. bibliog. index. $11.00. ISBN 026215014X. LC 73-19506.
Beginning with the fact that history has not been generous in bestowing recignition on mathematicians male or female, this study attends to the distinguished contributions of women to mathematics and astronomy. Biographical, historical, and mathematical in content, Osen's study is a graceful and informative treatment addressed to the general reader, covering ancient as well as modern mathematicians: Hypatia (370-415); The "Witch" of Agnesi (1718-1799); Emilie de Breteuil, Marquise du Châtelet (1706-1749); Caroline Herschel (1750-1848); Sophie Germain (1776-1831); Mary Fairfax Somerville (1780-1872); Sonya Corvin-Krukovsky Kovalevsky (1850-1891); Emmy (Amalie) Noether (1882-1935). Osen explores the cultural basis for women's supposed ineptitude for mathematics, terming the phenomenon "the feminine mathtique." Readers may also want to look at *Women and Mathematics: Research Perspectives For Change*, by Lynn H. Fox, et al. (U.S. Dept. of Health, Education and Welfare, National Institute of Education, Education and Work Group, 1977).

261   Ossoli, Sarah Margaret (Fuller) Marchesa d' [Fuller, Margaret], 1810-1850. **Love-Letters of Margaret Fuller, 1845-1846.** New York: Greenwood Press, 1969. 228p. $11.00. ISBN 0837114519. LC 69-14023.
Though Fuller's *Memoirs* provide a deeper insight into her thought and feeling, the *Love-Letters* written to James Nathan, a man whom she regarded as a spiritual counterpart, reveal Fuller's desire to be known by another. Nathan was a businessman. The letters convey much information about the daily ebb and flow of Fuller's life and its deeply contemplative quality.

262   Ossoli, Sarah Margaret (Fuller) Marchesa d' [Fuller, Margaret], 1810-1850. **Margaret Fuller, American Romantic: A Selection from Her Writings and Correspondence.** Ithaca, NY: Cornell University Press, 1970. 319p. bibliog. $3.95. ISBN 0801491002. LC 63-13082.
This edition (orig. 1963) of Margaret Fuller's writings, edited by Perry Miller (noted scholar of American intellectual history), contains general biographical material on Fuller and critical comments on her writing. Miller places her in the liberal tradition of New England as "one of the rigorous liberals of her age by criticizing most angrily the cowardice of liberals." Writings and correspondence are broken up into time periods by place: Cambridge, 1810-1833; Groton, Providence, Jamaica Plain, 1833-1850. Though this section concentrates on Fuller's letters and shows the private face of the woman, selections from her published work include excerpts from her *Dial* articles; her critiques of American literature in the *New York Tribune*; her foreign correspondent reportage for the *Tribune* from Europe; her study of Goethe; and her eloquent plea for woman suffrage, *Woman in the Nineteenth Century*.

263   Ossoli, Sarah Margaret (Fuller) Marchesa d' [Fuller, Margaret], 1810
       1850. **Memoirs of Margaret Fuller Ossoli.** By Ralph Waldo Emerson,
       William Henry Channing, and James F. Clarke. New York: B. Franklin,
       1972. (Repr. of 1884 ed.). 2v. in 1. $35.00. ISBN 0833712500.
       LC 72-82356.

Because this is the first biography of Fuller (1810-1850), the *Memoirs* is significant despite the distortions her contemporaries managed to inflict on her image
in the name of friendship and decorum. By slashing many important details
of her life from the *Memoirs*, Emerson, Channing, and Clarke immortalized
Fuller as a cold, egotistical, and grim individual. Though they included many
selections from her own journals and letters, interspersing these excerpts along
with their own comments on Fuller's life, character, and writings, many important
manuscripts were lost, disfigured, and destroyed in their endeavors. Nonetheless,
their account must be taken as one of the major sources even with its editing
problems and errors. Thomas W. Higginson, who was acquainted with Fuller
in his youth, saw his biography, *Margaret Fuller Ossoli* (1884), as an improvement
on the *Memoirs*, which he assessed as sentimental and unfair to Fuller. Higginson
was a good editor, and he handled the journal excerpts and correspondence
with skill in his portrait. The *Memoirs*, along with Higginson's biography, stand
as the important nineteenth-century published sources on Fuller.

264   Ossoli, Sarah Margaret (Fuller) Marchesa d' [Fuller, Margaret], 1810-
       1850. **Summer on the Lakes in 1843.** Nieuwkoop: B. De Graaf; New
       York: A. Schram, 1972. (Repr. of 1844 ed.). 256p. bibliog. $12.50.
       ISBN 0839001223. LC 72-86549.

It was *Summer on the Lakes in 1843*—Fuller's lyrical account of her summer in
the West and Midwest—that brought her to the attention of Horace Greeley.
Greeley made Fuller the literary critic for the *New York Daily Tribune*, launching
her into the world of popular journalism. Travel literature was very popular
during the nineteenth century, and Fuller's personal accounts of the great natural
wonders of the country met with critical success.

265   Peck, Mary Gray. **Carrie Chapman Catt: A Biography.** New York:
       H. W. Wilson, 1944; repr. New York: Octagon Books, 1975. 495p.
       index. $18.50. ISBN 0374963363.

This is the standard biography (orig. 1944) of one of the outstanding leaders of
the second generation of American suffragists, Carrie Chapman Catt (1859-
1947). Catt's activism in the Woman Suffrage Movement began in 1887, on the
eve of the reconciliation of the National Woman Suffrage Association and the
American Woman Suffrage Association. In 1890, Catt attended the first convention of the newly merged National American Woman Suffrage Association
(NAWSA) as part of the Iowa delegation, and over the subsequent ten years,
she established her reputation as a woman with extraordinary talents as organizer,
speaker, and leader. In 1900, the aging Susan B. Anthony chose Catt as her
successor to the presidency of the NAWSA, a post that Catt filled until 1904
and then again from 1915 until suffrage was won. Catt's national leadership
was noted for its flexible approach and its commitment to the pursuit of both
state-by-state action and a federal amendment. The string of state victories
during 1917-1918 under Catt's leadership is generally held to have been influential

in the eventual passage of the federal amendment (1918; ratification 1920). Eleanor Flexner has credited Catt with being next only to Susan B. Anthony in her contributions to the final suffrage victory. For a glimpse into Catt's own interpretation of the arduous suffrage struggle, see *Woman Suffrage and Politics*, which she co-authored with Nettie Shuler.

266   Peel, Robert, 1909- . **Mary Baker Eddy: The Years of Authority.**
       New York: Holt, Rinehart and Winston, 1977. bibliog. index. $14.95.
       ISBN 003021081X. LC 77-6275.
This is the third volume in the author's three-volume biography, the first and second of which are *Mary Baker Eddy: The Years of Discovery*, and *Mary Baker Eddy: The Years of Trial*. It covers the period from 1892 to Eddy's death in 1910.

267   Peel, Robert, 1909- . **Mary Baker Eddy: The Years of Discovery.**
       New York: Holt, Rinehart and Winston, 1966. 372p. bibliog. index.
       $7.50. ISBN 0030575559. LC 66-14855.
This is the first volume in the author's three-volume biography, the second and third of which are *Mary Baker Eddy: The Years of Trial*, and *Mary Baker Eddy: The Years of Authority*. Mary Baker Eddy (1821-1910) suffered a variety of nervous ailments from childhood onward and was attracted to the new theories of health and spiritualism prevalent in New England of the late nineteenth century. She was responsible for the founding (or "discovery," as she called it) of Christian Science, a church based on a doctrine that teaches the superiority of mind, the spirituality of humankind, and healing through a correct reading and understanding of the Scriptures. Most remarkable for her magnetism as a teacher, Eddy instructed hundreds of disciples (the majority of them women) whose subsequent efforts built a nationwide movement and an established church structure by the turn of the century. The "bible" of Christian Science is Eddy's *Science and Health*, first published in 1875. Eddy also wrote a brief autobiography entitled *Retrospection and Introspection* (1891 and later editions). The author of this trilogy, written over a period of twenty years, is himself a Christian Scientist. Volume 1 covers the years from Eddy's birth in 1821 to the publication of the first edition of *Science and Health* in 1875. A biographical chronology and extensive notes are included in each of the three volumes.

268   Peel, Robert, 1909- . **Mary Baker Eddy: The Years of Trial.** New York:
       Holt, Rinehart and Winston, 1971. 391p. bibliog. index. $8.95. ISBN
       0030867002. LC 73-31119.
This is the second volume in the author's three-volume biography, the first and third of which are *Mary Baker Eddy: The Years of Discovery*, and *Mary Baker Eddy: The Years of Authority*. It covers the years 1876-1891, the period of the expansion and solidification of the Christian Science movement.

269   Peters, Margot. **Unquiet Soul: A Biography of Charlotte Brontë.**
       Garden City, NY: Doubleday, 1975. 460p. bibliog. index. $12.50.
       ISBN 0385066228. LC 74-9461.
Peters writes an intelligent and perceptive biography of Charlotte Brontë. In a larger sense, this is a chronicle of Victorian womanhood and the experience

of being a genius in this confining milieu. "Charlotte Brontë's life and art were both an eloquent protest against the cruel and frustrating limitations imposed upon women and a triumph over them. Seen from this angle, the facts of her life fall into a new pattern, and it is this pattern that these pages propose to explore." This is a major contribution to scholarship on Brontë and to Victorian literary history and criticism.

270   Pétrement, Simone. **Simone Weil: A Life.** New York: Pantheon Books, 1976. 576p. bibliog. index. $15.00. ISBN 039449815. LC 76-9576.
Simone Weil (1909-1943), her biographer and close friend, Simone Pétrement, tells us, "would have preferred that people did not take a particular interest in her person and her life. On the contrary, she wanted them to examine her ideas and make an effort to find out whether or not they were true." Simone Weil's life, a life of sanctity and political radicalism in France, is intrinsically interesting, and Pétrement has set herself a difficult task in not allowing the life to overshadow the work. Though Weil's death was ascribed by medical authorities to suicide by willful starvation caused by mental illness, Pétrement's knowledge of Simone Weil and her philosophical writings suggests much more complex reasons for her death. Pétrement writes in the last chapter, "If there is an element of truth in the idea that she wanted to die, that element would perhaps consist in this: that her sorrow made her to a great extent indifferent to what might hpapen to her." Pétrement examines Weil's childhood, her early genius, and her revolutionary opposition to the social order in youth. From the beginning she considered it a great misfortune to be female and sought to sublimate her sexuality throughout her life. Important foci of the biography are her years at the École Normale, her year of factory work, her involvement in the Spanish Civil War, her retreat from the world into the inner space of mysticism (beginning in 1938), and throughout, her teaching and writing. Though Pétrement's is the definitive biography, those with serious interest in Weil will want to look at *Seventy Letters*, edited and translated by Richard Rees (New York: Oxford University Press, 1965), and *Simone Weil: A Friendship in Love*, by Jacques Cabaud (New York: Channel Press, 1964). Readers may also want to look at Megan Terry's dramatic rendition of the life of Somone Weil entitled *Approaching Simone*. Published by the Feminist Press (1973), the play is preceded by a critical introduction by Phyllis Jane Wagner. The volume also includes a biographical note on Terry and a bibliography of her plays.

271   Pinzer, Maimie, 1885- . **The Maimie Papers.** Old Westbury, NY: Feminist Press, 1977. 439p. index. $12.95. ISBN 0912670487. LC 77-21693.
This book of letters from a prostitute to an upper-class Boston matron sheds light on the personal, economic, and social forces that compelled many women to choose prostitution as a viable means of earning a living. These beautifully written letters chronicle the very difficult choices and experiences faced by Maimie, an extraordinary human spirit. Theodore Drieser's *Sister Carrie* provides a complementary fiction selection. (The letters were written 1910-1922, chiefly to Fanny Quincy Howe. Historical editor is Ruth Rosen; textual editor, Sue Davidson; with an introduction by Ruth Rosen.)

272   Plath, Sylvia, 1932-1963. **Letters Home: Correspondence, 1950-1963.**
        New York: Harper and Row, 1975. 502p. $15.00. ISBN 0060133724.
        LC 74-1849.

These were selected and edited with commentary and a lengthy biographical
introduction by Aurelia Schober Plath, the poet's mother. It is in the correspondence that the biography of Sylvia Plath (1932-1963) emerges—a strong and beautiful personality brimming with enthusiasm for living, and especially for writing.
The majority of these selected letters are to Sylvia Plath's mother, and from
the correspondence we have here, it would appear that mother and daughter
had superb rapport. The correspondence records the exhilaration of Plath's
writing success in college, the frequent despair she suffered as a result of overwork
and overstimulation, her plans for stories and poems, the bliss of her first years
with Ted Hughes, her experiences in England and Europe, her illnesses (emotional
and physical) during the period of coping with her two small children, and the
breakup of her marriage. Sylvia Plath wrote vivid and eloquent letters, letters
that spoke of events and people, but which are memorable and haunting for
their stunning rendering of the emotional moment up to her startling suicide
at the age of thirty. There are many interesting photographs of Plath as a girl
and young woman. Considerable controversy has arisen concerning Aurelia
Schober Plath's role in editing the letters.

273   Ray, Gordon Norton, 1915- . **H. G. Wells and Rebecca West.** New
        Haven, CT: Yale University Press, 1974. 215p. bibliog. $10.00. ISBN
        0300017537. LC 74-77990.

This is a well-documented love story of two extraordinary people. When they
met, Wells was famous, Rebecca, just beginning her career. The book illuminates
the struggle of the gifted young Rebecca West, who first attracted literary
attention by writing in the *New Freewoman*, an important weekly feminist
review (1911)—a struggle to maintain her own spirit and life as a writer while
carrying on an intense ten-year love affair with the dominating brilliant Wells.

274   Redinger, Ruby Virginia. **George Eliot: The Emergent Self.** New York:
        Knopf; distr. New York: Random House, 1975. 515, xxvp. bibliog.
        index. $15.00. ISBN 039449010X. LC 74-21301.

Though no one doing serious work on Eliot can omit turning to the definitive
biography by Gordon S. Haight, *George Eliot: A Biography* (Oxford, 1968),
the earlier Haight study, *George Eliot and John Chapman* (Yale, 1940), or to
the seven-volume edition of the letters edited by Haight, *The George Eliot Letters*
(Yale, 1954-1955), Redinger has written a fine and engaging biography that
seeks out the psychological roots of Eliot's genius—"the primal passionate store"
in Eliot's own words. The problem in uncovering early material is formidable
because of the lack of reliable documentation. Redinger makes a strong case,
however, for the theory that the George Eliot of fame and genius, a person of
serenity and gentle brilliance, was not at all the younger "impulsive and bitterly
frustrated" Mary Ann Evans of early family crises. Redinger carefully traces
early childhood dissatisfactions, which Eliot presumably worked out in her
fiction, interpreting many established facts in Eliot's life (e.g., her use of a
male pseudonym, her sensitivity about her unmarried state with Lewes) as
personal conflicts that may have influenced her to create characters who cannot

break out of their traditional feminine roles. Redinger sees Eliot's fiction as therapy through which she was able to free herself. Though Eliot did not write a formal autobiography, Redinger's psychological reading of the novels suggests that she has recorded much of her deepest self in her fictional creations.

275   Richards, Laura Elizabeth (Howe), 1850-1943, and Maud (Howe)
       Elliott, 1854-1948. **Julia Ward Howe, 1819-1910.** Dunwoody, GA:
       N. S. Berg, 1970. 2v. in 1. index. $20.00. ISBN 0910220247. LC
       78-11235.

The life experiences of Julia Ward Howe (1819-1910) gave her personal knowledge of the kinds of oppression experienced by nineteenth-century middle and upper class women and targeted by the woman's rights movement. Unlike suffrage leaders Elizabeth Cady Stanton—whose husband was for the most part supportive of her political commitments—and Susan B. Anthony—who retained the relative freedom of a single woman—Ward married a man violently opposed to any public activities by married women (despite her reformist ideas regarding other social questions). Ward's writing career, launched before marriage, was abruptly halted and her talents submerged during the course of 25 years of her married life. It was only at the age of 43 that a sudden unexpected fame following the publication of her poem "Battle Hymn of the Republic" encouraged Ward's exploration of possibilities for a wider life. She eventually channeled her energies into the post-war woman's rights movement, as a leader in the American Woman Suffrage Association and in the woman's club movement. Having only entered the public arena in her mid-forties, Ward was by the time of her old age the focus of great adulation, in frequent demand as a speaker as long as she was able and as a writer until her death in 1910. In 1908, she became the first woman ever elected to the American Academy of Arts and Letters. Richards and Elliott's Pulitzer Prize-winning biography, though an early one (originally 1916), remains a basic secondary source. Important sources for Ward's own writings are *Julia Ward Howe and the Woman Suffrage Movement*, edited by her daughter, Florence Howe Hall (orig. 1913; repr. 1969), and Ward's own *Reminiscences, 1819-1899* (Houghton Mifflin, 1899).

276   Robinson, Harriet Jane Hanson, 1825-1911. **Loom and Spindle: Or,
       Life Among the Early Mill Girls; With a Sketch of "The Lowell Offering"
       and Some of Its Contributors.** (Rev. ed.). Kailua, HI: Press Pacifica,
       1976. 128p. $7.95. ISBN 0916630013. LC 75-46389.

The women factory workers of the textile mills in Lowell, Massachusetts, have been a frequent focus for historical investigation for a variety of reasons. First, the history of their recruitment and integration into factory work provides a case-study in how an industrial labor force was created out of a rural population in the U.S. Second, the Lowell factories were touted as "model" workplaces, featuring attractive and airy mills, decent boarding facilities, religious facilities, etc. (though the women were working twelve to fourteen hours a day). Third, the women somehow found time to produce remarkable writings for their literary magazine, the *Lowell Offering*, which attracted international acclaim. Finally, the mill workforce was more than three-fourths women, at a time when factory work for women was considered controversial. It is of course this last factor that has made the Lowell factories an important topic for the new women's history and the renewed interest has resulted in the publication of new studies on the topic as well as the reissuing of works long out of print. Harriet Robinson's *Loom and Spindle* (1898) is, along with Lucy Larcom's *A New England Girlhood* (1889, repr. Peter Smith, 1973), a classic if somewhat over-rosey account of life in the mills by a woman who lived and worked there and wrote for the *Lowell Offering*. Despite the romantic light in which she casts the experience, a fair amount of information about living and working conditions at Lowell emerges haphazardly along the way. *Loom and Spindle*, a short reminiscence by Larcom, and an important article on mill magazines by Bertha M. Stearns (1930) are among the selections reprinted in a recent Arno collection, *Women of Lowell* (1974). Readers will also want to be aware of the recent publication of excerpts from the *Lowell Offering* edited by Benita Eisler (1977); Philip Foner's collection (*The Factory Girls*, 1977) of little known writings by more militant factory operatives who repudiated the *Lowell Offering* as a company organ, voicing their dissatisfaction in their own journals and periodicals; and the reprinted *The Golden Threads*, by Hannah Josephson (1949, reprint Russell and Russell, 1967).

277 Roosevelt, Eleanor (Roosevelt), 1884-1962. **Autobiography.** New York: Harper and Row, 1961. 454p. index. $15.00. ISBN 0060136154. LC 61-12222.

The *Autobiography of Eleanor Roosevelt* brings together three volumes of her previous autobiographical works: *This Is My Story*, which tells of Eleanor Roosevelt's somewhat tragic and unhappy early life as an orphan, her court-ship and marriage, her life as a young mother, and her introduction to national and state politics as the wife of a politician; *This I Remember*; and *On My Own*, which focuses on her experiences as United Nations delegate. The fourth segment, *The Search for Understanding*, contains Mrs. Roosevelt's impressions of foreign travel, especially her trips to the Soviet Union. Her political involvement during this time included her active support of Adlai Stevenson during the primary campaign of 1960 and finally, her participation in the campaign for Kennedy after he secured the nomination.

278 Roosevelt, Eleanor (Roosevelt), 1884-1962. **This I Remember.** New York: Harper, 1949; repr. Westport, CT: Greenwood Press, 1975. 387p. index. $25.00. ISBN 0837177022. LC 74-11884.

Eleanor Roosevelt's autobiography is remarkable for the common-sense perspec-tive and clear prose in which she renders the extraordinary events of her life as a public figure and for the simple, direct, and ungrudging way in which she characterizes her husband. Her modesty in chronicling her own unstinting public role from 1921 to 1925, a period that included FDR's governorship and three terms in office, marks her autobiographical style with extraordinary integrity. Perhaps most poignant are the last paragraphs of her memoir, in which she admits to the loneliness of her role as public figure: "on the whole, however, I think I lived those years very impersonally. It was almost as though I had erected someone a little outside of myself who was the president's wife. I was lost somewhere deep down inside myself. That is the way I felt and worked until I left the White House." More recent accounts of Eleanor Roosevelt's life include the non-essential and uninspired biography written by her son, Elliott

Roosevelt, *Mother R.: Eleanor Roosevelt's Untold Story* (Putnam, 1977), and the two engaging and laudatory Joseph Lash volumes, *Eleanor and Franklin* (Norton, 1971) and *Eleanor: The Years Alone* (Norton, 1972). Eleanor Roosevelt, a feminist in her own unique way, wrote *It's Up to the Women* (1932).

279   Rubins, Jack L. **Karen Horney: Gentle Rebel of Psychoanalysis.** New York: Dial Press, 1978. 362p. bibliog. index. ISBN 0803744250. LC 78-9339.

Psychoanalyst Jack Rubins spent seven years researching the life of Karen Horney (1885-1952), the eminent psychoanalytic therapist and theorist whose "revisionism" still unsettles disciples of orthodox Freudianism. Rubins notes that the expunging of her name and work from the history of psychoanalysis still continues, offset only recently by the upsurge of interest in her theories of the psychology of women due to the women's movement. Prior to Rubins's book, only two brief and incomplete biographical sketches were available (Joseph Natterson's in *Psychoanalytic Pioneers*, edited by F. Alexander, 1966; and Harold Kelman's *Helping People: Karen Horney's Psychoanalytic Approach*, 1971). Rubins fills in the account of Horney's life and the evolution of her work, from her birth near Hamburg toward the close of the Victorian era, through her psychoanalytic training in the Germany of the Weimar Republic, to her flight from Nazi persecution to the United States, where she remained until her death. Two chapters focus specifically on Horney's writings on women ("Feminine Psychology: Proud to Be a Woman" and "On Marital Problems," which have been collected in one volume entitled *Feminine Psychology* [1967]).

280   Ruddick, Sara, 1935- , and Pamela Daniels, 1937- , eds. **Working It Out: 23 Women Writers, Artists, Scientists, and Scholars Talk About Their Lives and Work.** New York: Pantheon Books, 1977. 349p. bibliog. $10.00. ISBN 0394409361. LC 76-54624.

This is a compelling book of extremely personal essays about working and life-styles by women who work because they want to and spiritually need to. *Working It Out* will be welcomed by women looking for some direction and looking to women who have "made it" to tell them how they have done it. Children, marriage, single life, the need for work space, going back to school, coping with sexism in academe: these are among the engrossing issues raised here. The majority of women represented here were born in the '30s and came of age in the traditional '50s; in many ways, their stories are of breaking out of old patterns. Among the contributors: Adrienne Rich, Catharine Stimpson, Alice Walker, Miriam Schapiro, Naomi Weisstein, Tillie Olsen. The essays range from "The Anomaly of a Woman in Physics" to "Learning to Work." The foreword is by Adrienne Rich.

281   Sand, George, pseud. of Mme. Dudevant, 1804-1876. **The Convent Life of George Sand.** Chicago: Cassandra Editions, 1977. (Repr. of 1893 ed.). 219p. $9.95. ISBN 0915864398. LC 77-10534.

Born Aurore Dupin, George Sand was educated between 1817 and 1820 at the English Augustinian Convent Rue des Fossés St. Victor. Apparently, she liked this life of the convent lived among her high-spirited friends within the sheltered walls and under the calming influences of the nuns. For one thing, the convent offered the young girl a respite from the feuding between her paternal grand-mother, Madame Dupin, and her difficult mother, the widowed Sophie Dupin. Sand's account of convent life is filled with recollections of girlhood friend-ships, religious fervor, and family attachments: "the convent was for me an earthly paradise. I was neither pupil nor nun, but something between the two, with absolute freedom in a place which I never left, even for a day, without deep regret. . . . I was surrounded by friends, a recognized leader in all pleasures, and the idol of the little girls."

282   Sand, George, pseud. of Mme. Dudevant, 1804-1876. **The Intimate Journal of George Sand.** London: Williams and Norgate, 1929; repr. New York: Haskell House, 1975. 198p. $11.95. ISBN 0838319394. LC 75-20492.

Most of the material in the *Journal Intime* derives from George Sand's life from her 29th to 36th year. The final comment, dated 1868, records the author's view of the journal and her life at age 65: "I happened to reread all this. I must have been quite in love with this book. I intended to fill it with beautiful things. But I have written nothing but foolishness. That is very evident to me from today." The "foolishness" to which Madame Sand refers are her very intimate accounts of life and love revealed through her journal to Alfred Musset; the Piffoël journal (Piffoël is a name she used for her philosophical self, an alter-ego with whom she carried on rational versus intuitive debates); and a scrapbook titled "Sketches and Hints," in which she wrote letters, impressions of people, and remembered conversations. Marie Jenney Howe's excellent feminist intro-ductory material and notes have been retained from the 1929 edition. Howe argues that the journal was George Sand's method of handling intense conflict in her personal life, a method that freed her to return to her creative writing after unburdening herself of her anxieties and obsessions.

283   Sanger, Margaret, 1879-1966. **Margaret Sanger: An Autobiography.** New York: Pergamon Press, n.d. $27.50. ISBN 0080187307.

Margaret Sanger is commonly acknowledged as *the* pioneer of the legalization and dissemination of birth control knowledge and devices. While this reputation has been qualified by some historians who argue that it denies the important roles played by other individuals, such as Emma Goldman, and by the birth control movement, Sanger's identification with the history of birth control can be seen as a product of her lifelong commitment to this single issue. Indeed, this single-issue emphasis has been the target of criticism by social historian Linda Gordon (*Woman's Body, Woman's Right*), who sees in it the foundation for Sanger's increasing conservatism over the years, ultimately delivering control over contraception into the hands of the medical establishment in exchange for the legitimacy that this brought. In this book, Sanger tells her own version of her life story and the history of the birth control movement, through the year 1938. Readers may also want to consult two recent books on Sanger: *Margaret Sanger: Pioneer of the Future*, by Emily Taft Douglas (1970) and *Birth Control in America: The Career of Margaret Sanger*, by David M. Kennedy (1970).

284   Sarton, May, 1912- . **The House by the Sea: A Journal.** New York:
       Norton, 1977. 287p. $8.95. ISBN 0393075184. LC 77-7490.
This passage captures the essence of this beautiful personal chronicle of stillness,
silence, solitude, and sociability: "I have learned in these last years to forget
the desk and everything on it as soon as I leave this room. The key to being
centered seems to be for me to do each thing with absolute concentration,
to garden as though that were essential, then to write in the same way, to meet
my friends, perfectly open to what they bring." This journal spanning a little
less than two years has much of beauty relating to aging and death, everyday
life and art.

285   Sarton, May, 1912- . **Journal of a Solitude.** New York: Norton, 1973.
       208p. $6.95. ISBN 0393074749. LC 72-13464.
Sarton begins this beautiful record of silence and slow movements, "I look out
on the maple, where a few leaves have turned yellow, and listen to Punch, the
parrot, talking to himself and to the rain ticking gently against the windows.
I am here alone for the first time in weeks, to take up my 'real' life again at
last. That is what is strange—that friends, even passionate love, are not my real
life unless there is time alone in which to explore and to discover what is
happening or has happened. Without the interruptions, nourishing and madden-
ing, this life would become arid. Yet I taste it fully only when I am alone here
and 'the house and I resume old conversations.' " Solitude, death, aging, depression: these are the subjects that Sarton chronicles. The unspoken question is—
how can we find the natural rhythm of life, an undistorted movement that
values observation, patience, simple routines? Quite simply, how can we find
peace in a complex world? Photographs of Sarton's country home accompany
the text.

286   Sarton, May, 1912- . **A World of Light: Portraits and Celebrations.**
       New York: Norton, 1976. 254p. $8.95. ISBN 0393075060. LC
       76-16796.
In her preface, Sarton confesses, "I have carried this book in my mind for twenty
years; I wanted to fill the gap between *I Knew a Phoenix* (that ends when I
was twenty-six) and *Plant Dreaming Deep* (that begins when I was forty-five)
by celebrating the great friendships that flowered during those years. How does
one grow? How does one change?" Observing that life has no still points,
Sarton tells us that writing of friends and the changing tides of friendship can
be painful. Particularly probing are her portraits of her parents. Of her father,
for whom she did not feel much love until her own middle age, she records,
"through my father I witnessed that if the vision were there, a man could work
eighteen hours a day, with joy, and never seem to tire. I understood that a talent
is something given, that it opens like a flower, but without exceptional energy,
discipline, and persistence will never bear fruit." From her mother, she learned
what it is to be a woman who "had to balance a thousand things into a complex
whole, and often felt torn among them." These observations shed enormous
light on Sarton's novels, which often pose the conflict of a woman artist between
commitment to her art and commitment to those closest to her. She returns
over and over again to the polarity of these two ways of living in the world

that represented her parents' opposite personalities. Among the friends about whom she writes are novelist Elizabeth Bowen and poet Louise Bogan.

287   Saxton, Martha. **Louisa May: A Modern Biography of Louisa May Alcott.** Boston: Houghton Mifflin, 1977. 428p. bibliog. index. $14.95. ISBN 0395257204. LC 77-23750.

Saxton takes a psychobiographical approach, which tends to be more critical than those of previous Alcott biographers, among them Madeleine B. Stern (*Louisa May Alcott*; orig. 1950, repr. University of Oklahoma Press, 1971) and Katharine Anthony (*Louisa May Alcott*; orig. 1938, repr. Greenwood Press, 1975). It is Saxton's contention that Louisa May Alcott's life was that of an unhappy and complex woman driven to produce fiction to make money so that she could support her family—her dependent and often ill mother and her Transcendentalist dilettante scholar father, as well as her sisters. Her successful career, which blossomed after *Little Women*'s publication (1869), was unusual for a Victorian woman. Perhaps because of this success, she sacrificed her emotional and sexual happiness and her physical health to make a home for the family. Interestingly, her father died at 88, only two days before Louisa May. Saxton reads her life as manifesting a self-destructive pattern. Constantly meeting the excessive demands of family, Alcott became addicted to morphine to overcome her own physical deterioration caused by mercury poisoning (which she had suffered as a result of contact with the drug calomel during her service as a nurse in the Civil War). Saxton writes, "With Bronson's [her father's] death her lifeline snapped. She was left without a conduit into which to pour her dedication, and her existence, built on self-sacrifice, was rendered without meaning." Both Stern and Saxton record Alcott's passing attraction to suicide. Saxton reads *Little Women* as a novel of "programmatic morality" and sees Alcott as submerging all her uncertainties and guilt in a plot "in which everyone is a caricature of some virtue or vice." Excellent notes and bibliographic details are provided.

288   Sayre, Anne. **Rosalind Franklin and DNA.** New York: Norton, 1975. 221p. bibliog. $8.95. ISBN 0393074935. LC 75-11737.

Sayre has produced a case-study of the process by which women's contributions to science are distorted or even obliterated. Rosalind Franklin (1920-1958) was one of the handful of scientists whose work ultimately culminated in the discovery of the molecular structure of deoxyribonucleic acid (DNA). The tale of the fast pace of the last year or so of discovery and of the competition between Franklin's team at King's College in London and the Cambridge team of James D. Watson and Francis Crick was told in 1968 by Watson in his popular book, *The Double Helix*. In this work, Rosalind appears in the unrecognizable form of an "unattractive, dowdy, rigid, aggressive, overbearing, steely, 'unfeminine' bluestocking," and is given the nickname "Rosy," which neither she nor her friends ever used. In introducing her, Watson commented, "the best home for a feminist is in another person's lab." Franklin died tragically of cancer at the age of 37. The series of factual errors and overall distortion in Watson's account have been reproduced and even improved upon since her death. Not only was she eliminated from consideration for the 1962 Nobel Prize awarded to the three other important DNA scientists—Watson, Crick, and Maurice Wilkins—but she has since then often been written out of the history of this momentous scientific discovery altogether (for example, by Linus Pauling in *Nature*). Sayre wrote this account, she says, because "Rosalind has been robbed, little by little; it is a robbery against which I protest."

289   Seifer, Nancy. **Nobody Speaks for Me! Self-Portraits of American Working Class Women.** New York: Simon and Schuster, 1976. 477p. $9.95. ISBN 0671223089. LC 76-11836.

Seifer has collected oral histories of ten working-class women who have been active politically—in neighborhood organizing, work with women, unions, Chicago politics, politics of the coal mines, the Civil Rights Movement. Seifer was concerned about working-class women's lack of an effective political voice, on the one hand, and about the ways in which the women's movement tended to alienate working-class women, on the other. She wanted to find out if important changes were happening to working-class women and, if so, how and why. The women she spoke with tell about their lives—their childhoods, education, marriage, children, work—and the experiences that made them eventually take an active political stance. Readers should also be aware of Lillian B. Rubin's *Worlds of Pain: Life in the Working-Class Family* (1976).

290   Sexton, Anne, 1928-1974. **Anne Sexton: A Self-Portrait in Letters.** Boston: Houghton Mifflin, 1977. 433p. index. $15.00. ISBN 0395257271. LC 77-21355.

Editors Linda Gray Sexton and Lois Ames sifted through more than 50,000 pieces of paper written by Sexton from her childhood to her death, 1928-1974. She was a tireless correspondent who wrote letters nearly every day, saving carbon copies as well as other memorabilia—invitations, scrapbooks, photographs. The sense of rejection that pervades her poetry comes through vividly in the correspondence. The letters reveal a personality of constantly shifting moods ranging from exhilaration to suicidal depression. Sexton's was a privileged childhood, a tempestuous marriage, and a tortured development as an artist. Those close to her expected her suicide. In a letter to her daughter, Linda, written in 1969 (anticipating her suicide), Sexton wrote, "I wrote unhappy— but I lived to the hilt." Though the complete correspondence will not be available for some time because of the sensitive personal issues it raises, this is a useful companion to the poetry. Wonderful photographs are included as well.

291   Shadegg, Stephen C. **Clare Boothe Luce: A Biography.** New York: Simon and Schuster, 1970. 313p. index. $7.95. ISBN 0671206729. LC 72-130489.

Clare Boothe Brokaw Luce (1903-) has excelled in many fields: congresswoman, ambassador, playwright, editor, critic—she has been all of these. Additionally, her exceptional beauty, her sense of fashion, and her wealth are commented on by Shadegg just as these qualities have been noted throughout her life. As the wife of *Time* magazine publisher, Henry Luce, she lived at the nexus of a journalistic elite. Such a person is subject to criticism and misunderstanding simply because her position affords more opportunities to err and to offend than does that of an individual living less in the public light. Born in 1903,

Clare Boothe knew the plight of too little money in her childhood and too much money in her young adulthood. One comes away from this biography feeling one has read a greatly extended *Time* magazine article, so crammed with money, power, achievements, and names of celebrities as it is. Nevertheless, Shadegg has tried to suggest the complexity and tragic circumstances in Luce's life that have contributed to her achievements, which are dazzling by any standard.

292   Shelley, Mary Wollstonecraft (Godwin), 1797-1851. **Mary Shelley's Journal.** Norman: University of Oklahoma Press, 1967. (Repr. of 1947 ed.). 247p. bibliog. index. $8.95. ISBN 0806101709. LC 47-31418.
The editor of this volume, Frederick L. Jones, takes Mary Shelley to task for her "failure to make even a reasonably complete record of events." He *is* grateful that, "in spite of these deficiencies . . . the journal is the richest mine of information about Shelley's daily life: where he lived, where he went and whom he saw from day to day." It has often been hard to find Mary, for critics see Percy even when Mary is writing about herself. Concerning the suicide of Shelley's first wife and the deaths of Mary's babies, she has omitted much. This may in itself say something about the personal tragedy and pain of Mary Shelley. More than anything else, this journal records the reading of the Shelleys. The journal begins in 1814, when Mary and Percy fled to France. Shelley had left pregnant wife and debts behind in England. The journal ends with entries in 1840, when a tranquil Mary records how the years have tamed her impetuous youthful spirit, enabling her to enjoy peace and the affection of her son. This edition contains the Richard Rothwell portrait of Mary (1841). A biography of Mary Shelley worth looking at is Muriel Spark's *Child of Light* (1977, repr. of 1951 edition).

293   Shorter, Clement King, 1857-1926. **The Brontës: Life and Letters.** New York: Haskell House, 1969. (Repr. of 1908 ed.). 2v. $39.95. ISBN 083830186X. LC 68-24918.
Shorter is essential reading for the letters of Charlotte Brontë and for an understanding of the Brontë family. He acknowledges his debt to the Gaskell biography and incorporates the letters and commentary of Gaskell into his own collection of previously unpublished letters, as well as the letters he had previously organized in a volume entitled *Charlotte Brontë and Her Circle* (orig. 1896; repr. Gale Research Company, 1969). It is difficult to understand the rationale for Gale's republishing of *Charlotte Brontë and Her Circle*, when Shorter tells us in *The Brontës: Life and Letters*, "during the eleven years that have passed since I first published *Charlotte Brontë and Her Circle*, correspondents from all parts of the world have forwarded me documents and letters which I am glad to add here, thus making this book, which I call *The Brontës: Life and Letters*, very largely a new work. Everything that was in the former work has been incorporated, and a quantity of extremely valuable new material has been added, including many hitherto unpublished letters. The placing for the first time of the whole of the correspondence in chronological order will, it is hoped be considered in itself sufficient to justify publication." In this volume, dating from Charlotte's thirteenth year as a girl at the parsonage to her last days as Mrs. Nicholls still at the parsonage in Haworth, appear 1,314 letters.

294   Showalter, Elaine, ed. **These Modern Women: Autobiographical Essays From the Twenties.** Old Westbury, NY: Feminist Press, 1978. 147p. bibliog. $4.95. ISBN 0912670460. LC 78-8750.

Showalter resurrects seventeen essays written by "women active in professional and public life" that appeared in *The Nation* in 1926-1927. These women, feminists all, were struggling with the issues of role conflict, sex-role stereotyping, birth control, the reconciliation of love and independence, and sexuality. Unlike the nineteenth-century feminists who often seemed content to rule out marriage or heterosexual relationships in their quest for equality and independence, the '20s women as a group expressed the "modern" view that successful heterosexual relationships could complement or even enhance successful careers. The essays which were intended by *The Nation* and progressive editor, Freda Kirchwey (1894-1976), to provide a profile of the modern woman and her notion of career, marriage, and children—were responded to in essays written by three psychologists of the day, whose judgments of those profiles ranged from supportive to anti-feminist. Mary Austin, Genevieve Taggard, and Crystal Eastman are among the well-known contributors, but there are many more obscure women who provide significant insights into the life experiences of feminists of the '20s. Showalter has written an illuminating and well-researched introductory essay about the 1920s as American "feminism's awakened age," as a period that witnessed the withering of the women's movement and the decline of political radicalism on the part of women.

295*   Sikakane, Joyce, 1943- . **A Window on Soweto.** London: International Defence and Aid Fund, 1977. 80p. ISBN 0904759172. LC 78-301493.

In South Africa, blacks are primarily defined in terms of their capacity for labor for the white minority elite. Women, old people, and children, who are limited in their capacity for hard labor, are regarded as "superfluous appendages," and every effort is made to force them out of the townships and into exile in the impoverished Bantustans (this deportation is called "repatriation"). This is but one small aspect of the brutal oppression described by Joyce Sikakane in her first book, *A Window on Soweto.* Sikakane was born in 1943 and brought up in Soweto. She worked as a journalist on the *World* and the *Rand Daily Mail* newspapers until she was detained for seventeen months under the Terrorism Act. Following her detention, she was served with a banning order, which forbade her return to journalism. In 1973, with increased government reprisals against "political agitators" threatening, Sikakane left for Britain. Her book combines a personal autobiographical account with a systematic description of life in Soweto. Another publication of the International Defence and Aid Fund that may be of interest is Hilda Bernstein's *For Their Triumphs and For Their Tears* (1975), which analyzes the particular suffering of women under apartheid and their resistance. Bernstein's and Sikakane's books are available from the International Defence and Aid Fund for Southern Africa, 104 Newgate Street, London EC1.

296   Sinclair, May. **The Three Brontës.** Norwood, PA: Norwood Editions, 1977. (Repr. of 1911 ed.). 296p. $15.00. ISBN 0848261852.

It is for the light that it sheds on Emily Brontë that this biography is important. Sinclair's biography draws heavily on *The Complete Poems of Emily Brontë*, edited by Clement K. Shorter (1902). Sinclair sees Emily as a mystic, pagan spirit and a superior literary talent to her sister Charlotte Brontë. Emily, a much more solitary figure than Charlotte, "left no record, not a note or a word to prove her authorship of *Wuthering Heights*," writes Sinclair. "Emily herself had no legend; but her genius was perpetually the prey of rumors that left her personality untouched."

297   Sklar, Kathryn Kish. **Catharine Beecher: A Study in American Domes-**
        ticity. New Haven, CT: Yale University Press, 1973. 356p. bibliog.
        index. $17.50. ISBN 0300015801. LC 73-77166.
This traces the life of Catharine Beecher (1800-1878), a woman who saw her task as "that of interpreting and shaping the collective consciousness of American women" to achieve "the unification of American culture around a new image of politically transcendent womanhood." Sklar notes that the middle decades of the nineteenth century have been seen by feminist historians as pivotal: it was then that both the Woman Suffrage Movement and the cult of domesticity emerged. In this book, Sklar attempts to assess that era through a study of Catharine Beecher, in whose writings and career these social currents met and did battle. Distressed by women's marginal status, Beecher urged a new female dominance grounded in domesticity, motherhood, and moral superiority. Critical of inadequate education for women, Beecher advocated and founded schools that would instruct women in the art of housewifery. A firm believer in the importance of women's social influence, Beecher rejected its expression in abolitionism and woman suffrage politics, arguing that women's influence should remain confined to the domestic sphere but be accorded greater weight. Sklar's study is to be recommended both as biography and as social history.

298   Smedley, Agnes, 1890-1950. **Portraits of Chinese Women in Revolution.**
        Old Westbury, NY: Feminist Press, 1976. $3.95. ISBN 0912670444.
        LC 76-18896.
The beautifully crafted portraits of Chinese women that Smedley has given us in this volume tell us much of the individual sufferings, dilemmas, and tragedies of women in China during the twentieth century against the political backdrop of revolution and dramatic political events. Smedley focuses with great compassion on the plights of peasant and radical women. She tells of women crippled by footbinding, of women forced into marriages, of wives killed by overwork. The theme throughout appears in Smedley's first sentence: "across the great historical stage on which the Chinese revolution is being played, appears and reappears the figure of a woman."

299   Sorell, Walter, 1905- . **Three Women: Lives of Sex and Genius.** Indian-
        apolis: Bobbs-Merrill, 1975. 234p. bibliog. index. $7.95. ISBN
        0672517507. LC 74-17644.
Sorell states that he chose to examine the lives of these particular three women—Alma Mahler-Werfel, wife of Gustav Mahler; Gertrude Stein; and Lou Andreas-Salome, lover of Rilke and Nietzsche and friend of Freud—because "they inspired some of the greatest artists of this century." He views them all as liberated women, yet finds them most compelling because of their attraction for "some of the most powerful pioneers of a world to come, men whose

magnitude of mind and boldness of vision changed the direction and meaning
of our existence." One can fault Sorell's point of view, though his understanding of these three contemporary women at their most notable in the first quarter
of the twentieth century and of their milieu—the intellectual, artistic world
of Vienna, Paris, Rome, Munich, and Berlin—is apparent and fully documented.
Clearly all three women shared the life goal of inspiring the men with whom
they associated, though in varying degrees and employing quite different personal
styles.

300   Standing, E. Mortimer. **Maria Montessori: Her Life and Work.** New
        York: New American Library, 1962. 382p. bibliog. index. $1.50.
This is a biography of the important Italian educator, Maria Montessori (1870-
1952), who developed a theory of learning and education based on the encouragement of spontaneous interest and self-discipline. This work written by a friend
and disciple, focuses more on the work than the life and is somewhat fanatical
in its enthusiasm for the Montessori method.

301   Stanton, Elizabeth (Cady), 1815-1902. **Elizabeth Cady Stanton: As
        Revealed in Her Letters, Diary and Reminiscences.** Edited by Theodore
        Stanton and Harriot Stanton Blatch. New York: Arno Press, 1969.
        (Repr. of 1922 ed.). 2v. bibliog. $25.00. ISBN 0405001142. LC
        77-79183.
"It is a settled maxim with me that the existing public sentiment on any subject
is wrong," Elizabeth Cady Stanton (1815-1902) was once heard to say. Stanton
devoted her talents as writer and orator, her passion, and her radical vision of
women's rights to the nineteenth-century feminist movement for more than
fifty years. For most of that half century, she worked in close collaboration
with Susan B. Anthony, whose superior organizational sense and greater freedom
as a single woman complemented Stanton's capacities. Stanton was responsible
(along with Lucretia Mott) for organizing the first woman's rights convention
in Seneca Falls, New York, in 1848. There she introduced a resolution calling
for woman suffrage. She went on to serve twenty years as president of the
National Woman Suffrage Association (1879-1890), two years as president
of the National American Woman Suffrage Association (1890-1892), and to
speak and write for woman suffrage right up until her death (she was co-editor
of Anthony's paper, *Revolution*). However, Stanton also consistently advocated
a feminist vision that went beyond the suffrage demand to an indictment of
the male power structure itself and of the many forms of woman's oppression.
This stance placed her in the radical wing of the movement (her *Woman's Bible*
(1895-1898; repr. 1972), for example, was repudiated by the NAWSA in 1896).
However, her radicalism had its own limits, as became clear when the exclusion
of women from the 14th and 15th Amendments after the Civil War led her to
advocate an "*educated* suffrage irrespective of sex and color." Thus her personal
and political history in many ways crystalizes the contradictions and cross-
currents of nineteenth-century feminism. These two volumes, edited by two of
her seven children, represent a key primary source on Stanton (along with the
massive *History of Woman Suffrage*, which she co-authored with Anthony,
Gage, and Harper). Volume 1 is a revised edition (1902) of her autobiography,
Eighty Years and More (1815-1897): Reminiscences of Elizabeth Cady Stanton

(orig. 1898; also available in reprint as a separate volume from Source Book Press, 1970). Collected in volume 2 are her letters (1839-1880) and selections from her diary (1880-1902). Other biographical sources on Stanton are Alma Lutz's *Created Equal: A Biography of Elizabeth Cady Stanton, 1815-1902* (orig. 1940; repr. Octagon Books, 1974), which has a substantial bibliography of manuscript and printed sources; and Mary Ann B. Oakley's *Elizabeth Cady Stanton* (Feminist Press, 1972), which is written from a contemporary feminist perspective but is directed at a young audience.

302   Stein, Gertrude, 1874-1946. **The Autobiography of Alice B. Toklas.**
       New York: Vintage Books, 1960; repr. Gloucester, MA: Peter Smith.
       252p. $2.45. ISBN 039470133X.

Probably one of the most famous contemporary women's autobiographies (1933), this is actually the autobiography of Stein written as if Toklas were telling the story. The figures of the dazzling cultural salon that Stein commanded— Picasso, Matisse, and others—glint throughout the work. But for many, the most compelling aspect is Stein's gift for revealing herself in wonderful and witty conversational style. "She [Stein] is passionately addicted to what the french call métier and she contends that one can only have one métier as one can only have one language. Her métier is writing and her language is english." Surely the most memorable moments in Stein's accounts are the colorful vignettes and the incidents that occurred in the Paris cafés, studios, and salons of her circle; but one also learns of the straight biographical details: growing up in California, studying philosophy under William James and Santayana, a brief stint at Johns Hopkins Medical School, her writing of experimental literature, her war efforts for the Allies. And always there is the presence of Alice, Stein's enduring lesbian relationship, conveyed as a sort of travelogue—"we met," "we traveled," "we enjoyed." Beautiful, simple, and always understandable writing.

303   Stein, Leon, 1912- , comp. **Fragments of Autobiography.** New York:
       Arno Press, 1974. 1v. (various pagings). $23.00. ISBN 0405060963.
       LC 74-3982.

Because of the expanded emphasis on the lives of ordinary women, this Arno reprint is especially worth collecting. "The short autobiographical pieces in this volume were written by women whose lives—in each case—were like no other lives: a scholar writing histories in a sanctum of male scholarship in Boston, a horse thief who made two mistakes, an Indian and a woman who crossed the continent by horse, another who ran for President of the United States, one who studied medicine in all-male Heidelberg, a pioneer of modern reform and an exchange about the South by four women. Included in this volume is a special lengthy section comprised of a series of articles that appeared in *The Nation* under the general titles 'These Modern Women' and 'Explaining Women.' World War I brought women into defense industries. In the period that followed, the feeling of liberation was augmented by psychoanalysis, the literature of disillusionment, the spread of bohemias and the general realization that true sex equality involved more than just the right to vote. Protected by anonymity, seventeen contributors to *The Nation*, during 1926 and 1927, depicted and analyzed their own problems and experiences against that background of

changing sex mores. A noted psychoanalyst, the propounder of behaviorism
and a popular doctor-author then analyzed the series" ("A Note about This
Volume"). The *Nation* articles have been brought out in a separate volume by
Feminist Press entitled *These Modern Women: Autobiographical Essays from
the Twenties*, edited by Elaine Showalter (1978).

304   Steiner, Nancy Hunter, 1933- . **A Closer Look at Ariel: A Memory
       of Sylvia Plath.** New York: Harper's Magazine Press, 1973. 83p. $8.95.
       ISBN 0061278157. LC 72-79718.
George Stade writes in his long and excellent introduction to this slim volume
written by a former roommate of Plath's at Smith College: "Sylvia Plath would
have been a good poet even if she had not committed suicide, but not exactly
the poet she has become. Our knowledge of her suicide comments on the poetry
as we read it." Steiner writes of the Smith milieu during the '50s and of Plath's
1954 return to the college after her suicide attempt. Steiner's experience of
Plath speaks of the impression Plath created as a "typical American girl, the
product of a hundred years of middle-class propriety," a young woman who
deplored exterior signs of rebellion in dress, manners, or language. Paradoxically,
it was her inner life, the life reflected in her poetry, that seethed with rage and
rebellion. This is a lucid, intimate glimpse of an important part of Plath's growth
and development as woman and poet.

305   Stewart, Eliza (Daniel), 1816-1908. **Memories of the Crusade.** New
       York: Arno Press, 1972. (Repr. of 1889 ed.). 535p. $24.00. ISBN
       0405044828. LC 72-2627.
Eliza "Mother" Stewart (nicknamed Mother for her work ministering to soldiers
during the Civil War) was an early and key leader in the women's temperance
crusade. Originally published in the 1880s, this is her account of the important
nineteenth-century struggle by women against the liquor interests and of their
organizing around the issue of the miseries suffered by women and their children
when their husbands and fathers drank. Readers might want to consult Flexner's
classic *Century of Struggle* for an analysis of the relationship between the
temperance struggle and the suffrage movement, and, in particular, of how
opposition to the former by the liquor interests spilled over into a formidable
opposition force against woman suffrage as well.

306   Szenes, Hannah [Senesh, Hannah], 1921-1944. **Hannah Senesh: Her
       Life and Diary.** New York: Schocken Books, 1972. 257p. $6.95.
       ISBN 0805234438. LC 77-179076.
Born in 1921 to a distinguished, assimilated Hungarian Jewish family, Hannah
Senesh became a Zionist at the age of seventeen, on the eve of World War II,
and left Hungary for Palestine soon after. In 1942, word was received from
Europe that confirmed the horrors taking place under Nazi terror. A plan was
conceived to parachute a select group of Palestinian Jewish members of the
British armed forces into Nazi-occupied Balkan countries and Hungary in an
effort to save the remaining Jews. Hannah Senesh immediately volunteered
for the mission, one of 32 eventually sent. She crossed the border into Hungary
on June 9, 1944. She was executed for "treason" in Budapest on November 7
of that year, at the age of 23. Hannah Senesh has since come to symbolize

Jewish sufferings and resistance during the Holocaust and has been called the "Joan of Arc of Israel." Included in this volume are her diary, letters, and selected poems (1934-1944); two essays by her mother, Catherine Senesh ("Memories of Hannah's Childhood" and "Meeting in Budapest"); "The Last Border," by Reuven Dafne (a fellow parachutist); and "How She Fell," by Yoel Ralgi.

307   Tarry, Ellen, 1906- . **The Third Door: The Autobiography of an American Negro Woman.** Westport, CT: Negro Universities Press, 1971. (Repr. of 1955 ed.). 304p. $15.25. ISBN 0837152003. LC 70-135613.
This is the autobiography of a deeply religious, black Catholic woman born and raised in the South. Writing in the mid-1950s, Tarry's tone is moderate and "reasonable," which won her praise from '50s reviewers. In part, her perspective seems the product of her religious outlook, in part, the product of the times. She writes of her childhood education in a Southern convent school, her conversion to Catholicism, her career as a journalist in the South and later in New York, her work in Harlem with Catherine de Hueck (founder of the interracial Friendship House) during the Depression, her founding of a similar institution in Chicago, and her work with the National Catholic Community Service during World War II. She concludes her account on an optimistic note.

308   Taylor, Susie King, b. 1848. **Reminiscences of My Life in Camp.** New York: Arno Press, 1968. (Repr. of 1902 ed.). 82p. $4.00. ISBN 0405018401. LC 68-29020.
"This charming little book provides vignettes of the Civil War viewed in retrospect by a black woman who participated in the conflict. Born a slave on one of the Georgia Sea Islands, Susie King Taylor grew up in antebellum Savannah. She learned to read and write in a clandestine school taught by a free colored woman, and her description of the subterfuges resorted to by Negro children to escape detection in their illegal quest for literacy is amusing and instructive. When Union forces attacked and occupied the Sea Islands in the spring of 1862, the young slave girl escaped with her uncle's family to the Yankees and freedom" (from the introduction by James M. McPherson). King was involved throughout her life in volunteer causes—as teacher, nurse, organizer of the Women's Relief Corps in Boston. This account covers the years 1861-1865, when King served as a nurse (Women's Relief Corps) with the 33d United States Colored Infantry.

309   Tobin, Kay, and Randy Wicker. **The Gay Crusaders.** New York: Paperback Library, 1972. repr. New York: Arno Press, 1975. 238p. bibliog. $10.00. ISBN 0405073747. LC 75-12349.
Tobin and Wicker interviewed sixteen gay activists during 1971-1972 about the history of their politicization. These interviews are written up as descriptive profiles, with liberal interspersing of direct quotations. The women featured here are Phyllis Lyon and Del Martin, founders of the Daughters of Bilitis (DOB); Ruth Simpson, active in the DOB and the Lesbian Center of New York; and Barbara Gittings, a founder of DOB's first chapter on the East Coast in New York City, editor of *The Ladder*, and coordinator (at the time of this book's publication) of the Task Force on Gay Liberation of the American Library

Association. The profiles are followed by a "Symposium," in which activists' responses to a series of controversial questions are grouped together.

310   Tomalin, Claire. **The Life and Death of Mary Wollstonecraft.** New York: Harcourt, Brace and Jovanovich, 1975. 316p. bibliog. index. $8.95. ISBN 0151515395. LC 74-14816.
Tomalin has been faulted by some scholars for writing a biography of Wollstone-craft with much subjective detail and undocumented analysis—for dabbling in psychohistory. Wollstonecraft's life particularly lends itself to psychography because of her unhappy affair with Gilbert Imlay and subsequent suicide attempts. Tomalin finds Mary's personal life a much richer field for comment than her writings; but, an examination of the literature on Wollstonecraft demonstrates that almost all work has focused on Mary Wollstonecraft's life. Nevertheless, Tomalin writes a lively biography and does not distort the essential facts; indeed, she carefully relates details. Care should be taken when reading Tomalin to question her speculations about Mary's actions and feelings with regard to specific incidents. She provides an excellent bibliography, a useful chronology, and a Wollstonecraft family tree.

311   Trautmann, Joanne. **The Jessamy Brides: The Friendship of Virginia Woolf and V. Sackville-West.** University Park: Administrative Committee on Research, Pennsylvania State University, 1973. 57p. $3.00. LC 74-621569.
"Virginia had a feminine womanliness; Vita had a masculine womanliness." In this way, Trautmann summarizes the complementary aspect of the friendship between the two. Trautmann's fine essay makes no claims for Vita Sackville-West that cannot be substantiated: Vita was a striking woman, a fine gardener, a dedicated but never dazzling writer and poet. She was devoted to her house ("Knole"), to her husband, to special friends, and to solitude. She and Virginia Woolf were devoted to each other; it probably helped that both had husbands who played similar supportive roles in the lives of their wives. "Androgynous" is the word that Trautmann uses frequently to describe the personal styles of Woolf and Sackville-West, their marriages, and their relationship to one another. This is a carefully-written essay on the development of a famous literary lesbian friendship, and the development of literature from that friendship (most notably, Woolf's *Orlando*). Trautmann edits the definitive volumes of Virginia Woolf's letters with Nigel Nicolson, Sackville-West's son.

312   Troubridge, Una Elena Taylor, Lady. **The Life of Radclyffe Hall.** New York: Citadel Press, 1961; repr. New York: Arno Press, 1975. 189p. $10.00. ISBN 0405073550. LC 75-12350.
First published as *The Life and Death of Radclyffe Hall*, this is the complete account of Hall's life written by her lover of over thirty years. The autobiograph-ical parallels between the fabulous Stephen Gordon in Radclyffe Hall's most sensational novel, *The Well of Loneliness* (1928), and Radclyffe Hall herself are fully explored by Troubridge. The identities of other characters in *Well* are revealed: Lady Troubridge is Mary, and Valerie Seymour is Natalie Clifford Barney. The book is a celebration of the love affair between Troubridge and Hall, which lasted until Radclyffe Hall's death in 1943. For an excellent analysis

of lesbianism and the *avant garde* in Paris among the expatriate community, see Bertha Harris's "The More Profound Nationality of Their Lesbianism: Lesbian Society in the 1920's," in *Amazon Expedition* (1973), edited by Phyllis Birkby, et al. This group included Djuna Barnes, Radclyffe Hall, Romaine Brooks, Natalie Clifford Barney, Colette, and Renée Vivien.

313   Van Doren, Dorothy (Graffe), 1896- , ed. **The Lost Art: Letters of Seven Famous Women.** Norwood, PA: Norwood Editions, n.d. $20.00.
In this volume (orig. 1929), Van Doren has gathered together representative letters of seven significant women who span a range of times and tempers: Lady Mary Wortley Montagu (1689-1762); Abigail Adams (1744-1818); Mary Wollstonecraft (1759-1797); Jane Austen (1775-1817); Jane Welsh Carlyle (1801-1866); Margaret Fuller (1810-1850); and Charlotte Brontë (1816-1855). Nicely written biographical material precedes each selection of letters.

314   Van Voris, Jacqueline. **Constance de Markievicz in the Cause of Ireland.** Amherst: University of Massachusetts Press, 1967. 384p. bibliog. index. $12.50. ISBN 0870230255. LC 67-11245.
This is a thorough biography of the Irish revolutionary, Constance de Markievicz (1868-1927). Born to English aristocratic parents and a life of wealth and privilege, Markievicz grew up and lived most of her life in Ireland and considered it her home. She becamse involved in the struggle for Irish independence and eventually became a leader of the Sinn Fein, a group committed to independence. During the heroic and ill-fated 1916 Easter Rebellion in Dublin, Markievicz led 120 rebels and was the last of the Sinn Fein leaders to surrender. Trial, conviction, and imprisonment followed; but she was one of only two leaders of the rebellion spared execution. Van Voris writes, "although she was always, in a sense, a second-in-command, an instrumental but not a determining figure in Irish politics, she was bound into the rebellion by connections with art, literature, theater, labor, suffrage, and youth movements. Consequently she is one of the best representatives of the whole course of rebellion. She is also a representative of the class and circumstances which made rebellion necessary." Van Voris includes a lengthy bibliography of primary and secondary sources on Markievicz and the Irish context. A shortened version of this bibliography has been published by the Feminist Press under the title *Constance de Markievicz* (1972).

315   Vorse, Mary Marvin Heaton. **Autobiography of an Elderly Woman.** Boston: Houghton Mifflin, 1911; repr. New York: Arno Press, 1974. 269p. $15.00. ISBN 0405061250. LC 74-3977.
"What does it mean to grow old, feel physical ability waning, yet retain a fierce sense of personal independence? This autobiography tells exactly what it means— in terms of life's daily routine, friendships, arguments, comforts. More especially it depicts the condescension of youth, the guarded impatience of a bright mind in an aging body and a spirit that youthfully refuses to be paced by oncoming chronological age. This book accomplishes it with great skill because the narrator, in recording her life and picturing her old age, is aided by her daughter, a gifted writer who became an outstanding labor reporter. 'I knew exactly how my mother felt about age, or rather about growing old,' said the daughter in her own autobiography years later. 'She never was old except in years and retained

her gusto for life until shortly before her death' " ("A Note about This Volume"). Her own autobiography is titled *A Footnote to Folly* (1935).

316   Wade, Mason, 1913- . **Margaret Fuller: Whetstone of Genius.** New York: Viking Press, 1940; repr. New York: A. M. Kelley, 1973. 304p. bibliog. index. $13.50. ISBN 0678031789. LC 72-122077.

Wade's biography has stood until recently as the most comprehensive and best of the Fuller biographies. Chevigny's biography of Fuller replaces Wade, to a certain extent, though her purpose is quite different from Wade's. Feminists may find Wade's emphasis on Fuller's sexual frustration before marriage to be a misguided analysis. Wade is correct, however, in his assessment of *The Memoirs of Margaret Fuller Ossoli*, in which her friends Emerson, William Henry Channing, and James Freeman Clark collaborated in 1852, as sentimental and inadequate: "these friends of Margaret, in their regard for her memory, inked out, scissored, or pasted over a third of the never-to-be-duplicated mass of material they had before them, and thus blocked the path for all who might follow them" (Wade's introduction). Wade is clearly appreciative of Fuller, but in terming Fuller "a whetstone of genius," he tends to bolster the argument of woman as inspiration rather than producer. Many consider Fuller a genius in her own right. A problem in using Wade as a scholarly source is his cavalier attitude about footnotes; there are none in the text and his bibliographical note does not clarify problems readers may have about sources, though Wade's approach does make for smooth reading.

317   Wardle, Ralph Martin, 1909- . **Mary Wollstonecraft: A Critical Biography.** Lincoln: University of Nebraska Press, 1966. 366p. bibliog. index. $3.75. ISBN 0803252110. LC 66-8869.

Originally published in 1951, this is considered one of the best and most reliable biographies of Wollstonecraft. Wardle takes a meticulous approach to the documentation that exists. He is sympathetic to Wollstonecraft and genuinely appreciates her mind and work. The chapter on *Vindication* is particularly fine. Wardle's technique has been to examine the extensive periodical literature about Wollstonecraft both during her life and soon after her death. He also carefully examined portions of Mary Wollstonecraft's correspondence unavailable to previous biographers. Wardle has great empathy for William Godwin, Mary's husband, and uses the epilogue to detail the reason behind Godwin's disastrous *Memoirs*, in which the learned man attempted to "explain" his dead wife to the public. A slightly patriarchal tone seeps into Wardle's account. Throughout he refers to Wollstonecraft as "Mary"; when referring to men, he uses surnames.

318   Waters, Ethel, 1900- . **To Me It's Wonderful.** New York: Harper and Row, 1972. 162p. $1.95. ISBN 0060692782. LC 76-183634.

Both *To Me It's Wonderful* and *His Eye Is on the Sparrow* (Doubleday, 1951; repr. Greenwood Press, 1978) are infused with Waters's deep religious faith, which was nurtured by both her Catholic background and her work for Billy Graham. Mainly, Waters is thrilled by her good fortune, which she believes is the work of the Lord—including such disparate experiences as starring in Carson McCullers's *Member of the Wedding* and singing at Tricia Nixon's and Edward Cox's wedding. "Sometimes I have to pinch myself to believe all the wonderful things my Lord has allowed to happen to me already in the 1970's. To me it's wonderful." The editors have included a discography in essay form highlighting Waters's performing career from the '20s to the present.

319 Wells, Anna Mary. **Miss Marks and Miss Woolley.** Boston: Houghton
     Mifflin, 1978. 268p. $10.95. ISBN 0395257247. LC 78-1391.
Mary Emma Woolley served as the president of Mt. Holyoke College from 1901 to 1937, a pioneer in the women's higher education movement and a very close friend of Jeannette Marks, who had been a student of Woolley's at Wellesley. The two lived together in an intense (though perhaps not physical) union, sharing a home for over 25 years. Woolley died in 1947 of cancer; Marks, in 1964, at the age of 89. These two single women lived lives zealously devoted to colleges for women, and it is probably little wonder that Woolley felt that her point had been lost when Mt. Holyoke appointed a male president in 1937, an action that deeply offended her and about which she issued strong negative statements. Wells has based her portrait of the two women and their lives together on papers donated to the college, which contained many packets of the letters between Marks and Woolley. She quotes extensively from these letters, which reveal something of the quality of this remarkable friendship between the kind and calm Woolley and the demanding and irascible Marks. Many fine photographs from the Mt. Holyoke College Library support this lively and carefully documented biography, filled with detail about the lives of American intellectual women in the late nineteenth and first half of the twentieth century.

320 White, Elizabeth Wade. **Anne Bradstreet: "The Tenth Muse."** New
     York: Oxford University Press, 1971. 410p. bibliog. $12.95. ISBN
     0195014405. LC 77-161893.
As the first English-speaking North American woman poet, Anne Bradstreet has received increasing attention during the last few years. However, her life and background have been virtually ignored except in passing introductions to her poetry. White's study is the definitive scholarly biography. Because of the dearth of factual information available on Bradstreet, White has looked to the poetry and prose "to examine in some detail the various episodes of her eventful life" (1612?-1672). A stunning intellect, an exemplary wife and mother, a traveler to the New World as a young woman, a poet who significantly shaped America's literary tradition, Anne Bradstreet was also a complex personality coping with the constraints of Puritan life and domesticity even as she struggled to find appropriate lyrical forms. White conveys these struggles admirably, skillfully interweaving biographical detail with critical analysis. The bibliography draws on an impressive corpus of manuscript and printed sources.

321 Whitney, Janet (Payne), 1894- . **Abigail Adams.** Westport, CT: Green-
     wood Press, 1970. 357p. bibliog. index. $16.25. ISBN 0837134358.
     LC 77-100190.
Abigail Adams, being a voluminous correspondent, is most vivid in her letters [see Adams, *New Letters of Abigail Adams, 1788-1801* (repr. 1973) or Fried-laender and Kline, ed., *The Book of Abigail and John: Selected Letters of the Adams Family 1762-1784* (Harvard U. Press, 1975)]. However, the Whitney biography (orig. 1947) is worth having. She draws Abigail Adams as a woman

who closely watched current events. While Whitney sees Adams chiefly in the role of virtuous wife and helpmate, acutely observing the world of men and power so close around her, Page Smith's *John Adams* (1962) translates Abigail's role as a partner in the much more active sense, shaping her husband's career and decisions through her valued counsel.

322   Wickes, George. **The Amazon of Letters: The Life and Loves of Natalie Barney**. New York: Putnam, 1976. 286p. bibliog. index. $10.00. ISBN 0399118640. LC 76-17302.

Wickes, an English professor and author of *Henry James and the Critics*, has written a detailed biography of the famous American expatriate lesbian writer, Natalie Clifford Barney (1877-1972). Barney's salon in Paris was a center for the expatriate lesbian community including Romaine Brooks, Renée Vivien, Colette, and Gertrude Stein; other salon visitors included Gide, Pound, and Joyce. Wickes appends a series of tributes to Barney written by friends and acquaintances. Barney's own writings are unfortunately available only in French. In *Adventures de l'esprit* (Editions Émile-Paul Frères, 1929; repr. Arno Press, 1975), Barney reminisces about many of her well-known acquaintances, among them Colette, Djuna Barnes, Stein, Brooks, Vivien, Oscar Wilde, Pierre Louÿs, and Marcel Proust. *Traits et portraits* (Mercure de France, 1963; repr. Arno Press, 1975) is a series of portraits of homosexual writers such as Stein and Gide and references to figures like Verlaine, Rimbaud, Sappho, and the Ladies of Llangollen; *Traits* also includes a strong defense of lesbianism and male homosexuality as normal lifestyles ("L'amour défendu").

323   Willard, Frances Elizabeth, 1839-1898. **Glimpses of Fifty Years: The Autobiography of an American Woman**. New York: Source Book Press, 1970. (Repr. of 1889 ed.). 698, 6p. $31.00. ISBN 0442810792.

This is the autobiography of a woman largely responsible for shaping the temperance movement in the United States in the final quarter of the nineteenth century. A popular speaker, exceptional political strategist, and deeply committed feminist, Willard saw the temperance movement as a way of politicizing women, and she fought continuously to broaden the movement to encompass other reform concerns. In her twenty years as president of the National Woman's Christian Temperance Union (WCTU), Willard did battle with its more conservative members in her efforts to commit the Union to the suffrage cause (this she achieved in 1880), as well as to such causes as labor, health, and prison reform. Willard's extraordinary influence waned after she was defeated in 1895 in her attempt to bring the temperance movement into the emerging Populist movement. After her death in 1898, the movement's focus narrowed considerably. Published in 1889, the autobiography provides an incomplete account of Willard's life. Other sources are Mary Earhart Dillon's *Frances Willard: From Prayers to Politics* (1944) and Ray Strachey's *Frances Willard: Her Life and Work* (1912). Willard's *Woman and Temperance* is currently available from Arno Press (orig. 1883; repr. 1972).

324   Williams, Ellen, 1930- . **Harriet Monroe and the Poetry Renaissance: The First Ten Years of Poetry, 1912-22**. Urbana: University of Illinois

Press, 1977. 312p. bibliog. index. $10.95. ISBN 0252004787. LC 76-45403.
Harriet Monroe (1860-1936) was the founder and first editor of *Poetry* magazine, which was born in Chicago in 1912 and marked a new age of poetry in the United States, publishing such writers as Ezra Pound, William Rose Benét, Joseph Campbell, Bliss Carman, Vachel Lindsay, Amy Lowell, Alice Meynell, William Vaughn Moody, and William Carlos Williams. Harriet Monroe was a poet-playwright, an essayist, and a journalist on the periphery of the literary world when she began *Poetry* at age 51. Ellen Williams's analysis of *Poetry* magazine and Harriet Monroe's influence as its guiding light is founded in meticulous research. She concludes of Monroe that "it required extraordinary intensity of purpose to survive without bitterness or compromise. As much as the poets of the movement, Harriet Monroe was a successful survivor of that time. Her testimony to the early years emphasized always the excitement and joy of a new age, a renaissance. It was her hope and her faith that *Poetry* had ushered in a great era of poetry, and that faith was justified."

325   Witke, Roxane. **Comrade Chiang Ch'ing.** Boston: Little, Brown, 1977. 549p. bibliog. index. $15.00. ISBN 0316949000. LC 77-935.
This is a very interesting biography because the Chinese Communist Party has never approved of individuals' histories, favoring instead collective history. Chiang Ch'ing—Mao's fourth and last wife, a member of the Politburo of the Chinese Communist Party, and an uncompromising life-long radical—is the subject of a biography by a Westerner that resulted in her political denouncement. There is much here of the oppression of women in China as revolutionaries, especially in the 1920s and 1930s.

326   Wollstonecraft, Mary, 1759-1797. **Letters Written During a Short Residence in Sweden, Norway, and Denmark.** Lincoln: University of Nebraska Press, 1976. 200p. bibliog. $11.50. ISBN 0803208626. LC 75-38056.
Wollstonecraft's lively observations of the northern countries written in 1795 to her lover, Gilbert Imlay, in London are all the more remarkable when one considers the personal situation of the writer during this period. Estranged from Imlay, with her baby and nursemaid in tow, under financial strain, Wollstone-craft managed to range over social, personal, political, literary, and scenic topics. The letters are at once a daily journal and a specimen of the travel literature so popular in the eighteenth century. There are many observations here about the plight of women as she observed injustices and lives of difficulty during her travels. The letters were first published in Joseph Johnson's 1796 edition; this edition has been edited by Carol H. Poston, who also wrote the introduction.

327*   Women's Co-operative Guild. **Maternity: Letters from Working-Women.** London: G. Beu and Sons, 1915. 211p. LC 16-12747.
Though unfortunately out of print and therefore hard to come by, this volume of letters represents valuable testimony about childbearing and childrearing experiences of British working-class women early in this century. Many of the

brief accounts are chilling, vividly portraying the reality of motherhood under conditions of poverty, medical neglect and ignorance, and unemployment.

328   Woodham-Smith, Cecil Blanche (Fitz Gerald), 1896- . **Queen Victoria, From Her Birth to the Death of the Prince Consort.** New York: Knopf; distr. New York: Random House, 1972. 486p. index. $12.50. ISBN 039448245X. LC 72-2235.

Victoria (1819-1901) became queen at age nineteen upon the death of her uncle. A carefully researched study of Victoria up to the death of Prince Albert (when Victoria was 42), this biography draws from Royal Archives material. Victoria's diaries were destroyed by her daughter, Princess Beatrice, after her death. While never taking a critical stance toward the Queen, Woodham-Smith meticulously documents the dependency of Victoria first on her advisors, later on her husband. Her adoration of Albert during their twenty-year marriage was legendary. For a more lively portrait of Victoria, see Lytton Strachey's *Queen Victoria.* Never much concerned with the improvement of the social conditions of her people, she allowed herself to be influenced greatly by Melbourne, who had a passionate distaste for reform. Nevertheless, she took a lively interest in foreign affairs, leaving the policy-making to husband and advisors.

329   Woolf, Virginia Stephen, 1882-1941. **The Diary of Virginia Woolf.** New York: Harcourt, Brace, Jovanovich, 1977- . index. ISBN 0151255970. LC 77-73111.

Edited by Anne Oliver Bell, with an introduction by Quentin Bell, volume 1 (1915-1919) of the projected five-volume project presents the complete text of the diaries from this period—in contrast to *A Writer's Diary*, edited by Leonard Woolf (1973), which attempted to present only excerpts. Between 1915 and 1941, Woolf recorded her daily thoughts in thirty separate books, all now housed in the Berg Collection of the New York Public Library. A member of the family circle, Bell has annotated the text, liberally drawing from the recollections and materials of family and friends; thus there is a wealth of biographical detail about Woolf's intimates and acquaintances. Quentin Bell calls the diary "a masterpiece" equal to Woolf's finest fiction. With the publication of the final volume "the *oeuvre* of Virginia Woolf will be complete and the critics may, if they so wish, sit down and assess it as a whole." The difference between the complete diary and *A Writer's Diary* is that the latter concentrated on the creative process, while the complete diary gives Woolf's running commentary on her family, friends, and world. Woolf's biographer, Quentin Bell, provides an excellent abbreviated introduction to the social and cultural milieu that Virginia Woolf inhabited. Major topics in the diary are literary life, Bloomsbury, the Hogarth Press, domestic details, friends, and briefly, her tranquil, harmonious life with Leonard.

330   Woolf, Virginia Stephen, 1882-1941. **The Letters of Virginia Woolf.** Edited by Nigel Nicolson and Joanne Trautmann. New York: Harcourt Brace Jovanovich, 1975. 3v. bibliog. index. v.1: $14.95; ISBN 0151509247. v.2: $14.95; ISBN 0151509255. v.3: $14.95; ISBN 0151509263. LC 75-15538.

Volume 1 (1888-1912) works through the childhood of Woolf, marked by the deaths of her mother in 1895 and her half-sister in 1897. Many of the letters in this volume are to her sister, Vanessa, and her dearest friends, Madge Vaughan, Violet Dickinson, and Lady Robert Cecil. *The Voyage Out* is the only novel she wrote during this period. The volume concludes when she marries Leonard Woolf at age thirty. Volume 2 (1912-1922) of these well-edited letters deals with the period when Virginia and Leonard founded the Hogarth Press; Virginia suffered from nervous breakdowns, and produced three of her most important novels. Much of the correspondence is to Vanessa and deals with household and servant problems. Volume 3 (1923-1928) begins when Virginia is 41 and well-launched in the literary world. These were the years of *Mrs. Dalloway, To the Lighthouse*, and *Orlando*, said to be inspired by her friendship with Vita Sackville-West. Many of the most personal letters in this volume are to Vita. Sometimes ill but never mad during this period, Virginia's correspondence provided an outlet for ideas and impressions, always witty and sometimes malicious, that she let fly from her pen as the mood struck. Volume 3 then becomes a chronicle of friendships both literary and intensely personal. Leonard is mentioned infrequently, a tribute perhaps to their steady marriage characterized by mutual support for each other's work. The indexing in all volumes is admirably set up so that one can find Woolf's views on almost any literary figure or event and trace her literary and personal friendships with some ease. The letters were first published under the title, *The Flight of the Mind*.

331   Woolf, Virginia (Stephen), 1882-1941. **A Writer's Diary. Being Extracts from the Diary of Virginia Woolf.** New York: Harcourt, Brace, Jovanovich, 1973. 355p. index. $3.65. ISBN 015698380X. LC 73-5737.
Selected and edited by Leonard Woolf, these excerpts culled from the diary kept by Woolf from 1918 to a few days before her death in 1941 will remain essential reading to those with an interest in Woolf's art and the creative process. Many consider this the greatest of Virginia Woolf's works. She is superb in recording the ups and downs of daily existence and the problems and pleasures she encounters in her writing. Leonard Woolf chose the selections here from 26 volumes of the diaries; his focus was to include passages in which she records feelings about her own reading and writing, and he warns that this must be borne in mind lest the reader get "a very distorted view of her life and her character." The complete diaries edited by Anne Olivier Bell have begun to appear, the first of five projected volumes covering 1915-1919 published September, 1977 (Harcourt, Brace, Jovanovich).

332   Zakrzewska, Marie Elizabeth, 1829-1902. **A Woman's Quest: The Life of Marie E. Zakrzewska, M.D.** Edited by Agnes C. Vietor. New York: Arno Press, 1972. (Repr. of 1924 ed.). 514p. bibliog. $22.00. ISBN 0405044860. LC 72-2630.
"Marie Elizabeth Zakrzewska (1829-1902) was born in Berlin. Her liberal-minded father had been dismissed from the Prussian army; her mother, descended from Lombardi gypsies, was compelled to put her to work learning domestic service at age thirteen. Five years later she obtained a job for her daughter in the charity hospital in which whe worked. By the time she was 23, Marie was chief midwife and professor. The remainder of her life, spent in America, is a record

of opposition overcome, of fierce dedication to medicine and the training of women doctors, of compassion tested among the poor in New York and in Boston, of the founding of two outstanding hospitals for women and children, and of steady battle against the ignorance, prejudice and poverty that shortened feminine life. Agnes C. Vietor, a Boston surgeon, based this biography on materials and letters given to her by Marie Zakrzewska" ("A Note about This Volume").

333   Zassenhaus, Hiltgunt. **Walls: Resisting the Third Reich—One Woman's Story.** Bsoton: Beacon Press, 1974. 248p. $9.95. ISBN 0807063886. LC 73-16443.

Zassenhaus chronicles a twelve-year nightmare of resistance that began when Adolf Hitler came to power in 1933 and the author was in high school in Hamburg, Germany. She came from a middle-class intellectual family all of whose members resisted Nazism. Because she was proficient in Scandinavian languages, she was assigned a job as a postal censor to read letters going in and out of Scandinavia. In this position, she learned much about the activities of the Gestapo, and about ghettos other than in Warsaw into which Jews had been driven by the Gestapo. This connection with postal censorship gave her an opportunity to resist and to help prisoners. She began by smuggling letters out of her department that were written by Jews requesting food and clothing from relatives in Scandinavia. Later she helped Norwegian prisoners by allowing mail to go through uncensored. This was a period of nerve-wrenching fear at a constant pitch, during which Zassenhaus combined resistance activities with premedical studies. A consistently absorbing personal account of courage and humanity, the book ends with Hitler's death and Zassenhaus's hairline escape from the clutches of the Gestapo. At 28, she records that she felt "ancient" and confused about where to take up life again, but firm in her resolution to become a physician.

Three major groups of materials are brought together in this chapter, reflecting literature ranging from the most theoretical approaches to the very practical: 1) the discipline of economics as conventionally defined in works like Brownlee and Brownlee's *Women in the American Economy*; 2) material on women workers, labor, and labor force participation, for example, Howe's *Pink Collar Workers* and Allen's *The Labor of Women in the Production of Cotton*; and 3) the burgeoning and sometimes disturbing new "how to get yours in the business world" genre (say, Hennig's *The Managerial Woman* and Harragan's *Games Mother Never Taught You*), as interesting for the trends they profile as the suggestions that they proffer for career advancement. Users will want to consult the Reference chapter for important bibliographies in the labor, economics, and business areas. Consult the Sociology section when looking for sources that emphasize the impact of women's work on the family, and History for books written by an historian that approach labor and economics in a heavily historical manner. The subject index provides additional access (e.g., Management, Labor Force Participation, and Agricultural Workers).

334   Abbott, Edith, 1876-1957. **Women in Industry: A Study in American Economic History.** New York: D. Appleton, 1910; repr. New York: Arno Press, 1969. 408p. bibliog. index. $17.50. ISBN 0405021011. LC 70-89714.
Rediscovered by the contemporary women's movement, this classic study is remarkable for the clarity of its analysis. Abbott's perspective on the issues of sexual inequality and women's employment has been crucial in helping to shape much contemporary feminist, and particularly socialist-feminist, historical thought. She begins with the premise that women have always worked, but that they have *not* always worked in wage labor. What is needed, therefore, in order to explain contemporary trends and problems, is a historical analysis of the changing forms, conditions, and relations of women's work. This Abbott does by presenting a history and analysis of the transition from the colonial period, when the home was the basic productive unit, to the period of the emerging factory system, the gradual removal of production from the home, and women's and men's increasing dependence on wage labor. Abbott is also important for her insistence on distinguishing between the situations, the needs, and the struggles of working-class and professional women. This is truly seminal work within women's history.

335   Allen, Ruth Alice, 1889- . **The Labor of Women in the Production of Cotton.** New York: Arno Press, 1975. (Repr. of 1933 ed.). 285p. bibliog. index. $19.00. ISBN 0405067615. LC 74-30616.
This study (originally 1933) reports on Allen's dissertation research on the lives and work of women living on Texas cotton farms on the eve of the Depression (1928-1930). Allen used a questionnaire, filled out for the most part in personal interviews, that asked women about their living conditions and their work (including childrearing, housework, field work for the family, and field work

for hire). Included in her sample of over 1,000 were white, black, and Mexican women; these groups are separately analyzed to facilitate comparisons. Her research provides a particularly rich case-study in the history of rural depopulation in the United States: the process by which agriculture was industrialized, family production eliminated, the small farmer uprooted, agricultural labor proletarianized, and the flood of newly superfluous rural labor released for industrial exploitation in the cities. Particularly important in Allen's study is the focus on how this transition affected women and on the part played in the process by racial and ethnic competition.

336   American Academy of Political and Social Science, Philadelphia.
       Women in the Modern World. Edited by Viva B. Boothe. New York:
       Arno Press, 1974. (Repr. of 1929 ed.). 396p. index. $21.00. ISBN
       0405060785. LC 74-3929.
This collection of articles was originally published in 1929 as a special issue
(on "Women in the Modern World") of the *Annals* of the American Academy
of Political and Social Science (volume CXLIII, May 1929). Thirty-six articles
consider the following major topics: The Genesis and Significance of the Woman
Movement; Woman's Contribution to the Modern Home; Woman's Work Outside
the Home—In Industry; Women in Business and the Professions; Some Achievements of Women as Creative Citizens; Social Attitudes Affecting Women's Work;
and The Integration of Women's Activities. Among the authors represented
here are: Willystine Goodsell, Theresa Wolfson, Mary Beard and Lorine Pruette.
The collection is very similar in foci and approach to the many recent surveys
of women's status, and historical comparisons would doubtless prove interesting.

337   Baker, Elizabeth (Faulkner), 1885- . **Technology and Woman's Work.**
       New York: Columbia University Press, 1964. 460p. bibliog. index.
       $15.00. ISBN 0231027478. LC 64-22559.
This is a study of technological change in the United States from the eighteenth
century to the present and its impact on women's status in the labor market.
Baker's historical focus will be of interest to those exploring current research
on job segregation by sex.

338   Bird, Caroline. **Everything a Woman Needs to Know to Get Paid What
       She's Worth.** New York: McKay, 1973. 304p. bibliog. index. $8.95.
       ISBN 0679503722. LC 73-79946.
This is a practical guide for women looking for better jobs at better pay, which
in most cases means jobs outside the "female job ghetto." Written in a question-
and-answer format, the book addresses issues of discrimination and how to
predict it; tactics for entering male-dominated fields; tactics for promotion;
self-employment; blue-collar work; and strategies for fighting discrimination
(affirmative action, legal action, and unions). A "Resource Section" at the end
lists publications and organizations that could help in the documentation of
discrimination, vocational choice, education and training, job hunting, becoming
self-employed, plus a list of feminist consultants and professional organizations
for management. Bird—in conjunction with her large staff—interviewed personnel
managers, executive recruiters, vocational counselors, government specialists,

and legal experts, in addition to several hundred working women in diverse jobs, in preparation for the writing of this book.

339   Blaxall, Martha, and Barbara Benton Reagan, 1920- , eds. **Women and the Workplace: The Implications of Occupational Segregation.** Chicago: University of Chicago Press, 1976. 326p. bibliog. index. $12.50. ISBN 0226058212. LC 76-10536.

The articles in this collection were first presented at a workshop conference on occupational segregation held at Wellesley College in May 1975; they were originally published as a supplement to the spring 1976 issue of *Signs: Journal of Women in Culture and Society* (vol. 1, no. 3, pt. 2). Among the contributions are: Jessie Bernard, "Historical and Structural Barriers to Occupational Desegregation"; Heidi Hartmann, "Capitalism, Patriarchy, and Job Segregation by Sex"; Francine Blau and Carol L. Jusenius, "Economists' Approaches to Sex Segregation in the Labor Market: An Appraisal"; and Marianne A. Ferber and Helen M. Lowry, "Women: The New Reserve Army of the Unemployed."

340   Boserup, Ester. **Woman's Role in Economic Development.** New York: St. Martin's Press, 1974. 283p. bibliog. index. $4.95. ISBN 0312886551. LC 70-118569.

Ester Boserup is concerned with the tendency of certain development patterns in the Third World to deprive women of their productive functions. Her goal in this study was to identify and explain pre-existing patterns in the sexual division of labor from the point of view of development policies. She consistently tries to relate changes in the sexual division of labor to other economic and political and social changes, such as changes in population density or in land use. The material is divided into three major sections: In the Village; In the Town; and From Village to Town.

341   Bosworth, Louise Marion. **The Living Wage of Women Workers: A Study of Incomes and Expenditures of 450 Women in the City of Boston.** New York: Longmans, Green, 1911; repr. New York: Arno Press, 1976. 90p. $7.00. ISBN 0405074778. LC 75-16459.

This study of the cost of living of working women was conducted from 1906 to 1911 in Boston. It is based on detailed records of the living expenses of 450 wage-earning women, collected through budget schedules and personal interviews. Among the women studied were (in descending order of numbers represented) clerical workers, factory workers, waitresses, saleswomen, professional women, and kitchen workers. The vast majority earned between $6 and $11 per week, although nearly 13 percent earned as little as $3 to $5 weekly. The material presented offers a detailed picture of the living conditions of women workers in a turn-of-the-century United States city, including information on homes and lodgings, nominal versus actual incomes, food, rent, clothing, health, savings and debts, and education and recreation. Numerous statistical tables are scattered throughout the text.

342   Braverman, Harry. **Labor and Monopoly Capital: The Degradation of Work in the Twentieth Century.** New York: Monthly Review Press, 1974. 465p. bibliog. index. $12.50. ISBN 0853453403. LC 74-7785.

This book has been hailed as the most important contribution to an analysis of capitalist labor process since Marx's *Capital*. Braverman's careful and critical analysis of changes in the occupational structure of the United States in the last century makes this work of specific as well as general relevance for women's studies, for he comes to argue that the most rapidly expanding working-class occupations in the present day are in the clerical and service sectors—i.e., "female occupations." This study makes substantial contributions to an understanding of structural determinants of women's experiences in the labor market.

343   Breckinridge, Sophonisba Preston, 1866-1948. **Women in the Twentieth Century: A Study of Their Political, Social and Economic Activities.** New York: Arno Press, 1972. (Repr. of 1933 ed.). 364p. $18.00. ISBN 040504450X. LC 72-2593.

This study of "women in the twentieth century" was actually written and first published in the early 1930s and, therefore, only speaks to changes that took place in the first three decades of the present century. The book was written by S. P. Breckinridge, then a professor of public welfare administration at the University of Chicago, first woman to pass the Kentucky bar and earn a doctorate in political science at the University of Chicago, pioneer in the professionalization of social work, and advocate of Progressive party policies on unions, slums, and legislation. Her study examines developments in "the activities and relationships of women other than those incidental to family life"—specifically, in women's organizations, in paid labor, and in politics.

344   Brownlee, W. Elliot, 1941- , and Mary M. Brownlee. **Women in the American Economy: A Documentary History, 1675-1929.** New Haven, CT: Yale University Press, 1976. 350p. bibliog. index. $17.50. ISBN 0300018975. LC 75-18168.

Patterns in the labor force participation of women yield significant information about the changing status of women and social opportunities open to them. This documentary history conveys "the diversity of women's attitudes toward work and the complexity of women's participation in the marketplace, particularly ingenuity, flexibility, shrewd adaptation, aggressiveness, and persistent search for a 'sense of self' that have characterized the contribution of women to the nation's economic life." Letters, speeches, diaries, recollections, and report literature provide the diverse literature for this patchwork of the American woman. Major sections include: Women in Preindustrial Society; Women on Farms; Women in Factories: The Industrial Revolution, 1820-70; Women in Factories: Continuing Industrialization, 1870-1929; Women in the Services: Home and Office; Women in the Services: The Professions; and Women as Consumers. The reader might also want to look at *America's Working Women* (R. Baxandall, et al.) and G. Lerner's two documentary collections, *The Female Experience* and *Black Women in White America*.

345   Chapman, Jane Roberts, ed. **Economic Independence for Women: The Foundation for Equal Rights.** Beverly Hills, CA: Sage Publications, 1976. 285p. bibliog. $17.50. ISBN 0803904444. LC 75-11129.

This collection of articles on women and economics is the first volume of the Sage Yearbooks in Women's Policy Studies, a series edited by the Center for

Women Policy Studies. The general topic is introduced by Martha Griffiths in an article, "How Much Is a Woman Worth? The American Public Policy," which discusses the low value placed on women's work in the United States, whether it be paid work in the labor force or unpaid labor in the home. Subsequent articles pursue this theme through investigations of blue-collar work, credit, labor unions, poverty, changes in the occupational structure, along with comparative studies on other industrialized countries and on underdeveloped countries. Among the authors represented here are Irene Tinker, Heather Ross, Pamela Roby, Barbara Wertheimer, and Carolyn Shaw Bell.

346   Conference on Women's Challenge to Management, Arden House,
       1971. **Corporate Lib: Women's Challenge to Management.** Edited by
       Eli Ginzberg and Alice M. Yohalem. Baltimore, MD: Johns Hopkins
       University Press, 1973. 153p. bibliog. $8.50. ISBN 0801814758.
       LC 72-12371.
This collection brings together the principal papers prepared for and the key presentations delivered at the Conference on Women's Challenge to Management held at Arden House, Columbia University, in 1971 and attended by representatives of business, government, and academia. Among the better-known contributors are Eli Ginzberg and William Goode, of Columbia University, Elizabeth Janeway, author, and Valerie K. Oppenheimer, of U.C.L.A.

347   Council on Economic Priorities. **Guide to Corporations: A Social
       Perspective.** Chicago: Swallow Press, 1974. 393p. $20.00. ISBN
       0804003300. LC 73-13212.
Of interest to women in this profile of gigantic corporations is the segment given for each one entitled "Equal Opportunity for Minority Groups and Women," which shows the corporation's employment record and briefly states hiring and training policy. Useful information on the corporation such as address, major products, consumer brands, financial data and disclosure will also interest women researching the American economic terrain. Corporations are listed for the following major industries: airline, automobile, chemical, oil, paper, and steel.

348   Council on Economic Priorities. **Women and Minorities in Banking:**
       Shortchanged/Update. New York: Praeger, 1977. 173p. bibliog.
       $16.50. ISBN 0030403367. LC 77-21469.
This Council on Economic Priorities survey of the status of women and minorities in the banking industry updates its 1972 study, *Shortchanged: Minorities and Women in Banking.* CEP reports important progress since 1971 in this study of employment practices in 24 leading banks across the country, but the improvement so far appears to be confined to the lower levels. Minorities have begun to be hired as tellers, and women are found as ground floor officers, but the executive suites remain uniformly white and male. This survey includes chapters on Employment in the Banking Industry; Minority Group Members; Women in the Labor Force; Regulation and the Quality of Enforcement; and Bank Profiles.

349   Dodge, Norton T. **Women in the Soviet Economy: Their Role in Economic, Scientific, and Technical Development.** Baltimore, MD: Johns Hopkins Press, 1966; repr. Westport, CT: Greenwood Press, 1977. 331p. bibliog. index. $21.00. ISBN 0837194679. LC 76-57945.

In this highly detailed empirical analysis, Dodge's concern is with utilization of "manpower resources"—specifically, the extent of the utilization of women in the labor force. He looks to the Soviet Union as an example of a social system that has, by comparison with the United States, massively mobilized women's productive potential, especially in the areas of science and technology. While Dodge's ideological biases are immediately apparent in his comments on "Soviet totalitarianism," the study is rich in data on the following topics: demographic factors affecting women's employment; women's participation in the labor force; social, economic, and legal factors affecting employment; family versus work; education and training; educational attainment; nonprofessional occupations; semiprofessional and professional occupations; professional attainment; and achievements in science and technology. Sources used included published Soviet materials, information gathered during Dodge's trips to the U.S.S.R., and interviews he conducted there. Statistical tables support the text throughout. Readers may want to consult the more recent, more comprehensive, and less technical *Soviet Women* (1975), by William Mandel.

350   Ewen, Stuart. **Captains of Consciousness: Advertising and the Social Roots of the Consumer Culture.** New York: McGraw-Hill, 1976. 261p. bibliog. index. $10.00. ISBN 0070198454. LC 75-34432.

This is a penetrating analysis of the growth of a monopoly economy during the last century and, more particularly, of the concomitant rise of mass production strategies, which required for their success continual expansion of consumption. The generation of mass consumption necessitated corporate access to the realm of "private life," where decisions about spending are made. This entire process is thus by its nature connected to questions of the family and sex roles. Ewen makes this explicit in part 3, "Mom, Dad and the Kids: Toward a Modern Architecture of Daily Life."

351   Garson, Barbara. **All the Livelong Day: The Meaning and Demeaning of Routine Work.** Garden City, NY: Doubleday, 1975; repr. New York: Penguin Books, 1977. 221p. $1.95. ISBN 0140043810. LC 76-49076.

At this time when more women than ever before are needing and demanding work in the paid labor force, it's important to be aware not just of whether they can get it, but also of *what* they get when they get it. While her focus is not exclusively on women, Barbara Garson is concerned with this question. She set off to interview workers in a variety of occupations to discover how they feel about their work. She spoke with men and women factory workers (at ping pong, tuna fish, cosmetics, auto, lumber, mink, and medical factories), with keypunchers, clerical workers, and typists. She writes in the aftermath of her interviews: "I expected to find resentment, and I found it. I expected to find boredom, and I found it. I expected to find sabotage, and I found it in clever forms that I could never have imagined. But the most dramatic thing I found was quite the opposite of non-co-operation. *People passionately want to work.*" What Garson repeatedly observed were the imaginative strategies devised by workers to enliven jobs that corporate management sought just as energetically to simplify, rationalize, trivialize. Garson is much influenced by another recent, ground-breaking book on work—Harry Braverman's *Labor and Monopoly Capital: The Degradation of Work in the Twentieth Century*— and one would do well to read the two together. Braverman provides a rigorous historical and theoretical framework for Garson's stories, which, in turn, bring to life the abstract arguments of Braverman.

352   Gordon, Francine E., and Myra H. Strober, eds. **Bringing Women into Management.** New York: McGraw-Hill, 1975. 168p. bibliog. $9.95. ISBN 0070238065. LC 75-1247.
Based on a conference for executives held April 18, 1974, at the Stanford University Graduate School of Business and entitled "Women in Management," this includes: "Introduction" (Arjay Miller); "Institutional Barriers" (Cynthia Fuchs Epstein); "Sex Differences and Their Implications for Management" (Carol Nagy Jacklin and Eleanor E. Maccoby); "Executive Man and Woman: The Issue of Sexuality" (David L. Bradford, et al.); "The Law" (Colquitt L. Meacham); "Bringing Women into Management: Basic Strategies" (Myra H. Strober); "Bringing Women into Management: The Role of the Senior Executive" (Francine E. Gordon); "Women into Management: Vignettes" (personal accounts by seven women); and "Conclusion" (Myra E. Strober and Francine E. Gordon).

353   Harragan, Betty Lehan. **Games Mother Never Taught You: Corporate Gamesmanship for Women.** New York: Rawson Associates; distr. New York: Atheneum, 1977. 334p. index. $10.95. ISBN 0892560193. LC 76-53673.
Harragan's thesis is that "learning the game skills *must* come first for ambitious women because mastery of business technical skills is only gained through playing with and against more accomplished players." This "how-to" book plots strategies for getting to "the top of the pyramid." All advice is given in terms of "selling yourself," "scoring," and "tricks." Still this will be useful for women who seek high paying positions in this milieu and who want to fit into the business world as it exists. Harragan covers the terrain in matters of office politics, jargon, salary negotiations, clothing, office protocol, and corporate hierarchical structures.

354   Hennig, Margaret, and Anne Jardim. **The Managerial Woman.** Garden City, NY: Anchor Press/Doubleday, 1977. 221p. bibliog. index. $7.95. ISBN 0385022875. LC 73-9161.
Hennig and Jardim examine the life and career histories of 25 women who had gained high level management positions in business and industrial sectors of the economy by 1970. Part 1 explains patterns of difference in the styles of female and male managers. Part 2 focuses on "twenty-five women who made it." Essential reading for women interested in management positions. A major thesis of the book: "unless people not only are, but believe that they are, equally able or competent to compete, they will not willingly or successfully integrate themselves with more powerful individuals and groups."

355   Howe, Louise Kapp. **Pink Collar Workers: Inside the World of Women's Work.** New York: Putnam, 1977. 301p. bibliog. $8.95. ISBN 0399115887. LC 76-41300.

Louise Howe wanted to deepen her understanding of women's work in the United States and felt that the women's movement and the mass media had both emphasized the professional woman and the woman in traditionally "male" occupations to the exclusion of more typical women. Since 1900, over half of women workers have been in occupations in which at least two-thirds of the workforce is female; somewhere between 30-40 percent have been in occupations in which 80 percent or more is female. Howe set out to learn from women in traditional "female" occupations how they view their work and their lives and what changes they would like to see. The approach is largely descriptive and anecdotal, based on interviews. But she includes a statistical portrait of the female labor force in an appendix, and her bibliography can refer readers to sources taking different empirical approaches. Howe looks at women beauticians, sales workers, waitresses, office workers, and homemakers. Interested readers may also want to look at Studs Terkel's *Working: People Talk about What They Do All Day and How They Feel about What They Do* (Pantheon Books, 1974).

356   Jongeward, Dorothy, et al. **Affirmative Action for Women: A Practical Guide.** Reading, MA: Addison-Wesley, 1973. 334p. bibliog. $8.95. ISBN 0201032937. LC 73-10592.

This handbook on affirmative action is intended both for management of organizations forming affirmative action plans and for women interested in their status in the workplace. The collection goes beyond a narrow, legalistic analysis of affirmative action to consideration of the larger social context of working women. Chapters include: The Organization Woman: Then and Now; Women's Lack of Achievement: Then and Now; Legislation and Litigation: Impact on Working Women; Women in Government and Affirmative Action; Women in Organized Religion; Working Black Women: A Strategy for Change; The Obstacle to Women in Management; Bank of America's Affirmative Action Seminar; Seminars for Career Women: Combining Awareness Training with Transactional Analysis; What Do I Want to Do Next?; Women in Psychotherapy; and How to Eliminate Sexist Language from Your Writing: Some Guidelines for the Manager and Supervisor.

357   Katzell, Mildred E., and William C. Byham, eds. **Women in the Work Force.** New York: Human Sciences Press, 1972. 76p. bibliog. $10.95. ISBN 0877050627. LC 74-184155.

The proceedings of a conference sponsored by the Division of Personnel Psychology of the New York State Psychological Association, Nov. 1970 (New York), form a book with the theme that organizations need to change in the ways they utilize the skills of women. The presentations covered legal, social, and union pressures for change and reviewed the basic attitudes and stereotypes that speakers perceived as preventing women from assuming proper roles and being treated on a par with men. This conference (one of the pioneer sessions on these topical issues) concentrated more on issues definition than upon prescribing how to translate commitments into action. Among the edited papers:

Employment Implications of Psychological Characteristics of Men and Women;
What is Labor Doing about Women in the Work Force?; What Management is
Doing about Women in the Work Force; What Government is Doing about
Women in the Work Force; and Where Do We Go from Here? Presenters included
a psychologist, an attorney, professors, and administrators from the public and
private sectors.

358   Kreps, Juanita Morris. **Sex in the Marketplace: American Women at
       Work.** Baltimore, MD: Johns Hopkins Press, 1971. 117p. bibliog.
       $2.75. ISBN 0801812771. LC 75-155165.
A condensed review of what the author considers to be the quintessential
literature on women's labor force participation, this book also explores the
basics of when women work, at what jobs, and under what arrangements.
The author states that much more data are needed on the worklives of women
in order to assess and have impact upon the equality-of-sexes issue. A bibliography covers materials written mostly before 1970. Chapters include: The
Demand for and Supply of Women Workers; A Case in Point: Women in the
Academic Profession; and Home and Market Work in Lifetime Perspective.

359   Kreps, Juanita Morris, ed. **Women and the American Economy: A
       Look to the 1980's.** Englewood Cliffs, NJ: Prentice-Hall, 1976. 177p.
       index. $8.95. ISBN 0139623248. LC 76-4105.
This is a collection of eight papers on the history of women in paid employment
in the United States, current issues relating to women's employment and
questions for the future. The papers served as background material for partici-
pants in the American Assembly, which met in the fall of 1975 in Harriman,
New York. Among the authors represented here are Juanita Kreps, William
Chafe, Karl Taenber, James Sweet, Isabel Sawhill, and Martha Griffiths.

360   Lobsenz, Johanna. **The Older Woman in Industry.** New York: Scribner,
       1929; repr. New York: Arno Press, 1974. 281p. bibliog. index. $16.00.
       ISBN 0405061102. LC 74-3961.
"Johanna Lobsenz directed her skills as an interviewer and writer to disclosing
the fate of older women who had to continue working in order to support
themselves. Based on scores of interviews conducted in Manhattan, the book
analyzes a problem of tremendous emotional impact. In her explorations, which
excluded the professions, the author found general agreement among production
employers and job agencies that in the late '20s, 'older women' meant women
after age 35. This is a pioneer study of a kind of double discrimination that
persists—discrimination because of age and because of sex" ("A Note about This
Volume," L. Stein and A. K. Baxter, eds.). Lobsenz looked at factory work,
clerical and general office work, sales, and domestic work. Among the topics
she discusses are: the problem as the older woman herself sees it; the problem
as employment managers and employment agencies see it; the role of the state;
and social dimensions of the problem.

361   Loring, Rosalind, and Theodora Wells. **Breakthrough: Women into
       Management.** New York: Van Nostrand Reinhold, 1972. 202p. bibliog.
       $8.95. ISBN 0442248903. LC 72-7926.

Women are forcing changes in court, in government regulations and on the job (where demand is far in excess of the supply of female managers, say the authors), and the issue is not if women will move up, but when and how. They cite the proposed 27th U.S. Constitutional Amendment as one of the foundation stones for future change and claim that development of other such bases for change in the United States is rapidly gaining momentum. The intended audience of the book includes male executives, and the hoped-for result is "more women in management NOW." Among the chapters: Guidelines for Immediate Action; Managerial Climate; Our Sex-Role Culture; Managers, Marriages and Mates; Working Relationships That Work; and Future Implications. The authors fault futurists for failing to see how substantially women will affect organizational life, even more so than technological change and zero population growth. They assume ERA passage. The appendix includes excerpts—those that concern women in management—from Revised Order No. 4, useful for readers unfamiliar with affirmative action program requirements. Also in this section is a sample survey questionnaire that would be useful for any organization wishing to assess employees' perceptions of and feelings about the organization in which they work.

362   Lyle, Jerolyn R., and Jane L. Ross. **Women in Industry: Employment Patterns of Women in Corporate America.** Lexington, MA: Lexington Books, 1973. 164p. bibliog. index. $11.00. ISBN 0669861243. LC 73-1012.

The researchers looked at 246 large firms and discovered that, in 1970, only six percent of the managerial positions were held by women. Unlike Hennig and Jardim's *The Managerial Woman* (1977), Lyle and Ross did not find recognized patterns for moving into managerial jobs or clearly defined managerial styles characteristic of female executives. Chapters are: Occupational Discrimination in Industrial and Non-Industrial Firms; Women in the Managerial Elite; The Role of Federal Government in Equal Employment Opportunity. The annotated bibliography of readings on women is especially good on areas such as occupational choice, women's participation in the labor force, and legal issues in employment, though the literature clusters around the late '60s and early '70s.

363   MacLean, Annie Marion. **Wage-Earning Women.** New York: Macmillan, 1910; repr. New York: Arno Press, 1974. 202p. bibliog. $13.00. ISBN 0405061110. LC 74-3962.

This study of 400 firms employing 135,000 women was one of the first projects undertaken by the National Board of the Young Women's Christian Association, organized in 1906. The study was launched on the rationale that the work of the YWCA among working women would benefit from an investigation of the conditions of these women's lives. Investigators looked at working conditions, living conditions, and social backgrounds of women in paper, shoe, textile, paper goods, garment-making, buttons, and beer industries; in department stores and the mills; hop and fruit picking from New York to Chicago, the Middle West to Oregon and California; and in the coal fields of Pennsylvania. Two final chapters consider "Uplifting Forces" (trade unions, legislation, social settlements, working girls' societies, the YWCA) and "Suggestions for Improvement."

364   Molloy, John T. **The Woman's Dress for Success Book**. Chicago: Follet,
       1977. 189p. $9.95. ISBN 0695808109. LC 77-81320.
Molloy calls himself "a wardrobe engineer," and his design is intended for
businesswomen and wives of businessmen. The basic principle of this "reference
work" is that, "the right clothes can help a woman enormously in achieving
success in her business and social life." Chapters: The Mistakes Women Make
and How to Correct Them; Instant Clothing Power for the Business Woman;
The Success Suit; Packaging Yourself; Dressing for the Job; Selling Yourself
and Other Important Items; Dressing to Attract Men; The Company Spouse.
Molloy bases his formulas on research he conducted with a large sample of men
and women. His suggestions are geared to help women choose clothes appropriate for the occasion and occupation (e.g., dressing for the jury if you are a
lawyer) and for the geographical area (e.g., Southern California accepts infor-
mality). This could be useful to women who aspire to success in a milieu that
defines clothing as the index of a person's worth. More significant, perhaps,
are the findings Molloy has identified about the perceptions of women seeking
"success" in the world of affairs. Diagrams, sketches, and lists of the plan
are given in case a woman should miss the point.

365   Nye, Francis Ivan, 1918- , and Lois Norma Wladis Hoffman, 1929- .
       The Employed Mother in America. Chicago: Rand McNally, 1963;
       repr. Westport, CT: Greenwood Press, 1976. 406p. bibliog. index.
       $23.00. ISBN 0837187842.
This collection brings together articles from the fields of sociology, social
psychology, economics, and child development. Originally published in 1963,
the book is clearly of the pre-women's movement era. In general, the articles
begin from the premise that there is something problematic about women who
are both mothers and in the paid labor force, and the problem tends to be located
more in the woman and her familial relationships than in the structure of
society. The subject headings grouping the articles are indicative of this perspec-
time: Why They Work; Effects on the Children; The Husband-Wife Relationship; and Adjustment of the Mother. The importance of the volume today lies
in the fact that it has been a starting point for much of the more recent work
on the subject. Furthermore, despite the overall skeptical tone, much of the
evidence reported in this collection refutes dire predictions about the negative
impact of maternal employment on children and marriage.

366   Oppenheimer, Valerie Kincade. **The Female Labor Force in the United
       States: Demographic and Economic Factors Governing Its Growth and
       Changing Composition.** Berkeley: Institute of International Studies,
       University of California, 1970; repr. Westport, CT: Greenwood Press,
       1976. 197p. bibliog. index. $14.25. ISBN 0837188296. LC 76-4536.
This is an important study of changing patterns in women's labor force participation over the course of this century. Oppenheimer analyzes statistical data
on changing demographic characteristics of women workers (increasingly more
are married and mothers) and on sex segregation in the labor market. Her most
significant contribution lies in the demonstration of the existence of different
labor markets for men and women and of the often neglected or underplayed
importance of *demand* for female labor as a determinant of *supply*. She concludes

that "perhaps the best explanation for the overall increase in female labor force participation in recent years is that there has been an increase in the *demand* for female workers which has, in turn, stimulated an increase in the *supply* of women to the labor market."

367   O'Neill, William L., comp. **Women at Work.** Chicago: Quadrangle Books, 1972. 360p. bibliog. $10.00. ISBN 0812902165. LC 72-182506. O'Neill has reprinted here two accounts about women's work that provide an interesting contrast between the sweatshop exploitation working-class women faced at the turn of the century and the masked exploitation of contemporary service jobs. Dorothy Richardson's *The Long Day: The Story of a New York Working Girl* (1905) is an account by a middle-class woman forced by circumstance to support herself at unskilled jobs. Though Richardson's story is as rich in snobbish moralizing as it is in significant detail about the lives of her co-workers, O'Neill views it as "the best place to begin studying the condition of working women in, or just before, the Progressive era that I know of." Elinor Langer, an author published in such magazines as the *Nation* and the *Atlantic*, chose to work as a customer's service representative for the New York Telephone Company from October to December 1969. Her account, "Inside the New York Telephone Company" (1970), depicts the working conditions, the likes and attitudes of her co-workers within a job situation requiring employee identification with the company.

368   Rapoport, Rhona, and Robert Norman Rapoport, 1924- . **Dual-Career Families Re-examined: New Integrations of Work and Family.** New York: Harper and Row, 1977. 382p. bibliog. $4.95. ISBN 0060905212. LC 77-150829. A sequel to *Dual-Career Families* (1971) by the Rapoports, this book is essentially a study of five English families, drawn from a series of sixteen subject families characterized by both spouses pursuing active careers and family lives. Influenced by studies of women in the labor force in the United States, the authors' speculations about such participation in England offer interesting comparisons for U.S. researchers in these subject areas, especially with the wide-ranging sociological impact as the percentage of dual-career families increases. The authors present ideas about implications for social policy relevant to families in which both spouses are pursuing careers, especially in the realm of equal-opportunity legislation. It is argued that change can come through a synergism of efforts by innovative managers and politicians destroying myths and promoting realities. Women's freedom to achieve in careers will improve, the book posits, in a milieu featuring shorter working hours, more flexible patterns of employment, more work sharing, more male commitment in the home, and more understanding of the impact of dual-career families upon a nation's economy. The Rapoports' latest book is *Working Couples* (Routledge and Kegan Paul, 1978), a compilation of essays on the subject of dual-career families. Another study on this topic is Lynda Lytle Holmstrom's *The Two-Career Family* (1972).

369   Salmon, Lucy Maynard, 1853-1927. **Domestic Service.** New York:
       Arno Press, 1972. (Repr. of 1897 ed.). 307p. bibliog. index. $15.00.
       ISBN 0405044453. LC 72-2766.
Originally published in 1897, this book reports the findings of Lucy Maynard
Salmon's large-scale study of domestic workers during 1889-1890. While Salmon's attempted stance of objectivity sometimes seems to cover for a primary
identification with the employer, her book is nonetheless a gold mine of data
on this key "female" occupation of the nineteenth century. In chapters 2
through 4, Salmon offers historical background on domestic service in North
America, a history she divides into three periods: first, the colonial period,
during which service was performed by transported convicts, indented white
servants, blacks, and Indians; second, from the Revolution to about 1850,
when indented servants were replaced by "free labor" in the North and by
slaves in the South; and third, from 1850 to 1890, during which period domestic
service was revolutionized by successive waves of immigration from Ireland,
Germany, and China, and by the abolition of slavery in 1863. Salmon emphasizes the impact of industrialization on household production and division of
labor and how changes in these have, in turn, altered the conditions of domestic
service. The balance of her study is an analysis of her statistical findings, based
on approximately 2,000 questionnaires (about two-thirds from employers,
one-third from employees). Included are data on wages, percentages of foreign
and native-born workers, geographic distribution, percentage of women (foreign
and native-born), male/female wage differentials, and problems and advantages
of domestic service from the point of view of employers, on the one hand, and
employees, on the other. Salmon concludes with an assessment of possible
"remedies" (none of a very revolutionary character), although it is never quite
clear how she defines the nature of the problem. She does note that at the close
of the nineteenth century, a significant number of other occupations are beginning to compete for women workers.

370   Schindler-Rainman, Eva, and Ronald Lippitt. **The Volunteer Community:**
       Creative Use of Human Resources. (2nd ed.). La Jolla, CA: University
       Associates, 1975. 176p. bibliog. index. $7.50. LC 75-18516.
In a time when many women activists and underemployed and unemployed
women are beginning to ask themselves, "why work for nothing when the rewards
often come back in the form of being treated as a substandard individual?," this
book may strike a negative chord. It purports "to be a useful resource, stimulus,
and guide for staffs and volunteers in public and private agencies offering
volunteers an opportunity to serve; for the organizers and leaders of cause
movements; for consultants doing organizational development work with agency
decision makers; for professors in professional schools and sequences such as
social work, health, medicine, psychology, psychiatry, nursing, religion, public
administration, etc.; for leaders in business and labor; and for anyone interested
in voluntarism as a vital part of an active democratic society" (introduction).
This brief treatment takes into account the changing profile of the volunteer
worker, who may, in fact, be compensated for on-the-job expenses while performing volunteer work. An extensive bibliography is included covering all
facets of volunteerism, its mechanisms, and its human resources.

371 Schultz, Theodore William, 1902- , ed. **Economics of the Family:
Marriage, Children, and Human Capital.** Chicago: University of Chicago
Press, 1975. 584p. bibliog. index. $12.95. ISBN 0226740854. LC
73-81484.

The articles and commentaries brought together in this collection were the
basis for two conferences on the economics of the family (in 1972 and 1973).
The approach adopted here represents the application of "human capital theory"
to an analysis of fertility, marriage, and household management. This new
approach extends premises about "economic man"—i.e., that human beings
are rational decision-makers who take stock of their resources, desires, and risks
and come to economic decisions about investment and expenditures accordingly—
to the realm of the family. Thus, children are here viewed as forms of "human
capital"—investments with predictable costs and benefits—as is the housewife's
time spent in household production and/or employment. What this amounts to
is an application of the rationalizing, cost/benefit approach to human affairs
that is characteristic of capitalist management, to the most intimate realm of
human relations. While there is much here that is disturbing, the analysis deserves
attention—first, because it is attracting proponents within academia and government, and, secondly, because it poses an interesting contrast to feminist analyses
of the sexual division of labor, childbearing and rearing, housework, and so on.
Fundamental to this contrast is human capital theory's failure to raise questions
both about the overall social structure in society that sets the context and limits
for family decision-making and about the priorities that this structure represents.

372 Schwartz, Eleanor Brantley. **The Sex Barrier in Business.** Atlanta:
Georgia State University, 1971. 116p. bibliog. $6.95. ISBN
0884060136. LC 79-174757.

The author presents an overview of women's roles from ancient times to the
American Civil War and summaries of their post-Civil War participation in labor
and management. Results of a survey of executive opinions of women in management reveal stereotypical attitudes as well as sanguinity about women's contributions and competence. Also reviewed are Title VII of the Civil Rights Act of
1964 and actions brought under that discriminatory practices legislation. The
author posits that women can bring about stronger reforms than in the past if
they will fully exercise their legal rights. Despite an optimism for the future,
Dr. Schwartz concludes that the greatest amount of work is yet to be done to
reduce the level of prejudice and discrimination and to increase the utilization
of American womanpower. A copy of the survey questionnaire form is included
in the appendix.

373* Seear, B. N. **Re-Entry of Women into the Labour Market after an
Interruption in Employment.** Paris: Organisation for Economic Co-
operation and Development, 1971. 135p. LC 77-854859.

This study was initiated by OECD to evaluate major factors affecting women's
re-entry into employment and resulted in findings about the need for women to
return to employment; steps being taken to provide information, training, and
other assistance; and the effectiveness of measures taken in terms of women's
on-the-job satisfaction and economic contribution. A most helpful foldout
recapitulative table summarizes several policy and practice factors pertaining

to the re-entry phenomenon for the United States and eight other Western industrial nations. Factors include nondiscrimination policies, availability of vocational guidance, financial support provision, levels and trends of participation rates, and employment outside traditional occupations. Chapter 3 presents commentaries and conclusions on developments in the nine collaborating countries: Canada, Denmark, West Germany, France, Italy, Netherlands, Sweden, United Kingdom, and United States.

374   Seed, Suzanne. **Saturday's Child: 36 Women Talk About Their Jobs.** Chicago: J. P. O'Hara, 1973. 159p. $7.98. ISBN 0879558032. LC 72-12599.
Women from such fields as the arts, communication, science, business, and government discuss their jobs, job requirements, and job selection. Interviews and photos were by Suzanne Seed.

375   Sobel, Lester A., ed. **Job Bias.** New York: Facts on File, 1976. 190p. index. $10.95. ISBN 0871962446. LC 76-41984.
A section on women handles ERA, federal action, court decisions, academic discrimination, and discrimination cases among other issues. Useful graphs and tables such as "Employment by Occupation Group & Sex," and "Number of Women Candidates for Public Office and Women Elected Officials: 1972 and 1974" are included as well.

376   Splaver, Sarah. **Nontraditional Careers for Women.** New York: J. Messner, 1973. 224p. bibliog. $6.25. ISBN 0671326198. LC 73-5384.
Discusses over 500 careers for women in such fields as law, medicine, science, math, engineering, creative arts, business, manual trades, and government services.

377   Stromberg, Ann, and Shirley Harkess, eds. **Women Working: Theories and Facts in Perspective.** Palo Alto, CA: Mayfield, 1978. 458p. bibliog. index. $7.95. ISBN 0874843014. LC 77-89921.
This is a volume of readings on the sociology of women's work in the United States by scholars in the fields of sociology, economics, psychology, and history. Articles for the most part present summaries of their topics rather than new empirical research, making the collection appropriate for introductory or intermediate-level college courses. Topics include the demographic characteristics of women workers, the position of minority women workers, male/female wage differentials, legal remedies for discrimination, sex-role socialization and achievement, the relation between women's work inside the home and in the paid labor force, plus analyses of women's experiences in male-dominated professions, in female-dominated professions, in temporary clerical work, "blue-collar" and service occupations, domestic service, and housework. Among the contributors: Carolyn Shaw Bell, Francine D. Blau, Elizabeth M. Almquist, Joan Acker, Isabel V. Sawhill, Joann Vanek, and Constantina Safilios-Rothschild. Bibliographic notes follow each selection to direct interested readers to further sources.

378   Sweet, James A. **Women in the Labor Force.** New York: Seminar Press, 1973. 211p. bibliog. index. $14.50. ISBN 012785813X. LC 72-7704.

This is principally an analysis of cross-sectional demographic data from the 1960 United States Census of Population. Specifically, it is based on a sample of married women under the age of sixty who are living with their husbands, who do not live on farms, and who are not members of secondary families. The following variables were evaluated: labor force participation, family composition, family history, economic status, and a group of "other" variables, including age. A review of the literature on factors influencing the employment of wives is included in chapter 1. White/non-white differences are discussed in chapter 3 in the context of the relationship of labor force activity to family composition and age of the woman. A background in statistics will help the reader better to understand chapter 4, a multivariate analysis of employment status in relation to the family status variables—education, family economic pressure, and age. Also, some aspects of marital and fertility history are examined in relation to current employment. Chapter 5 is concerned with the interactions between economic characteristics and the family life cycle in their effects on current employment. The author concludes that in developing a theory of labor force participation of wives and designing policies related to the employment of women, it is important to examine the interactions of family status, family income adequacy, and education, and to include stages in the family life cycle in any model of the employment of wives. A bibliography is included. The methodology used by Sweet may provide ideas for researchers who wish to analyze data that are more recent than those in this study.

379   Task Force on Working Women. **Exploitation from 9 to 5: Report of the Twentieth Century Fund Task Force on Women and Employment.** Lexington, MA: Lexington Books, 1975. 200p. bibliog. $13.50. ISBN 0669960993. LC 74-14614.

Representatives from the fields of law, business, economics, government, education, and labor came together as a task force (1971) to consider and make recommendations on: affirmative action and the means of enforcing it; the responsibilities of labor unions; the government's role as provider of jobs, welfare, social security, and job training; and social policy issues such as child care, educational equality, and the role of the media. The authors who pulled the material together are Adele Simmons, Ann E. Freedman, Margaret C. Dunkle, and Francine Blau. The bibliography is an excellent one, pointing the way to government publications and to periodical literature that regularly address the issues of the status of working women in the United States.

380   Thomas, Sherry, and Jeanne Tetrault. **Country Women: A Handbook for the New Farmer.** Garden City, NY: Anchor Press, 1976. 381p. bibliog. $12.95. ISBN 0385030347. LC 75-32296.

The cover of this book expands the title: "how to negotiate a land purchase, dig a well, grow vegetables organically, build a fence and shed, deliver a goat, skin a lamb, spin yarn and raise a flock of good egg-laying hens, all at the least possible expense and with a minimum reliance on outside and professional help." It is copiously illustrated. The bibliography identifies such diverse items as publication information for *Dairy Goat Journal* and *The United Stand Privy Booklet.*

381   Tilly, Louise A., and Joan Wallach Scott. **Women, Work, and Family.**
       New York: Holt, Rinehart and Winston, 1978. 274p. bibliog. index.
       $12.95. ISBN 0030333261. LC 74-19821.
The purpose of *Women, Work, and Family* is to explore the impact of industrialization on women's work. Tilly and Scott approach this problem by analyzing
women's work in England and France since the eighteenth century. They
discover that, while women's work shifts in three centuries from being largely
household and farm labor in the eighteenth century to factory wage-earning
in the nineteenth and finally to low-skilled bureaucratic and involving consumer
skills in the twentieth, women's work always originates in and contributes to
the family unit. Women's work can only be studied meaningfully in the context
of the family, they conclude. With thoughtful organization, Tilly and Scott
have synthesized much of the most important scholarship on women's work.
Their graphs and charts are clear and helpful, and the bibliography is explicitly
oriented toward undergraduate use. *Women, Work, and Family* should become
an essential textbook, in addition to being a piece of solid and lucid scholarly
analysis.

382   Trahey, Jane. **Jane Trahey on Women and Power: Who's Got It? How
       to Get It?** New York: Rawson Associates, 1977. 265p. index. $8.95.
       ISBN 0892560290. LC 77-77891.
Written in a breezy, "how to" style, this volume is laced with common sense,
tinged with humor, and has a tone of urgency. Trahey wants to increase the
wallop of those women already in the corporate hierarchy and to enlarge their
representation in the ranks of decision makers. She avers that one can acquire
power in corporations by starting work early, staying late, working at home,
and placing family considerations second, but that going into business for
oneself is the ultimate power trip. Guidelines are given for avoiding rip-offs
by idea thieves, handling interviews and salary negotiations, getting promotions,
dressing appropriately, how to choose the correct automobile, and dealing with
the realities of sex and liquor. In chapter 8, she profiles nine successful women
and projects the thesis that mothers and other significant female relatives were
dominant influences, as contrasted with Margaret Hennig's (*The Managerial
Woman*) findings that her 25 female subjects were predominantly influenced
by their fathers. Of Trahey's sample, seven had mothers who worked either
full- or part-time; the mothers in Hennig's study were usually not gainfully
employed. Trahey is president and owner of an advertising agency.

383   United States. President's Commission on the Status of Women.
       **American Women: The Report of the President's Commission on the
       Status of Women and Other Publications of the Commission.** Edited
       by Margaret Mead and Frances B. Kaplan. New York: Scribner, 1965;
       repr. Washington: Zenger, 1975. 274p. bibliog. index. $11.95. ISBN
       0892010045. LC 75-33325.
The introduction and epilogue are by Margaret Mead, but the Report is commonly
known as the Petersen Report, after Esther Petersen, then Assistant Secretary
of Labor, who served as executive vice chairman of the Commission on the
Status of Women. The text of this 1965 publication (which grew out of John
Kennedy's establishment of a commission on the status of women in 1961)

is interesting for the report and recommendations of the Commission, for the membership of the Commission itself, and for the basic assumptions it makes about the "typical" American woman (for example, "that both males and females attain full biological humanity only through marriage and the presence of children in the home, whether these are born to a couple or are adopted by them"). In addition to documenting the history of past inequities that women have experienced and the gains they have made in American society, the report outlines the status of women with regard to education, home and community, employment, protective labor legislation, social insurance and taxes, civil and political rights, and public office. Recommendations of the committee call for such broad reforms as the reexamination of educational goals for girls and women as well as equal opportunity for women in hiring, training, and promotion, with encouragement of part-time and flex-time possibilities for employed women and appropriate legislative reform to end sex discrimination. Valuable statistical material is contained here.

384*   Walker, Kathryn E., 1917- , and Margaret E. Woods. **Time Use: A Measure of Household Production of Family Goods and Services.** Washington: Center for the Family of the American Home Economics Association, 1976. 328p. bibliog. index. ISBN 0846107015. LC 75-46524.

Walker and Woods report here on the results of their ambitious study of time use patterns in household production. Feminists have long emphasized the lack of recognition and compensation accorded to women's work in the home. Walker and Woods's research lays the foundation for a concrete assessment of the nature of household work and the contributions of different family members to it. Based on a 1967-1968 survey of households in an urban-suburban community in upstate New York, *Time Use* analyzes the total time spent by all household workers for all household work and for each separate task (e.g., food preparation, care of family members, care of the house, care of clothing, marketing, and management). Data are also provided on the contribution of each type of household worker (husband, wife, young children, older children, and others), and on how these contributions vary (in size and as a proportion of the total time spent) according to whether the wife is employed outside the home, whether she is employed full- or part-time, and by number and ages of children. Among the interesting findings reported here are the following: that the average time that housewives spend on household work has not been drastically reduced by the last fifty years' development of appliances; that wives, employed or not, were the principle household workers (62 percent of total time spent if employed, 72 percent if not); and that husbands' relatively small contributions did not vary substantially according to their wives' employment status or the number and age of children. Readers who are put off by statistical tables will find the results summarized in accessible language within the body of the text. Readers may be interested in the work by Oli Hawrylyshyn, *The Economic Value of Household Services: An International Comparison of Empirical Estimates* (Praeger, 1978).

385   Wallace, Phyllis Ann, ed. **Equal Employment Opportunity and the AT&T Case.** Cambridge, MA: MIT Press, 1976. 355p. bibliog. index. $16.95. ISBN 0262230739. LC 75-34095.

"The essays draw heavily on the materials made available during a two-year public hearing on the employment patterns of the American Telephone and Telegraph Company (AT&T), the largest private employer in the country." As a result of the AT&T case, which involved racial, sexual, and national origin discrimination, a total of 38 million dollars was awarded to the victims. But perhaps more significantly, the entire framework of institutional discrimination was thoroughly examined. Issues surfaced such as equity in the work place, allocation of occupational roles, and toleration of tradeoffs between efficiency and equity. Among the impressive essays here are Kenneth Boulding's "Toward a Theory of Discrimination"; Judith Long Laws's "The Bell Telephone System: A Case Study"; Felix Lopez's "The Bell System's Non-Management Personnel Selection Strategy"; and Laws's "Psychological Dimensions of Labor Force Participation of Women."

386   Wetherby, Terry, ed. **Conversations: Working Women Talk About Doing a "Man's Job."** Millbrae, CA: Les Femmes, 1977. 269p. $4.95. ISBN 0890879222. LC 76-53343.

Conversations brings together transcribed interviews of 22 women in "non-traditional" or "male" occupations. Among the occupations represented here are: butcher, grain elevator manager, welder, truckdriver, mill supervisor, dairy officer, law school dean, top fuel race car driver, pesticides inspector, and neuropathic physician. The conversations range over topics such as how the women ended up in their particular jobs, what they actually do on the job, problems they face as women, and their family situations. Each interview is prefaced by a brief introduction written by Wetherby.

387   Williams, Marcille Gray. **The New Executive Woman.** Radnor, PA: Chilton, 1977. 233p. index. $9.95. ISBN 0801965284. LC 77-2473.

A feminist book, this is not. It does have many practical points on the conduct of life executive-style and should be available for women interested in business careers. Chapters include: Dealing with Male Chauvinism; Whatever You Do, Don't Cry; Managing Other People; Learning to Leash Your Libido; Traveling for Business; The New Etiquette; Dressing for Success. The author has adopted a male model for the appropriate conduct of women in business.

EDUCATION

Materials with education as a central focus—even when the secondary focus is historical, sociological, or economic—come together in this section of the bibliography. Several major clusters of material indicate the scope of this chapter: sex discrimination in higher education, women's studies theory and syllabi, historical treatises on women's education, broad surveys and histories of women's education in modern times and antiquity, and counseling handbooks for women. Contemporary works on sexism in primary and secondary schools and comparative studies and histories of daycare also figure prominently in the Education section. Users should note the title index for full access to the important Female Studies series. Additional education materials will be found in the Reference section of this bibliography. Beyond this bibliography, ERIC and CIJE (*Current Index to Journals in Education*), as well as the bibliographic services and files of WEECN (Women's Educational Equity Network), provide ongoing assistance in periodical and report literature dealing with contemporary women-related educational issues.

388   Abramson, Joan. **The Invisible Woman: Discrimination in the Academic Profession.** San Francisco: Jossey-Bass, 1975. 248p. bibliog. index. $12.95. ISBN 0875892566. LC 74-32627.
Joan Abramson's own incredible experience within academia provides the starting point for her inquiry into how sex discrimination takes place within the world of universities and colleges. Part 1 is a case-study of her own history, including her sex discrimination suits against the University of Hawaii. In part 2, she examines the "myth of merit" as the operating premise of academia, the white male backlash, and relations between academic women. Part 3 offers information on and critical analysis of methods of appeal available to women who are discriminated against.

389   Ahlum, Carol, and Jacqueline Fralley, comps. **High School Feminist Studies.** Old Westbury, NY: Feminist Press, 1976. 157p. bibliog. $5.00. ISBN 091267024X. LC 76-373858.
Ahlum and Fralley also authored *Feminist Resources for Schools and Colleges* (1973), updated by Froschl and Williamson (1977). As the first published collection of women's studies materials, bibliographies, and syllabi designed for high schools, this is indeed a benchmark publication. The introduction by Florence Howe identifies goals of a feminist curriculum: "the ultimate purpose of women's studies hearkens back to its primary source—the women's movement: to improve the status of women in the society, to render to women the dignity and social justice due to them." Arlow and Froschl review the dismal treatment of women in high school literature and United States history texts. Their criticisms are bolstered by an extensive bibliography. The heart of the book is the presentation of syllabi and course outlines for history, literature, and interdisciplinary courses—25 contributions from around the United States.

390   Astell, Mary, 1666-1731. **A Serious Proposal to the Ladies.** New York: Source Book Press, 1971. (Repr. of 1701 ed.). 162p. $9.50. ISBN 0442810547. LC 77-134177.

" . . . since GOD has given Women as well as Men intelligent Souls, why should they be forbidden to improve them?" So wrote the English author, Mary Astell, in the early eighteenth century. Astell had an unusual upbringing for a woman of her time, in that her uncle instructed her in Latin and French, logic, mathematics, and natural philosophy—an education she further pursued as an adult in London. She was ridiculed for her views on women and especially on the education of women. *A Serious Proposal to the Ladies* ("for the advancement of their True and Greatest INTEREST, by a Lover of her SEX," reads the full title of the 1701 edition) develops suggestions for the improved education of women in the context of an institution that she alternately calls a monastery and a "Religious Retirement."

391   Astin, Helen S., 1932- , ed. **Some Action of Her Own: The Adult Woman and Higher Education.** Lexington, MA: Lexington Books, 1976. 180p. bibliog. index. $14.50. ISBN 0669005673. LC 75-43476.

This collection of articles comes out of a study of fifteen continuing education for women programs, the administrators, the women students, and their families. The primary foci of the study were: 1) demographic characteristics of the women students; 2) development and structure of the programs; 3) impact of the programs on the parent institutions; 4) impact of the programs on the women; and 5) impact on the women's families. Data were collected primarily through interviews and questionnaires. Articles by Helen Astin, Carole Leland, Joseph Katz, and Jessie Bernard present the results and conclusions of the study. A preliminary chapter by Elizabeth Cless gives an historical account of the continuing education for women movement.

392*   Astin, Helen S., 1932- . **The Woman Doctorate in America: Origins, Career, and Family.** New York: Russell Sage Foundation, 1969. 196p. bibliog. index. LC 79-90261.

Though this study is by now somewhat out of date, it remains a classic in the field of sociology and for the study of higher education for women. The basic question informing the research was whether professional education is "wasted" on women. Astin's study followed up over 1,600 women who had received their doctorates in various fields in 1957-1958, and her results dispell many myths, showing that the majority of women were employed and stable in their employment patterns. Ten years after receiving their degrees, over half had achieved the status of full or associate professor, many of them having at the same time married and raised children. Astin reports here on the women's family backgrounds and early career decisions, career development, and work patterns; occupational achievements and awards; use of leisure time; and obstacles to career development (including family responsibilities and sex discrimination). Also included are brief autobiographical sketches by six woman doctorates—a professor of English, a pharmacologist, a sociologist, a historian, a physiologist, and a psychologist—that speak to the important influences and dilemmas in these women's lives and careers. In a final chapter, Astin discusses implications of the findings and policy recommendations.

393   Beecher, Catharine Esther, 1800-1878. **A Treatise on Domestic Economy.**
       Saint Clair Shores, MI: Scholarly Press, 1976. (Repr. of 1848 ed.).
       $45.00. ISBN 0403065291.

Another classic work by Beecher on the subject of "domestic economy," this
was sparked by her discovery in the course of extensive travel of "the deplorable
sufferings of multitudes of young wives and mothers, from the combined influence of *poor health, poor domestics, and a defective domestic education.*"
She suggests that these ills can be alleviated if domestic economy is placed
"on an equality with the other sciences in female schools. This should be done
because it *can* be properly and systematically taught (not *practically,* but as a
science), as much so as *political economy* or *moral science,* or any other branch
of study. . . . Are not the principles that should guide in constructing a house,
and in warming and ventilating it properly, as important to young girls as the
principles of the Athenian Commonwealth, or the rules of Roman tactics?"
The present work is intended as a textbook for female schools, and it discusses
women's responsibilities, preparation of food and drinks, clothing, cleanliness,
exercise, manners, children, housework, charity, and more.

394   Beecher, Catharine Esther, 1800-1878, and Harriet Elizabeth (Beecher)
       Stowe, 1811-1896. **The American Woman's Home: Or, Principles of
       Domestic Science.** Saint Clair Shores, MI: Scholarly Press, 1976.
       (Repr. of 1869 ed.). $35.00. ISBN 040306532.

This classic treatise on the principles of "domestic science" is dedicated "to
the women of America, in whose hands rest the real destinies of the Republic,
as moulded by the early training and preserved amid the maturer influences
of home. . . . " As has frequently been noted, the rise of "domestic science"
coincided not just with the expanding authority of science, but also, ironically,
with the *decline* of the home as the productive unit, the decline in the birth
rate, and hence the decline in domestic work as a whole. As such, "domestic
science" served as an ideological rationale for continued belief in "woman's
sphere" in the face of its actual transformation. Among the topics that Beecher
and Stowe discuss are: The Christian Family; Scientific Domestic Ventilation;
Cleanliness; Domestic Manners; Good Temper in the Housekeeper; The Care
of Servants; and The Care of the Homeless, the Helpless, and the Vicious.

395   Bennett, John, curate of St. Mary's, Manchester. **Strictures on Female
       Education: Chiefly as It Relates to the Culture of the Heart.** New
       York: Source Book Press, 1971. (Repr. of 1795 ed.). 115p. $9.50.
       ISBN 0442810598. LC 74-134179.

Reprinted in this volume are four essays originally published in 1795: 1) "Con-
taining a slight survey of the treatment of women in different ages and nations
of the world, and an investigation of the causes, which have contributed to the
obvious and shameful negligence in their education"; 2) "Observations on the
manner, in which the treatment of this sex will be influenced by, and will recipro-
cally influence the taste, the sentiments, the habits and pursuits, the manners,
the morals, the publick and the private happiness of a people"; 3) "A Disquisi-
tion concerning the nature, quality and extent of female talents, and the comparative difference of understanding in the sexes"; 4) "Reflections on the dangers
and insufficiency of Boarding Schools, considered as a mode of Female Education."

396   Bernard, Jessie Shirley, 1903- . **Academic Women.** University Park:
       Pennsylvania State University Press, 1964. 331p. bibliog. index.
       $11.50. ISBN 0271730501. LC 64-15066.
This is an early sociological study on a topic that has, since the contemporary
women's movement, attracted enormous attention: the comparative status,
performance, and rewards accruing to men and women in academia. This book
is still commonly cited and is a good place to start with this topic. However,
it has a curiously dated tone (1964). There's a seeming assumption that women
choose their position within academia, and Bernard hastens to inform her
readers that she is not a feminist and has never experienced professional discrimination. Thus the book has another interesting dimension (beyond its stated
focus) as an indicator of the change in social climate in the last fifteen years.

397   Boas, Louise (Schutz). **Woman's Education Begins: The Rise of the
       Women's Colleges.** Norton, MA: Wheaton College Press, 1935; repr.
       New York: Arno Press, 1971. 295p. bibliog. index. $18.00. ISBN
       0405036949. LC 74-165705.
A volume in the Arno reprint series on American education, this study delves
into the early seminaries for women, with emphasis given to developments in
Massachusetts and New York. Basing her research almost entirely on primary
sources, Boas places women in the context of social, domestic, and religious
currents that shaped early higher education for women in America. Her chapter
on curriculum is recommended, as is the bibliography, which points the way
to many primary-source materials.

398   Burton, John, 1745 or 1746-1806. **Lectures on Female Education and
       Manners.** New York: Source Book Press, 1970. (Repr. of 1793 ed.).
       2v. in 1. $15.00. ISBN 0442819587. LC 72-134181.
Published in London in 1793, this is a series of lectures for young female
students on the subject of those duties and manners "which may be strictly
called feminine." Included among the topics are the following: The Influence
of the Female Sex in Society; On the Duties of Wives; On the Duties of Mothers;
Female Accomplishments (e.g., needle work, drawing, music); On Beauty and
Dress; Reading Recommended; On Female Manners; On Pleasure; On the Necessity
of Governing the Temper; Forgiveness of Injuries; Of Courtesy, Affability, and
Complacency; On Pride; On Affectation; and On Evil-Speaking.

399   Carnegie Commission on Higher Education. **Opportunities for Women
       in Higher Education: Their Current Participation, Prospects for the
       Future, and Recommendations for Action.** New York: McGraw-Hill,
       1973. 282p. bibliog. $5.95. ISBN 0070101027. LC 73-14726.
This is a good summary and analysis of the status of women in higher education—
as students, faculty members, administrators, and nonfaculty academic employees—
including their backgrounds, the mechanisms of discrimination, sex-role barriers
to women's advancement (e.g., exclusive responsibility for childraising), relative
productivity of men and women and relative rewards received, and recommendations for change (from affirmative action to the provision of sliding-scale
fee child-care services). Arguments are amply illustrated with relevant statistical
data.

400*   Chmaj, Betty E. **American Women and American Studies.** Pittsburgh,
       PA: Women's Free Press; distr. Pittsburgh: Know, 1971. 258p. LC
       70-31571.
This is an anthology of materials by, about, or relevant to university women in
the field of American studies. Part 1 reports on the responses received to a
questionnaire on sex discrimination sent out to women in the American Studies
Association in 1971. The results are discussed in relation to an overview of the
status of women in academia and in American studies. Part 2 reproduces 27
course syllabi relevant to women's studies developed by professors all over the
country in the fields of American studies, literature, history, sociology, politics,
and economics. Part 3, titled "Collage," is a miscellany of excerpts from articles,
bibliographies, book reviews, sexist textbooks, and more.

401   Chmaj, Betty E., and Judith A. Gustafson. **Image, Myth and Beyond:**
       American Women and American Studies, Vol. Two. Pittsburgh, PA:
       Know, 1972. 404p. $6.00. ISBN 0912786205.
This is the sequel to Chmaj's *American Women and American Studies* (1971)
and is organized along similar lines. Part 1 further explores the status of women
in universities in general and in the field of American studies in particular. It
also includes some responses to volume 1, including the resolutions of the
American Studies Association. Part 2 reproduces more course syllabi, plus reports
on a number of women's studies programs and programs in continuing education. Part 3, which Chmaj considers the most important part of the present
volume, reprints a collection of articles relevant to women's studies.

402   Clarke, Edward Hammond, 1820-1877. **Sex in Education; Or, A Fair**
       Chance for the Girls. Boston: J. R. Osgood, 1873; repr. Buffalo, NY:
       Heritage Press, 1974. 181p. bibliog. $14.50. ISBN 0884710114.
       LC 73-19407.
Edward Hammond Clarke, physician and author, noted for his skillful use of
drugs in treatment, specialized in diseases of the eyes and the nervous system.
He believed that the women's rights movement was responsible for many nervous
problems suffered by women. He wrote *Sex in Education* (1873) to prove that
women were constitutionally unable to withstand the same mental and physical
strain as men and that, therefore, coeducation was a fatal policy that should
be replaced where instituted with sex-specific education. Readers will want to
look at the replies to and critiques of Clarke collected by Julia Ward Howe in
one volume entitled *Sex and Education* (1874), which express the point of view
that Clarke's book "seems to have found a chance *at* the girls, rather than a
chance *for* them." John and Robin Haller's *The Physician and Sexuality in
Victorian America* (1974) is a historical analysis of the emergence in nineteenth-
century America of the physician as moral counselor on issues pertaining to
the relations between the sexes and sexual inequality.

403   Conable, Charlotte Williams, 1929- . **Women at Cornell: The Myth of**
       Equal Education. Ithaca, NY: Cornell University Press, 1977. 211p.
       bibliog. index. $12.50. ISBN 0801410983. LC 77-3117.
"I would found an institution where any person can find instruction in any
study"–so reads the Cornell University motto, a quotation from the founder,

Ezra Cornell. Situated in upstate New York, forty miles from Seneca Falls
(home of the first women's rights convention in 1848) and in a prevailing climate
of social reform, Cornell did in fact open its doors to women four years after
its establishment in 1868. Charlotte Conable's book is an account of how the
original commitment to equal education for men and women was progressively
eroded from the 1880s on, until Cornell emerged as a decidedly male-dominated
institution, at which women were a numerical minority, were accorded second-
class status, and were counseled into "appropriate" fields such as home economics.
Any significant challenge to this state of affairs had to wait until the late 1960s,
when women began to organize and make demands on the university.

404   Cross, Barbara M., ed. **The Educated Woman in America: Selected
       Writings of Catharine Beecher, Margaret Fuller, and M. Carey Thomas.**
       New York: Teachers College Press, 1965. 175p. $6.50. ISBN
       0807712213. LC 65-23578.
Cross says of these three extraordinary educated women: "they lacked the
grace of acquiescence: thorny, critical, at odds, they were not typical women."
Her interesting introduction briefly outlines the ambitions of each woman.
Each recognized that women lacked equality but as domestic reformer, intellectual, and educational innovator, each went about her visions for American women
quite differently. This is a useful little volume for introducing the work of three
pioneers of American feminist social philosophy.

405*   Daniels, Arlene Kaplan, 1930- . **A Survey of Research Concerns on
       Women's Issues.** Washington: Association of American Colleges, 1975.
       43p. bibliog.
Daniels addresses the need for systematic research on women's issues: "although
the number of studies about women has increased in the past several years,
they are often underfunded, sporadic and isolated from other relevant studies."
Among the research issues she identifies as critical are: the educational system,
marriage and the family, health and the life cycle, finance, voluntarism, politics,
careers, continuing education, and old age. She provides a useful appendix
listing specific print "Resources: Research on Women's Issues." The book is
available from the Association of American Colleges, 1818 R. St., N.W., Washington, DC 20009.

406   Davies, Emily, 1830-1921. **Thoughts on Some Questions Relating to
       Women, 1860-1908.** Cambridge, MA: Bowes and Bowes, 1910; repr.
       New York: AMS Press, 1973. 227p. $12.00. ISBN 040456741X.
       LC 73-14557.
Emily Davies, a pioneer in the reformation of the male-dominated English
educational system, advanced the cause of women seeking higher education in
Britain during the last half of the nineteenth century. This book represents
selections from her writings and public lectures, 1860-1908. Among the selections: "Female Physicians" (1861); "Medicine as a Profession for Women"
(1862); "Home and the Higher Education" (1878); "Women in the Universities
of England and Scotland" (1896); and letters to the *Times* and the *Spectator*
on women's suffrage written by Davies during 1907 and 1908.

407   Farnsworth, Marjorie Whyte, 1921- . **The Young Woman's Guide to An Academic Career.** New York: Richards Rosen Press, 1974. 112p. $4.80. ISBN 0823902862. LC 73-80357.

Farnsworth, a professor of biology, writes from a personalized missionary perspective "to inform all eager women graduates of the perils and rewards of an academic career." Emphases are on "the absolute necessity" of the Ph.D.; the shoals of sexism, which must be navigated to be accepted as a "serious" graduate student; the hazards and horrors of student assistantships and qualifying examinations; job hunting in the academic community; and the importance of publishing. This is also a "how to" primer on research activities, handling students, committees, faculty meetings, and colleagues. A final lesson is on avoiding "faculty wives" and knowing the differences between colleagues and friends. If you can handle the obnoxious tone of this book and bear in mind that "the academic realities" presented by Farnsworth are one woman's view, this guide does have some issues that people considering academic careers should mull over.

408   Feldman, Saul D. **Escape from the Doll's House: Women in Graduate and Professional School Education.** New York: McGraw-Hill, 1974. 208p. bibliog. index. (Carnegie Commission on Higher Education). $9.95. ISBN 0070100691. LC 73-12829.

A revision of the author's thesis (University of Washington), this report is a well-documented state-of-the-art summary of women in graduate education that offers predictably grim data. Chapters include: Women in Higher Education: A Historical Perspective; Masculine and Feminine Academic Disciplines: Their Characteristics; The Ascent to the Ivory Tower: Men's and Women's Plans for Academic Careers; Dedication to Graduate Study: Beliefs and Behavior; External Constraints: Marital Status and Graduate Education. Among the appendices are the methodology and questionnaires used for the study. Readers may also wish to look at Lewis C. Solmon's *Male and Female Graduate Students: The Question of Equal Opportunity* (Praeger, 1976).

409   Frankfort, Roberta, 1945- . **Collegiate Women: Domesticity and Career in Turn-of-the-Century America.** New York: New York University Press, 1977. 121p. bibliog. index. $10.50. ISBN 0814725635. LC 76-53614.

A significant title in the literature of women's higher education, Frankfort's book makes the point that even the colleges created solely for the education of women fostered "the cult of domesticity" and a Victorian notion of women's sphere. It is useful to read this book along with Conable's *Women at Cornell* (1978), which examines the issue of women's progress at a coeducational institution. Two important characters in the history of the "seven sister" schools are Alice Palmer, president of Wellesley from 1881-1887, and M. Carey Thomas, who ran Bryn Mawr until 1922. Both were strong leaders whose personal ideologies shaped their institutions and, in the long run, shaped overall educational patterns of women in a sexist society.

410   Frazier, Nancy, and Myra Sadker. **Sexism in School and Society.** New
       York: Harper and Row, 1973. 215p. bibliog. $6.95. ISBN 006042172X.
       LC 72-11496.

Nancy Frazier, a journalist who writes books for children, is responsible for
the four chapters of this volume that address general issues of sexism in society:
the women's movement, black women's liberation, marriage, child care, work,
sanctions against "deviant" women, and sexist ideologies and science. Myra
Sadker, a professor of education, offers more concrete analyses of sexist practices in education, from elementary school through high school to university.
A final chapter by Frazier proposes a program for change in educational practices, and Sadker has composed a questionnaire for educators to examine their
own sexist preconceptions and expectations. An annotated bibliography on the
women's movement and sexism in education is appended. The book is somewhat
dated, but it offers a good introduction to feminist educational issues that have
been further explored and developed since Frazier and Sadker's writing in 1973.
One more recent study (though of much narrower focus) is Gross and Trask's
The Sex Factor and the Management of Schools (Wiley, 1976). Gross and Trask
conducted an empirical study of men and women school principals to explore
the impact of sex on role performance, conception of tasks, orientation to
managerial responsibilities, career histories and aspirations of the subjects,
and operation and productivity of their schools.

411   **The Gay Academic.** Edited by Louie Crew; written by Ellen M. Barrett,
       et al. Palm Springs, CA: ETC Publications, 1978. 444p. bibliog. index.
       $15.00. ISBN 0882800361. LC 75-37780.

Written by 22 authors representing a variety of fields—history, library science,
literature, linguistics, philosophy, psychology, religion and theology, science,
sociology, and political science—this collection of 26 original essays "is intended
as a sampler" of issues and scholarship representative of gay individuals in academe.
Of special interest to women: Barbara Gittings's "Combatting the Lies in Libraries"; Julia Stanley's "Lesbian Separatism: The Linguistic and Social Sources
of Separatist Politics"; Karla Jay's "Male Homosexuality and Lesbianism in
the Works of Proust and Gide"; and Ellen M. Barrett's "Gay People and Moral
Theology."

412   Gersoni-Stavn, Diane, comp. **Sexism and Youth.** New York: R. R.
       Bowker, 1974. 468p. bibliog. index. $11.50. ISBN 0835207102.
       LC 73-21651.

Although the 1974 copyright date will immediately call attention to the fact
that much has been done in the field of children's literature very recently,
Gersoni-Stavn's collection of articles is an outstanding gathering of the literature
on sexism in children's books. An incredible range of sources on this topic will
be found here, from Sandra and Daryl Bem's "Training the Woman to Know
Her Place: The Power of a Nonconscious Ideology" to Jo Freeman's "The
Social Construction of the Second Sex." Early research reports (e.g., *Dick
and Jane As Victims,* annotation no. 447) are excerpted here. The
attention to media is excellent, from "Film Resources for Sex-Role Stereotyping"
to Letty Cotlin Pogrebin's "Toys for Free Children." The compiler of this
anthology, a former editor for *School Library Journal,* knows children's books.

Her praised bibliography ("Reducing the 'Miss Muffet' Syndrome: An Annotated Bibliography") appears in this volume, a standard work.

413   Gianini Belotti, Elena. **What Are Little Girls Made Of? The Roots of Feminine Stereotypes.** New York: Schocken Books, 1976. 158p. bibliog. $7.95. ISBN 0805236309. LC 76-9136.

This translation of *Dalla parte delle bambine* has an introduction by Margaret Mead, who points out that the Italian version of sex-role stereotyping serves to accentuate the common thread occurring in English, French, and American versions of this same problem. "It emphasizes, more than any book I know, the way in which a world on the verge of radical change makes a last stand against that change. The books I read as a child, seventy years ago, had no such monotonous stereotyping; they were about groups of children, bright lively girls and bright lively boys, exploring the world. The monotonous compulsion which insists that there are appropriate interests for little girls and little boys is new; it is partly due to the mass production of school materials and toys, and partly due to the role of the urban and suburban women who have moved into an urban environment and have become consumers without productive functions." This book explores attitudes toward children and stereotyped behaviors that are enculturated from birth to secondary schools. Although legal improvements in women's status are necessary and important, the author believes that it is "psychological structures which taint all woman's attempts with guilt; which make her feel she has failed as a woman if she does enter [the] world, or alternately failed as an individual, if she chooses to realize herself as a woman." Chapters: Expecting the Baby; Early Childhood; Games, Toys and Children's Literature; Educational Institutions: Nursery, Primary and Secondary Schools.

414   Ginzberg, Eli, 1911- , et al. **Educated American Women: Life Styles and Self-Portraits.** New York: Columbia University Press, 1971. 220, 198p. bibliog. index. $13.50. ISBN 0231030274. LC 73-31186.

"This book is based almost entirely on the information and evaluations . . . elicited from a group of educated and talented women [fellowship winners] about the unfolding of their lives and careers." The sample of the group surveyed indicates a wide range of lifestyles from the traditionalists to innovators. A group that spans these two roles in the study are designated as "transitionalists." The three major trends identified as important in changing the lifestyle of the educated woman are: 1) the expansion of the job market and the pressures to end discriminatory hiring practices; 2) the women's movement, which has created positive attitudes toward married working women and 3) increased educational opportunities for women.

415   Goodsell, Willystine, 1870-1962, ed. **Pioneers of Women's Education in the United States: Emma Willard, Catherine Beecher, Mary Lyon.** New York: AMS Press, 1970. (Repr. of 1931 ed.). 311p. bibliog. index. $14.95. ISBN 0404028640. LC 78-121279.

This volume includes biographies of the three educators with selections of their works. An introductory essay is included, "Women's Education in America Before 1820." Willard (1787-1870), who adhered to the philosophy of her age that men and women were endowed with different talents, was opposed to political participation for women. Her famous work is *Plan for Improving Female Education* (1819). Catharine Beecher (1800-1878) committed herself to the challenge of persuading the country to send teachers to the West and to establish normal schools in recently settled areas. She supported herself by her writing: *A Treatise on Domestic Economy* (1841), *The Evils Suffered by American Women and American Children: The Causes and the Remedy* (1846). Mary Lyon (1797-1849), founder of Mount Holyoke Female Seminary, was deeply religious and firmly convinced that woman's role was a teaching role at home or in the classroom. She supervised every detail of the funding, building, and education process at Mt. Holyoke and insisted firmly on student participation in the domestic work of the campus. Her "Principles and Design of the Mount Holyoke Seminary" (1837) appears in this volume. An excellent biographical source for all three women is *Notable American Women*. Goodsell has written an earlier and more general work on women's education that contains some interesting historical material, *The Education of Women: Its Social Background and Its Problems* (Macmillan, 1923).

416   Gray, Eileen, 1922- . **Everywoman's Guide to College.** Millbrae, CA: Les Femmes, 1975. 168p. bibliog. index. $3.95. ISBN 0890879036. LC 75-10576.

Gray gears her approach to older women returning to school. Her first chapter (Today's Unprecedented Opportunity) deals with special programs for returning women, a survey of returning women, and the profile of re-entry women. Other chapters: The Difficult Decision to Become a Student; How to Finance Yourself in School; How Women Have Been Socialized to Fail; The Two-Year College; Choosing a Four-Year College; Graduate School; Special Programs for Returning Women; Occupational Outlook for Women College Graduates in the 1980s. Gray's style is simple and direct, with much helpful information. She includes appendix materials on academic vocabulary, resource centers for women specializing in educational and career counseling, and a bibliography featuring reports, bulletins, directories, newsletters, and search services.

417   Guttentag, Marcia, and Helen Bray. **Undoing Sex Stereotypes: Research and Resources for Educators.** New York: McGraw-Hill, 1976. 342p. bibliog. index. $8.95. ISBN 0070253803. LC 76-49036.

The central questions upon which this study rest are: what can be done to make a classroom nonsexist? what works in helping students to adopt nonstereotyped views? Four hundred children in three school systems were involved in the study, which revealed that children are very sexist about opposite-sexed peers. "The book contains nonsexist curriculum packets which have been evaluated for practicality and effectiveness by use in actual classrooms. Background materials, resource agencies, and bibliographies are provided to help administrators and teachers achieve nonsexism in their classrooms." The approaches are geared to early childhood classes, middle grades, and junior high school.

418   Hale, Sarah Josepha (Buell), 1788-1879. **Manners; Or, Happy Homes and Good Society All the Year Round.** New York: Arno Press, 1972. (Repr. of 1868 ed.). 377p. $18.00. ISBN 0405044615. LC 72-2606.

"From her mother, Sarah Josepha Buell Hale (1788-1879) received a classical education at home. Married at 25, she bore five children in nine years before being widowed. She then turned to writing, became editor in 1827 of the *Ladies' Magazine* and in 1836 of *Godey's Lady's Book*, published in Philadelphia. *Manners; Or, Happy Homes and Good Society All the Year Round* summarizes the credo that established her as arbiter of good conduct for half a century: the home, not the public arena, was woman's battleground; her weapons were education, conversation, delicacy, femininity, and the power to persuade; and her role was that of God's moral agent on Earth" ("A Note about This Volume," A. K. Baxter and L. Stein, eds.). Though the lifestyle advocated by Hale was clearly attainable only by a small minority of privileged women, this classic treatise on etiquette and home economics is valuable as an indicator of prevailing nineteenth-century ideology of the "good life" and of woman's place, an ideology whose power and influence were not limited to the upper class.

419   Harrison, Barbara Grizzuti. **Unlearning the Lie: Sexism in School.** New York: Liveright, 1973. 176p. bibliog. $6.95. ISBN 0871405598. LC 72-97486.

Harrison's book is a case history of a particular school at a particular time—the Woodward School in 1971, a private, multi-racial elementary school in Brooklyn, New York. In 1970, a group of feminist parents began to identify and question sexist attitudes that they felt existed at Woodward. A number of parents and teachers rejected the feminist findings at first; but significantly, the Sex-Roles Committee was able to raise consciousness and to make some headway in changing curriculum and attitudes (e.g., elective karate was introduced; the librarian became more aware of sexism in book selection; teachers began to read aloud more books with positive images of female characters; staff became more aware of sexist remarks to students). Because it offers specific suggestions (rather than merely theory) and documents changes that can occur even in an initially resistant climate, the book is an important primer for remedying sexism in schools. Frazier and Sadker's *Sexism in School and Society* (Harper and Row, 1973) is complementary reading to the Harrison and offers a more intensively documented approach to the issue of sexism in the elementary school.

420   Harway, Michele, 1947- , and Helen S. Astin, 1932- . **Sex Discrimination in Career Counseling and Education.** New York: Praeger, 1977. 154p. bibliog. index. $16.95. ISBN 0030218268. LC 77-7829.

Harway and Astin report here on their research into career counseling for women. Fundamental to their perspective is the belief that socialization in our society reflects sex-role stereotypes that devalue women and discourage their achievement strivings. The authors believe that sex-role rocialization shapes the young woman's development, the training and outlook of career counselors, and tests and other materials used in counseling situations. These hypotheses were tested against relevant research and theoretical literature and data from statistical sources. Chapters in this volume are: Socialization; Women's Access to and Participation in Education; Training of Counselors; The Counseling Process;

Results of Counseling; Alternatives to Traditional Counseling; and Implications and Recommendations.

421 Hoffman, Nancy, et al., eds. **Closer to the Ground: Women's Classes, Criticism, Programs–1972.** Old Westbury, NY: Feminist Press, 1972. 235p. bibliog. $5.00. ISBN 0912670266.
One can read successive volumes in the *Female Studies* series as a continuing history of the women's studies movement. *Closer to the Ground (Female Studies VI)* presumes a knowledge by the reader of the reasons behind a woman-centered curriculum. It does not justify the legitimacy of women's studies courses. Rather, it explores with increased specificity "classes, feminist criticism, and a profile of one women's studies program." Very particular pedagogical issues surface in the three major segments of this volume: I. The Radical Perspective on Women's Studies; II. Women's Studies in the Classroom; and III. Feminist Criticism. Articles are diverse: on Gertrude Stein, women's autobiographies, Charlotte Brontë's feminism, Joan Didion, Christine de Pisan, and more.

422 Howe, Florence. **Female Studies: Two.** Pittsburgh, PA: Know, 1970. 165p. bibliog. $5.00. ISBN 0912786027. LC 72-89971.
Female Studies: Two was collected by the Commission on the Status of Women of the Modern Language Association, and the collection of 66 syllabi and courses is greatly expanded from the seventeen items presented in *Female Studies: One.* This is an invaluable aid in developing new courses, improving old ones, and building up women's studies collections.

423 Howe, Florence. **Seven Years Later: Women's Studies Programs in 1976.** Washington: National Advisory Council on Women's Educational Programs, 1977. 104p.
Howe distinguishes women's studies *programs* from the women's studies courses that began appearing in the late sixties on the basis that the emerging programs have entered a new stage characterized by increased legitimacy, maturity, and responsibility. They are, additionally, more permanent, usually with a line budget, a paid administrator, and a curriculum that moves through committees and is recognized in an official catalog. Howe reviews here fifteen women's studies programs–Bennett College, Brooklyn College (CUNY), University of Hawaii, University of Kansas, University of Massachusetts (Amherst), University of Minnesota, University of New Mexico, Northeastern Illinois University, University of Pennsylvania, Portland State University, San Francisco State University, Sarah Lawrence College, University of South Florida, University of Tennessee, and University of Washington–inquiring into 1) their current state with respect to faculty, students, curricula, classrooms, internal governance structures, and administrative relationships to their home universities; 2) their impact on their campuses and in their communities; and 3) what they reveal to be the dominant issues and needs critical to the future of women's studies. Included in an appendix are informational profiles and curricula of the fifteen programs.

424   Howe, Florence, ed. **Women and the Power to Change.** New York: McGraw-Hill, 1975. 182p. bibliog. index. $8.95. ISBN 0070101248. LC 74-17374.

Sponsored by the Carnegie Commission on Higher Education, this volume of essays explores the male-oriented bias of the American university from the personal perspectives of four activist intellectuals in the academic women's movement committed to the university as a force for change and growth. Essays include "Toward a Woman-Centered University," by Adrienne Rich; "Inside the Clockwork of Male Careers," by Arlie Russell Hochschild; "A View from the Law School," by Aleta Wallach; "Women and the Power to Change," by Florence Howe. The Howe essay addresses the women's studies movement as a key factor in changing the pattern of women's education. Howe is a proponent of strengthening the power positions of women in fields where they dominate (e.g., education) so that these fields will be ripe for innovation.

425   Howe, Florence, and Carol Ahlum, eds. **Female Studies III.** Pittsburgh, PA: Know, 1971. 181p. bibliog. $5.60. ISBN 0912786035. LC 72-89971.

This compendium offers 54 new course designs and seventeen programs. The first thirty pages reprint *Guide to Female Studies, No. 1.* Courses are listed under the headings: Education, Home Economics, Law, Nursing, Social Work, Theology, City Planning, Economics, History, Literature, Political Science, Psychology, Sociology and Anthropology. A separate section lists inter-disciplinary courses. Program descriptions for seventeen colleges and universities speak to the problems, objections, and questions encountered by scholars in women's studies, in some cases, and give specific program statements and goals in others. Almost every description deals substantially with the question: what is women's studies? This volume is enlightening reading for those contemplating a women's studies curriculum, as approaches can be contrasted and compared.

426   Howe, Julia (Ward), 1819-1910, ed. **Sex and Education: A Reply to Dr. E. H. Clarke's "Sex in Education."** New York: Arno Press, 1972. (Repr. of 1874 ed.). 203p. $9.00. ISBN 0405044631. LC 72-2608.

Sex in Education; Or, A Fair Chance For the Girls was published in 1873 by a well-known physician, Edward Hammond Clarke. Clarke took the position that coeducation was a grave mistake in social policy due to the unequal physical and mental capacities of men and women. Many replies to Clarke appeared soon after his book's publication, and Julia Ward Howe, eminent suffrage leader, published a selection of these in one volume in 1874, along with testimony from Vassar, Antioch, Michigan University, Lombard University, and Oberlin. These are deeply felt arguments for equality in education and coeducation.

427   Komarovsky, Mirra, 1906- . **Women in the Modern World: Their Education and Their Dilemmas.** Boston: Little, Brown, 1953; repr. New York: Irvington Publications, 1971. 319p. bibliog. index. $24.50.

This classic study addresses the questions: how should women be educated? and, what are they being educated for? Komarovsky argues that creative solutions for women's problems begin with higher education, which determines the intellectual temper and tone of the entire society. Though she calls for a blurring of boundaries defining masculine and feminine roles, she believes that "full-time and demanding careers will continue to be difficult for all but exceptional mothers." Komarovsky makes liberal use of case material. One notes that she pioneered in recognizing the need for improved vocational guidance, flexible work schedules, child care, retraining courses, and educational programs designed for older and reentry students. Major chapters: Women's Education under Fire; The Homemaker and Her Problems; Home Plus a Job; Can College Educate for Marriage and Parenthood?; Toward a Philosophy of Women's Education. Much has happened because of the women's movement that makes Komarovsky appear moderate, even mild, in her approach to women's education. For 1953, though, certainly entrenched in a decade of domesticity, *Women in the Modern World* was a vanguard book.

428   Leiner, Marvin. **Children Are the Revolution: Day Care in Cuba.** New York: Penguin Books, 1978. bibliog. index. $2.50. ISBN 014004874X. LC 77-18817.

Leiner offers as an epigram the following statement by the famed nineteenth-century Cuban patriot and poet, José Marti: "we work for children because children know how to live, because children are the hope of the world." Leiner and his family lived in Cuba during 1968-1969, and his three children attended Cuban schools. He reports here on his investigations into the evolving system of day care in revolutionary Cuba, a system, he argues, that demonstrates "what can be done with the education of children in emerging countries if funds and resources are combined with dedication and commitment." Building from a pre-revolutionary base of virtually non-existent facilities, Cuba has developed an extensive and expanding system of daycare—free to families of working mothers, admitting babies as young as 45 days old, administered by the Federation of Cuban Women, and staffed by paraprofessionals. Leiner shows how these developments are explicitly connected in Cuban politics to goals of women's liberation as well as of expanded education and production. Readers will want to consult another recent study of education and childcare in Cuba—Karen Wald's *Children of Che: Childcare and Education in Cuba* (Ramparts Press, 1978).

429   Leslie, Eliza, 1787-1858. **Miss Leslie's Behaviour Book: A Guide and Manual for Ladies.** New York: Arno Press, 1972. (Repr. of 1859 ed.). 336p. $15.00. ISBN 0405044658. LC 72-2611.

"Eliza Leslie's (1787-1858) youthful literary ambitions found varied fulfillment. But in 1828 she produced a bestseller—a book of 75 recipes she had learned at Mrs. Goodfellow's Philadelphia cooking school. While her juvenile stories, game books, and magazine sketches met with regular success, she achieved her greatest readership with cook books—*The Domestic Cookery Book* reaching 38 editions by 1851. She quickly expanded into the fields of domestic economy and personal etiquette. Generations of American women not only cooked as she said they should, they also behaved as this grand dame told them to behave" ("A Note about This Volume," A. K. Baxter and L. Stein, eds.). As with most books on "domestic economy" and etiquette (see, for example, Sarah Hale and Catharine Beecher), Leslie's treatise is of value primarily as an indicator of prevailing ideology of "woman's place" in nineteenth-century America, as a prescriptive work. Her subtitle here reads: "A Guide and Manual for Ladies as regards their conversation; manners; dress; introductions; entree to society; shopping; conduct in the street; at places of amusement; . . . ," etc.

430   Mitchell, Joyce Slayton. **Other Choices for Becoming a Woman.** (Rev. ed.). New York: Delacorte Press, 1976. 258p. bibliog. $7.95. ISBN 0440067952. LC 76-5588.

This book is a series of essays on the theme of choice, especially written for high school women. Themes explored in the essays by professionals from many fields are: Who Chooses?; Sexual Choices; Relationship Choices; Beauty Choices; Turning-On Choices; Spiritual Choices; Educational Choices. Resource information is provided in the last section.

431   Pottker, Janice, and Andrew Fishel, eds. **Sex Bias in the Schools.** Rutherford, NJ: Fairleigh Dickinson University Press, 1977. 571p. bibliog. index. $27.50. ISBN 0838614647. LC 74-200.

This reader comprises articles that document sexist practices in the schools. Articles are included on the following topics: Preschool and Elementary Education; Secondary Education; Textbooks; Role Formation: Occupational, Social, and Political; Counseling; Policymakers; Higher Education; State and Local Studies of Sex Bias in Public Education; Opinion Pools; and Sex Differences in Educational Attainment. Thirty-seven contributors are represented, from a variety of disciplines including education, sociology, engineering science, educational psychology, psychology, guidance and counseling, political science, and social work. Among them are James S. Coleman, Ruth E. Hartley, Lynne B. Iglitzin, Carole Joffe, Carol Kehr Tittle, and Elaine Walster.

432*   Robinson, Lora H. **Women's Studies: Courses and Programs for Higher Education.** Washington: American Association for Higher Education, 1973. 48p. bibliog. $2.00.

An excellent bibliography on the genesis and development of women's studies as a discipline is a very useful feature of this short document, which gives an overview and background of the field. Programs are identified and examples of program development are sketched. The section of women's studies courses describes single and multidisciplinary approaches, gives examples of program offerings, degree programs, and student response. "Program Operation" covers organizational structure, personnel utilization, and extracurricular programming. Florence Howe's *Seven Years Later: Women's Studies Programs in 1976* (1977) should be consulted for the latest information on developments in this field.

433   Rosenfelt, Deborah Silverton, comp. **Going Strong: New Courses/ New Programs.** Old Westbury, NY: Feminist Press, 1973. 236p. bibliog. $5.00. ISBN 0912670274.

Female Studies VII (*Going Strong*) notes the growth spurt in women's studies from 600 courses and twenty programs in 1971 to 2,000 courses and over eighty programs. Volume VII is closely related to *Female Studies III* (1971), which presented course descriptions and syllabi. Criteria for inclusion of these later syllabi have included innovative approaches over earlier courses and more comprehensive approaches in terms of race, culture, class, and nationality. Courses cluster around these headings: Interdisciplinary; Humanities and Arts;

Social Sciences; Sciences; Vocational/Professional/Applied and Miscellaneous (consciousness-raising, for example). Format for the arrangement of these later materials has improved over the 1971 *Female Studies*, too. These courses can be mined for their bibliographies, which are excellent and keyed to specific questions. Twelve diverse women's studies programs are described, preceded by a November 1973 list of women's studies programs across the country.

434   Rosenfelt, Deborah Silverton, ed. **Learning to Speak: Student Work.** Old Westbury, NY: Feminist Press, 1975. 244p. bibliog. $5.00. ISBN 0912670398. LC 76-365622.

The *Female Studies* series has chronicled the growth of women's studies, collecting syllabi, program descriptions, bibliographies, and describing feminist pedagogy in essays on women's studies. The present work produces in a published format the writings of students in women's studies courses across the country. Perhaps the most important trend to note in the work produced here is the attention to personal experience. Autobiographical and journal writing is significantly represented. Thematically, the mother and grandmother emerge as the most dominant images. There is research, too: an analysis of roles of women in Scottish ballads, a discussion of women and the Mormon church, an essay on young women in China. Creative work clusters around the topics of sisterhood, lesbianism, divorce, and the women's movement. The collective autobiography, "Through the Looking Glass Finally," by The Women's Biography Collective at Sonoma, concertizes 23 voices, a moving collective expression of women's experiences.

435   Rossi, Alice S., 1922- , and Ann Calderwood, eds. **Academic Women on the Move.** New York: Russell Sage Foundation, 1973. 560p. bibliog. index. $12.50. ISBN 087154752X. LC 73-76761.

Many of the most important academic women in the movement have contributed essays to this volume. Studying the position of women in higher education: Jo Freeman, Helen Astin, Pepper Schwartz, Florence Howe, and Carol Ahlum, to name a few. Topics range from higher education's woman dropout to the faculty wife; from career profiles of women doctorates to women's studies; from the black woman in the university to institutional variations affecting the status of academic women. This volume of essays will provide a good theoretical starting point for an analysis of the sex discrimination patterns operant in academe.

436   Rousseau, Jean Jacques, 1712-1778. **Emile.** New York: E. P. Dutton, 1974. 444p. $5.00. ISBN 0460005189. LC 75-319528.

Acquaintance with this book is crucial to an understanding of the eighteenth-century French writer, Jean-Jacques Rousseau, as it seriously calls into question much of the traditional interpretation of his work as well as the characterization of him as "radical egalitarian." Most of the book is concerned with Rousseau's prescription for the proper education of Emile, his prototype for the natural man. A smaller section treats the question of the "Education of Girls." The contrast between the two sections (as well as between *Emile* and his *Discourse on the Origin and Foundations of Inequality*) is quite revealing.

437   Schramm, Sarah Slavin, ed. **Female Studies VIII.** Pittsburgh, PA: Know, 1975. 221p. $6.10. LC 72-89971.

This sample of strategies that have been used successfully to get courses formal recognition and, in some cases, to get women's programs and women's studies departments established should be considered essential reading for those interested in pedagogical approaches to women's studies. Among the types of resources to be found here are: syllabi, bibliographies, and names and addresses.

438   Showalter, Elaine, and Carol Ohmann. **Female Studies IV: Teaching About Women.** Pittsburgh, PA: Know, 1971. 71p. bibliog. $2.60. ISBN 0912786043. LC 72-89971.

Twelve essays on teaching female studies have been gathered under the auspices of the Modern Language Association Commission on the Status of Women. Essentially this is a primer on women's studies as a discipline and as a pedagogical issue. Contents: "Introduction: Teaching About Women, 1971," by Elaine Showalter; "Crisis: Women in Education," by Ruth Crego Benson; "Teaching Women's Studies—Some Problems and Discoveries," by Wendy Martin; "A Class of Our Own," by A. White; "All Male Students and Women's Liberation," by Mary Tyler Knowles; "Teaching Woman's History Experimentally," by Bryan Strong; "The Arthur and Elizabeth Schlesinger Library on the History of Women in America, Cambridge, Massachusetts," by Ann Douglas Wood; "Other Special Collections on Women in American Libraries"; "Special Collections on Women Writers in American Libraries"; and "An Annotated Bibliography: Anthologies of Women's Studies and Women's Liberation," by Ella Kusnetz and Carol Ohmann.

439   Siporin, Rae L., ed. **Female Studies Five.** Pittsburgh, PA: Know, 1972. 116p. bibliog. $5.25. ISBN 0912786051. LC 72-89971.

Consists of the proceedings of a conference held at the University of Pittsburgh, November 5-7, 1971, titled "Women and Education: A Feminist Perspective," cosponsored by the Modern Language Association and the University of Pittsburgh. Seventeen essays are printed here addressing issues on women, education, sexism, and female studies. A sampling of the essays: Agate Nesaule Krouse, "A Feminist in Every Classroom"; Catharine Stimpson, "Women as Scapegoats"; Judith P. Stelboum, "Woman's Studies at a Community College—A Personal View"; Nancy Reeves, "Feminine Subculture and Female Mind"; Sheila Tobias and Ella Kusnetz, "Teaching Women's Studies: An Experiment at Stout State"; Susan S. Sherwin, "Women's Studies as a Scholarly Discipline: Some Questions for Discussion."

440   Stacey, Judith, et al., comps. **And Jill Came Tumbling After: Sexism in American Education.** New York: Dell, 1974. 461p. bibliog. $1.75. ISBN 0440321115.

This is a basic reader in the issues of sex discrimination in education. Essays address the following topics: the comparative intellectual capacities and achievements of men and women; sex-role socialization at home and at school; sexism in high school and college; the teaching profession; and the feminist response. Among the many contributors are Florence Howe, Matina Horner, Philip Goldberg, Patricia Sexton, Ruth Hartley, Carol Tittle, M. Carey Thomas, Elaine Showalter, Mary Ellmann, and Alice Rossi. Suggestions for further reading and lists of resources for action and information, audio-visual resources, and legislation and governmental resources are appended.

441   Steinfels, Margaret O'Brien, 1941- . **Who's Minding the Children? The History and Politics of Day Care in America.** New York: Simon and Schuster, 1973. 281p. bibliog. index. $8.95. ISBN 0671215973. LC 73-14093.

The result both of extensive conversations with day care teachers, directors, and parents and of observance of children in day care situations, this study traces contemporary notions of day care, the legislative history of day care, and the history of the day care itself, differentiating the kindergarten from the day nursery movements. Commercial centers, franchise day care units, cooperative enterprises, and non-profit day care facilities are examined, often with lengthy quotations from interviews. Steinfels's discussion of day care underscores the complexity of the issue; questions involving the future of the family cannot be handled easily. The conclusions her study arrives at are: day care is a political question; it is a necessity; it should be considered a normalized segment of our lives, not a welfare device; the future of day care and the future of the family should be linked discussions; day care should be expanded in such a way as to insure quality training of teachers and quality programs; the emphases in day care should be educational and developmental rather than custodial; day care centers should not be the only setting for child-care services; day care should provide a format for new child-rearing practices and lifestyles that are child-centered and family-centered.

442*   **Storefront Day Care Centers: The Radical Berlin Experiment.** Edited by an authors' collective. Boston: Beacon Press, 1973. 177p. ISBN 0807031682. LC 72-75544.

Katia Sedoun, Valeria Schmidt, and Eberhard Schultz have assembled a history of the radical day care center movement (in which all three were actively involved) in Berlin, 1968-1970. The first storefront day care centers were founded by members of the Women's Liberation Action Group within the Student Federation of Social Democrats (SDS). The impetus for the project was the women's sense of frustration at being excluded from politics due to a lack of childcare; the goal of the day care programs was to create anti-authoritarian, political education for the children. The editors combine their own account with a series of documents (speeches, magazine articles, government reports, SDS pamphlets) to sketch the history of the day care movement and its connection with the student movement; the history of public reaction, culminating in press hysteria about "commie" schools and eventual cut-off of government funds; and a description of the centers' program of non-authoritarian child raising and their system of parental involvement.

443   Tobias, Sheila, ed. **Female Studies One.** Pittsburgh, PA: Know, 1970. 73p. $2.60. ISBN 0912786019. LC 72-89971.

Valuable as a reference tool as well as a document of social history, this anthology of seventeen syllabi and courses offered in Female Studies during 1969-1970 was a pioneer effort. The division of courses runs: Interdisciplinary; History; Psychology and Sociology; Political Science; Literature.

444*   United States. Congress. House. Committee on Education and Labor.
Special Subcommittee on Education. **Discrimination against Women:
Congressional Hearings on Equal Rights in Education and Employment.**
Edited by Catharine R. Stimpson. New York: R. R. Bowker, 1973.
558p. $14.95. ISBN 0835206084. LC 72-13703.

This is the transcript of the 91st Congress hearings (1970) on discrimination
against women in education and employment, edited by Catharine R. Stimpson.
Among those presenting testimony at the hearings were Pauli Murray, Bernice
Sandler, Lucy Komisar, and Shirley Chisholm. Testimony of these women and
others comprises the first part of the volume. Part 2 reprints documents on
women and work, the law, education, the professions, government action,
and model remedies.

445   **Women on Campus: The Unfinished Liberation.** New Rochelle, NY:
Change Magazine, 1975. 256p. $7.95. ISBN 0915390035.

Most of the essays in this book have appeared in *Change Magazine* and are
written by distinguished women writers. These interesting essays present a
composite portrait of women in academic life, looking at their participation in
higher education from perspectives as various as that of the underemployed
academic wife who cannot find a job to that of the highly motivated college
woman who cannot get a Rhodes scholarship. Contents include: Catharine R.
Stimpson, "The New Feminism and Women's Studies"; Jean Collins, "The
Feminist Press"; Cynthia Secor, "Lesbians—The Doors Open"; Elizabeth Janeway,
"Women on Campus: The Unfinished Liberation"; Kate Millett, "Women and
War"; Caroline Bird, "Women's Lib and the Women's Colleges"; Pat Durchholz
and Janet O'Connor, "Why Women Go Back to College"; and Elisabeth Hansot,
"A 'Second-Chance' Program for Women."

446   Women on Words and Images (Society). **Channeling Children: Sex
Stereotyping in Prime-Time TV: An Analysis.** Princeton, NJ: Women
on Words and Images, 1975. 84p. bibliog. $2.50. ISBN 096007242X.
LC 75-568.

To answer the question—"what is television telling our children about the
masculine and feminine roles of adults?"—trained observers viewed prime-time
family dramatic television programs, recording the data on individual episodes,
noting occupations, female/male behaviors, and social issues raised in plots.
Although the conclusions that the data suggest relating to sexism are not
surprising, the suggestions this study makes on combatting the worst effects
of sex stereotyping will be helpful for parents and teachers. The study concedes
that the networks are powerful, but adds that the public is also powerful.
"People do have power: the power to complain, to praise, to pressure—most
of all, the power to teach children to be critical of all stereotypes, and to demonstrate through their own lives the values of equality for all people." In a different
study, Women on Words and Images reported their findings on sex-role stereotyping found in readers in a booklet, *Dick and Jane as Victims* (1972), a study
that effected changes in consciousness among educators, parents, textbook
publishers, authors, and illustrators.

447 Women on Words and Images (Society). **Dick and Jane as Victims: Sex Stereotyping in Children's Readers.** Princeton, NJ: Women on Words and Images, 1975. 57p. bibliog. $2.00. ISBN 096007241. LC 74-77374.

In this classic in the documentation of sex-role stereotyping in current school readers, the authors state that knowing in what ways readers portray girls and boys will suggest how children perceive their roles in the society. "Grade school readers are a top priority area for change, since they influence children at their most vulnerable and malleable stage of development." Their sample included 134 elementary school readers from fourteen publishers; they supported their study statistically, through content analysis and picture analysis. Not surprisingly, they found that readers are filled with vapid, unrealistic stories in which girls do not excel. The interesting table material inventories sample quotations, occupational models for males and females, and biographical materials on males and females, all culled from the readers.

448 Woody, Thomas, 1891- . **A History of Women's Education in the United States.** New York: Science Press, 1929; repr. New York: Octagon Books, 1966. 2v. bibliog. index. $42.50. ISBN 0374987408. LC 66-17495.

A much cited scholarly source on women's education in the United States from colonial times to the 1920s, Woody's book presents massive amounts of documentation on girls' schools, female academies and seminaries, women in the teaching profession, girls' high schools, vocational education for women, physical education, higher education for women, and the early leaders of women's colleges, coeducation, and the women's club movement. Serious research on any historical aspect of women's education begins with Woody. In the first volume, Woody gallops through the world history of women's position and education from ancient times before warming to his subject of American education.

The fine arts represents an underdeveloped area of women's studies materials. Identified materials suggest the patchwork of the available literature: broad surveys of the work of women artists whose names may often be unfamiliar, interviews, and essays about contemporary women artists by feminist art historians and critics. Books of reproductions of women artists' and photographers' works have been included, as have been biographical treatments of noted women artists and photographers. Feminist critical film surveys and anthologies appear here as do some biographical materials on women and film, both on filmmakers and images of women in film. Little has been written about the contributions of women to music, but some finding aids are included here as well as women's song books. *Chrysalis* magazine has done significant work in identifying materials by and about women artists and provides ongoing assistance in the area of contemporary women artists. The archival copies of the now-defunct *Feminist Art Journal* contain worthwhile interviews with and articles on women artists and their contributions. Increasingly special issues of periodicals appear underscoring the contributions of women to the arts. For assistance in locating special issues on women and the arts, researchers will want to look at *Women's Studies Abstracts*, which covers feminist and women's studies periodicals, and the special issues bibliographies produced by *Canadian Newsletter of Research on Women* for identification of general scholarly journal special issues focusing on women and the fine arts.

449   Adair, Casey, and Nancy Adair. **Word Is Out: Stories of Some of Our Lives.** San Francisco: New Glide Publications, 1978. bibliog. $6.95. ISBN 0912078618. LC 78-8395.
This book is based on the recent film of the same name, a riveting documentary about the lives of 26 gay people (male and female) of widely divergent age, background, and lifestyle. Included here are: an in-depth commentary on the making of the film by one of its six filmmakers, Nancy Adair; complete transcriptions of the 26 interviews from the film; a substantial bibliography; and over 100 photographs. Another recent book offering transcriptions of interviews with lesbians (solely) is Laurel Galana and Gina Covina's *The New Lesbians: Interviews with Women Across the U.S. and Canada* (Moon Books; distr. Random House, 1977). Galana and Covina, founders of *Amazon Quarterly*, interviewed twenty lesbians across the U.S. and Canada, ranging in age from 21 to 62 and coming from varied backgrounds.

450*   Alloy, Evelyn. **Working Women's Music: The Songs and Struggles of Women in the Cotton Mills, Textile Plants, and Needle Trades, Complete with Music for Singing and Playing.** Somerville, MA: New England Free Press, 1976. 43p. bibliog. $2.50. LC 77-772037.
Mainly this is a songbook with tunes such as: "I Cannot Be a Slave," "The Factory Girl," "Bread and Roses," "The Mill Mothers Lament," and "Ballad of the Blue Bell Jail." But there is interesting accompanying text on women workers and the music that accompanied labor activism. Many of these songs

were born out of tragedy: for example, "Mamenu" (or the Triangle Victims), written after the Triangle Shirtwaist Factory fire in 1909, in which 140 Jewish and Italian young women perished. This type of material is difficult to locate, so the footnotes and bibliography will be helpful even though they are brief. *Working Women's Music* is published by The New England Free Press, 60 Union Square, Somerville, MA 02143.

451   Beauvoir, Simone de, 1908- . **Brigitte Bardot and the Lolita Syndrome.** New York: Arno Press, 1972. 37, 52p. $9.00. ISBN 0405039123. LC 78-169346.

A sophisticated pictorial essay about the French film star, Beauvoir's analysis explores Brigitte Bardot as androgyne, nymph, and child-woman and admires her for her authenticity. Beauvoir maintains that it is Bardot's independent spirit on and off screen that accounts for her unpopularity among the French public, and she contrasts attitudes on women's dependence in France and America that demonstrate the reasons for Bardot's popularity in the States.

452*   Berkeley Women's Music Collective. **Berkeley Music Collective Songbook.** Oakland, CA: Women's Press Collective, 1975. 1v. (unpaged).

Music and lyrics to raise feminist consciousness are the *raison* behind this songbook, which contains music for voice and piano as well as guitar chord progressions.

453*   Brooks, Romaine, 1874-1970. **Romaine Brooks, Thief of Souls.** By Adelyn D. Breeskin. Washington: Published for the National Collection of Fine Arts by the Smithsonian Institution Press; [for sale by Supt. of Docs., U.S. Govt. Print. Off.] 1971. 143p. bibliog. index. LC 79-150515.

Romaine Brooks was an American lesbian artist who became part of the expatriate circle in Paris early in this century that included intellectual and artistic figures such as Natalie Barney (Brooks's lover of fifty years); Radclyffe Hall and her lover, Una Troubridge; Collette; Marcel Proust; Paul Valéry; and others. Brooks was highly acclaimed for her portraits and abstract, stylized line drawings in Paris, London, and New York during 1910-1935. Just prior to her death in 1970, Brooks donated the majority of her work to the National Collection of Fine Arts in Washington, which then assembled her first exhibition in thirty to forty years. This volume, which is the catalog to that exhibition, reproduces 68 portraits and drawings (two in color), providing full background information on each. Brief biographies of portrait subjects are also provided. Joshua C. Taylor (director of the National Collection) writes a short critical introduction, and Adelyn D. Breeskin (curator of contemporary art) is responsible for an article on Brooks's biographical and artistic history. A substantial bibliography of books, exhibition catalogs, and periodical and newspaper articles is included. Arno Press has recently reprinted a 1952 French booklet of illustrations and criticisms of Brooks's work entitled *Portraits, Tableaux, Dessins* (orig. Braun and Cie, 1952; repr. Arno Press, 1975). This collection might possibly be more easily acquired than Breeskin's, but its reproductions are smaller and inferior in quality.

454　Carter, Ernestine. **The Changing World of Fashion: 1900 to the Present.** New York: Putnam, 1977. 256p. bibliog. $25.00. ISBN 0399119698. LC 77-309.

An illustrated history of fashion for women in the twentieth century, punctuated by quotations on the subject from well-known contemporaries. Though the book bills itself as social history, it does not consciously analyze fashion as an expression of the social forces that structure women's lives and that are the concern of women's studies. The graphics are most to be recommended.

455　Cheney, Joyce, 1950- , et al., eds. **All Our Lives. A Woman's Songbook.** Baltimore, MD: Diana Press, 1976. 200p. bibliog. $6.50. ISBN 0884470083. LC 76-22564.

Collected here are a series of contemporary songs (representing artists such as Hazel and Alice, Peggy Seeger, Malvina Reynolds, Holly Near, Anne Romaine, Alix Dobkin, Meg Christian, and others), traditional songs that are by or about women (e.g., "What Shall I Do With This Baby-o?," "Beware, O Take Care," etc.), and political songs from the past (e.g., "Bread and Roses," "Which Side Are You On?"). Music and lyrics are written out; historical introductions to the songs and artists are provided; and illustrations are used throughout. At the end of the book, the editors have compiled a list of relevant publications, records, tapes, and songbooks.

456　Chryssa, Varda, 1933- . **Chryssa.** By Pierre Restany. New York: H. N. Abrams, 1977. 274p. bibliog. index. $45.00. ISBN 0810903660. LC 77-1916.

This enormous, expensive and beautiful tome is called by *Choice* magazine "the most complete study to date of the work of Chryssa," a Greek-born sculptor best known for her work in neon. The text by Pierre Restany, a French art critic, describes and analyzes the evolution of Chryssa's work, an evolution the reader can trace visually through the book's 201 plates, seventy in color. Also included are many fascinating photographs of the artist at work among bits and pieces of sculpture. There is another much briefer and less expensive study of Chryssa available by Sam Hunter, professor at Princeton University (*Chryssa*; H. N. Abrams, 1974; $7.95); Hunter's volume includes 55 illustrations (twelve in color) plus a brief essay on the artist.

457　Cole, Doris. **From Tipi to Skyscraper: A History of Women in Architecture.** Boston: i press; distr. New York: Braziller, 1973. 136p. bibliog. $4.95. ISBN 091322202X. LC 73-80932.

Only 2 percent of practicing architects in the United States are women; less than one-half of the women with architectural degrees are registered architects; and the percentage of degrees granted to women is decreasing as the profession grows. Cole's book is intended to "first, document the historic contributions of women to American architecture; second, analyze the underlying social and economic reasons for the present situation; and third, propose ways of correcting and improving this situation by attracting more women to the profession of architecture." Cole discusses women's contributions in Native American culture, in the utopian communes of the Shakers, in the nineteenth century and into the present. Cole is herself a registered architect, having studied at the Harvard Graduate School of Design.

458   Cunningham, Imogen, 1883-1976. **After Ninety.** Seattle, WA: University of Washington Press, 1977. 111p. bibliog. index. $14.95. ISBN 0295955597. LC 77-73306.

Begun before her death at 93, this book is a tribute to the strength of aging. The aged San Francisco photographer sought out individuals who were in the process of confronting the aging process, assembling a gallery of people whose faces manifest a variety of responses to life and age: fear, nobility, joy, strength, wisdom, puzzlement. Hers is a commitment to beauty found in the most ordinary things, and this book is a compassionate essay on the beauty of the human spirit as reflected in the aging face. Margaretta Mitchell writes an eloquent introduction to Imogen Cunningham's work and to her philosophy of art and life. Very few of the photographs here are republished from her earlier work. The brief bibliography focuses on recent articles about the photographer and cites articles that speak to Cunningham's perception of the woman as artist.

459   Cunningham, Imogen, 1883-1976. **Imogen! Imogen Cunningham Photographs, 1910-1973.** Seattle, WA: Published for the Henry Art Gallery by the University of Washington Press, 1974. 110p. bibliog. $20.00. ISBN 0295953322. LC 74-2490.

Spanning a career of 63 years, the photographs here chronicle not only the development of Imogen Cunningham's unique photographic style, but also the development of the medium itself. As the technology moved from glass plates to sheer film, from larger, slower cameras to smaller, quicker cameras that used faster, more sensitive film—Imogen's work also changed, moving away from the gauzy romanticism of early work to the clarity and directness that have come to characterize her contemporary photographs. Imogen Cunningham was a West Coast photographer, a friend of photographers such as Edward Weston, Ansel Adams, and others of the f/64 Group. She has photographed many famous people but seems to prefer ordinary subjects whose faces interest her. The photographs in this volume are arranged as follows: Early Years in Washington, 1910-15; Northern California Portraits, 1921-36; Artists, Actors, Writers, 1923-40; Plants, 1923-46; Later Portraits, 1953-73; and Heads, Legs, Hands, 1965-73. A list of her exhibitions is provided, along with a selected bibliography of interviews and articles about her work.

460   Ferlita, Ernest, and John R. May. **The Parables of Lina Wertmuller.** New York: Paulist Press, 1977. 104p. bibliog. index. $3.95. ISBN 0809120488. LC 77-83562.

Lina Wertmuller's films have consistently succeeded in winning acclaim, provoking controversy, and eluding simple political categorization. They go to the heart of issues of sex and class. Yet more often than not, feminists and socialists find them disquieting. Ferlita and May argue that Wertmuller seeks fundamentally to disturb and provoke, and that therefore, her art is best understood as *parable.* While myth establishes the possibility of reconciliation and solution in the world, parable is essentially subversive. In part 1, the authors briefly sketch Wertmuller's life, career, and the critical response to her work. In part 2, they consider her films: *All Screwed Up*, 1973 ("Images of World"); *Swept Away*, 1974, and *Love and Anarchy*, 1972 ("Images of Woman"); *Let's Talk About Men*, 1965, *The Seduction of Mimi*, 1971, and *Seven Beauties*, 1975 ("Images of Man"). These discussions are followed by a brief interview with Wertmuller conducted by Ferlita in 1976. Three appendices list Wertmuller's works, reviews of her films, and general articles on Wertmuller.

461   French, Brandon, 1944- . **On the Verge of Revolt: Women in American Films of the Fifties.** New York: Ungar, 1978. 194p. bibliog. index. $9.95. ISBN 0804422206. LC 78-4294.

The '50s, sometimes called the twentieth century's "decade of domesticity," saw the production of films that represented women outside of their domestic roles. Brandon French, a Yale professor of English and a filmmaker, looks at films such as *Some Like It Hot, The Country Girl, Marty, The Nun's Story, Picnic, Mr. Allyson,* and *Shane* and finds an ambiguous representation of women, one in which marriage, sex roles, motherhood, and topical issues such as alcoholism and ambition, were not clearly defined or synchronized with societal mores during the '50s. French's historical and sociological film analysis is accompanied by an excellent bibliography, photographs, and film rental information.

462*   Harksen, Sibylle. **Women in the Middle Ages.** New York: A. Schram; distr. New York: Universe Books, 1975. 65p. bibliog. ISBN 0839001487. LC 74-8793.

The representation of women in various styles of art and life in the Middle Ages comprises a significant portion of this visually beautiful book with 112 plates. Harksen finds that in many cases women did wield important economic clout in the Middle Ages in the areas of food production, textile industries, and middle-class family enterprises. In politics, Harksen turns to notable women— Blanche of Castile, Joan of Arc, and Eleanor of Aquitaine, among others. Nuns, saints, and abbesses were particularly significant feminine figures in medieval times. As for literature, "in no other part of mediaeval civilization has the woman played so large a part as in literature, not only as celebrated by the poets but also herself as poetess." The bibliography provides an excellent background reading list of the Middle Ages and woman's place in that milieu.

463   Harris, Ann Sutherland, and Linda Nochlin. **Women Artists, 1550-1950.** Los Angeles: Los Angeles County Museum of Art; New York: Knopf, 1977. 367p. bibliog. index. $15.00. ISBN 0394411692. LC 76-39955.

This beautiful catalog is based on the first international exhibition of art by women, organized by the two art historian authors of this volume—Harris and Nochlin—and assembled in 1977 by the Los Angeles County Museum of Art. (It was also exhibited in Austin, Pittsburgh, and Brooklyn.) Included are works, chronologically arranged, of 84 European and United States painters spanning the period 1550-1950. Harris and Nochlin collaborated in writing a lengthy historical introduction. The main body of the text consists of short biographical sketches and critical assessments of each featured artist; bibliographies of literature on the artist as well as information on exhibitions and collections of work by the artist are further specified in a section at the end. Black and white plates (172 in all) illustrate the work of each painter, some of whom are additionally represented in the 32 stunning color plates. The exhibition featured both well-known artists (such as Käthe Kollwitz, Mary Cassatt, Frida Kahlo, and Georgia O'Keeffe) and the more obscure (e.g., Vanessa Bell, Anne Vallayer-Coster, and Anna Dorothea Lisiewska-Therbusch). An early source on the history of women artists is Clara Erskine Clement's *Women in the Fine Arts: From the Seventh Century B.C. to the Twentieth Century A.D.* (orig. 1904; repr. Hacker Art Books, 1974).

464   Haskell, Molly. **From Reverence to Rape: The Treatment of Women in the Movies.** New York: Holt, Rinehart and Winston, 1974. 388p. index. $10.00. ISBN 0030076064. LC 72-91580.

Haskell's analysis of the various images of women that the movies have projected reveals that the sexism of the old Hollywood was not nearly as oppressive as the movie politics of the early 1970s. Haskell's approach is steeped in film scholarship. "The Big Lie" that she identifies as the pervasive reality on and off screen is a belief in woman's basic inferiority. The number of films analyzed and stars mentioned is dazzling, but the message is a grim one, indicting female stereotypes that have had enormous cultural significance. Chapters include: The Twenties; The Thirties; The Woman's Film; The Forties; The Fifties; and The Europeans. Haskell is particularly disparaging of women in films during the last decade (1964-1974). Though she identifies a long list of actresses who have played strong parts, she points to the stereotypical roles they were assigned— "whores, quasi-whores, jilted mistresses, emotional cripples, drunks." The excellent indexing here makes materials on specific movies and actresses readily accessible. Rosen's *Popcorn Venus* and Mellen's *Women and Their Sexuality in the New Film* are useful to consult along with Haskell.

465   Hess, Thomas B., and Elizabeth C. Baker, 1934- , eds. **Art and Sexual Politics: Women's Liberation, Women Artists, and Art History.** New York: Macmillan, 1973. 150p. bibliog. $1.95. LC 72-85182.

These essays originally appeared in *Art News*, volume 69, no. 9, 1971. Included are "Why Have There Been No Great Women Artists?," by Linda Nochlin; "Great Women Artists," by Thomas B. Hess; "Why Have There Been No Great Women Artists?—Ten Replies," by Elaine de Kooning (painter), Bridget Riley (painter), Louise Nevelson (sculptor), Eleanor Antin (conceptual artist), Suzi Gablik (painter), Sylvia Stone (sculptor), Marjorie Strider (sculptor), Lynda Benglis (sculptor), and Rosemarie Castoro (painter); "Sexual Art-Politics," by Elizabeth C. Baker; and "In the University," by Lee Hall. Over seventy black and white illustrations are included.

466   Kalmus, Yvonne, et al., eds. **Women See Men.** New York: McGraw-Hill, 1977. 122p. $12.95. ISBN 0070046972. LC 77-8860.

Edited by Yvonne Kalmus, Rikki Ripp, and Cheryl Wiesenfeld, with an introduction and text by Ingrid Bengis and art direction by Geri Davis, *Women See Men* follows Kalmus and Davis's earlier *Women See Women* (Crowell, 1976). Here, 98 photographs by 68 women photographers depict men and boys in a variety of lifestyles and postures. The volume attempts to answer the questions of whether women really see men and, if they do, how. An interesting point made by the editors is that women photographers in their nude photographs of men tend to "wish to please the subject—proud possessor that he is of the male genitalia" (afterword). The portraits, on the other hand, seem to present particular problems for the women photographers. Though technically quite good, they lack in feeling and intimacy. Another, quite similar photographic collection, featuring the work of several photographers whose work appears in *Women See Men*, is *Women Photograph Men*, edited by Dannielle B. Hayes (Morrow, 1977); it offers 118 male images.

467   Kay, Karyn, and Gerald Peary, eds. **Women and the Cinema: A Critical Anthology.** New York: E. P. Dutton, 1977. 464p. bibliog. index. $8.95. ISBN 0525474595. LC 77-71301.

"These essays dealing with women, both past and present, and their participation in film constitute an extremely well thought out anthology whose selections represent a wide range of critical opinion on the position of women both in front of the camera and behind it" (*Choice*, 14 [1977], p. 1655). Articles often are reprints from such respected journals as *Sight and Sound, Focus*, and *The Velvet Light Trap*, and they offer fine writing dealing with women and film. In eight groups, they cover actresses, women in production, women in political films, and feminist film theory. Karyn Kay teaches Women in Film at Livingston College, Rutgers University; Gerald Peary lectures on film in the English Department of Livingston College.

468   Kendall, Alan, 1939- . **The Tender Tyrant, Nadia Boulanger: A Life Devoted to Music.** Wilton, CT: Lyceum Books, 1977. 144p. index. $8.95. ISBN 0915336170. LC 76-27098.

Composer, pianist, conductor, teacher, music critic: Nadia Boulanger's life (b. 1882) has been totally committed to music. Numbered among her students have been David Diamond, Aaron Copland, Hugo Cole, and Yehudi Menuhin. Considered one of the great music teachers of the twentieth century, she has had close friendships with Igor Stravinsky and Serge Koussevitsky. Properly speaking, this is not a biography. Boulanger apparently had neither the time nor the inclination to provide biographical information about herself to the author. Her reputation as "the tender tyrant" derives from her well-known temper. The account concentrates on her extraordinary achievements in the classical music world and her dedication to the philosophy that music and life are one and the same thing.

469   Kollwitz, Käthe (Schmidt), 1867-1945. **Prints and Drawings of Käthe Kollwitz.** New York: Dover Publications, 1969. 32p. bibliog. $5.00. ISBN 0486221776. LC 73-76286.

This collection of Kollwitz's prints and drawings is to be recommended for its moderate cost and the size of its 83 reproductions (12x10 inches). Although the compiler, Carl Zigrosser, includes a critical and bibliographic essay on the artist, the reader with a further interest in Kollwitz's life should look to Martha Kearn's *Käthe Kollwitz: Woman and Artist* (1976) and Mina and Arthur Klein's *Käthe Kollwitz: Life in Art* (orig. 1972; repr. Schocken Books, 1975).

470   Lippard, Lucy R. **From the Center: Feminist Essays on Women's Art.**
New York: E. P. Dutton, 1976. 314p. bibliog. index. $6.95. ISBN
0525474277. LC 76-150915.

Lucy Lippard applies a personal, feminist art criticism to the work of contemporary women artists. Her first book of essays was *Changing* (1971). Since then, Lippard notes, her criticism has moved away from comparing the work of women artists to the works of men because she feels that women are not attempting to do the same things as men, nor has the art of women entered mainstream art consciousness. In these essays, Lippard addresses herself to issues of sexual politics in art, feminist imagery, and the women's art movement. Essays on the work of specific women focus on Irene Siegel, Eva Hesse, Adrian Piper, Jo Baer, Joan Mitchell, Hanne Darboven, Ree Morton, Jackie Winsor, Mary Miss, Judy Chicago, May Stevens, Louise Bourgeois, Rosemarie Castoro, Faith Ringgold, Yvonne Ranier, and on the art films of Nancy Graves, Nancy Holt, and Rebecca Horn.

471   Medsger, Betty. **Women at Work: A Photographic Documentary.** New
York: Sheed and Ward, 1975. 212p. index. $14.95. ISBN 083620610X.
LC 75-1658.

Medsger captures the diversity of women's working experience in America in her candid photographic essay about women and the jobs they do. It is a wide range of traditional and non-traditional work experiences that she photographs: acupuncturist, bank officer, cabinetmaker, coal miner, teacher, meat packer, surgeon—to name a few. This book should be available to girls and women in every type of library and career counseling center. Beautiful photographs attempt to depict human rather than "feminine" qualities.

472   Mellen, Joan. **Women and Their Sexuality in the New Film.** New York:
Dell, 1975. 237p. $1.25. ISBN 0440393426.

Like Molly Haskell (*From Reverence to Rape*, 1973), Mellen believes that in current films, "the language of independent women may be reluctantly allowed, but the substance goes unaltered." Mellen's analysis indicts the bourgeois view of women fostered by, and which in turn sustains, schools, media, churches, and state. She argues that the women's liberation movement of itself cannot liberate images of women on film unless the filmmaker is a revolutionary who sees the imperative of overthrowing enslaving social forms. Specific films and directors are discussed throughout the text. Chapters are: Bourgeois Woman: A Disturbance in Mirrors (work of Bergman, Bertolluci, Buñuel, and others); Female Sexuality in Films (Pakula, Perry, Nichols, and others); Lesbianism in the Movies (Aldrich, Metzger, Chabrol, and others); Bergman and Women; Sexual Politics and Bertolucci's "Last Tango in Paris"; The Moral Psychology of Rohmer's Tales; Makavejev and Reich; Buñuel's "Tristana"; Visconti's "Death in Venice"; Outfoxing Lawrence: Novella Into Film; The Mae West Nobody Knows; and Counter Revolt: "Up the Sandbox." Many stills illustrate the text. Readers may also want to look at Mellen's *Big Bad Wolves: Masculinity in the American Film* (Pantheon Books, 1977).

473   Meltzer, Milton, 1915- . **Dorothea Lange: A Photographer's Life.**
        New York: Farrar, Straus and Giroux, 1973. 380p. bibliog. index.
        $15.00. ISBN 0374143234. LC 78-5509.

Of her art, Dorothea Lange (1895-1965) said, "you put your camera around
your neck in the morning, along with putting on your shoes, and there it is,
an appendage of the body that shares your life with you. The camera is an
instrument that teaches people how to see without a camera." This solidly
researched biography has drawn on over 250 pages of transcribed interviews
with Dorothea Lange and 100 interviews with family, close friends and colleagues
of this woman who made documentary photography (especially of Depression
victims and rural and immigrant workers) an art. As she was crippled by polio,
scarred by a difficult family background, withdrawn, and isolated in her youth,
the story of her breaking from her past and succeeding in the world of photography
is compelling reading. The text is documented by seventy or so of her photographs, the most renowned of which is "Migrant Mother." Her personal life
was complex and strained over the years, her personality a strong one, her
working relationships intense. See her photographs in *Dorothea Lange Looks
at the American Country Woman: A Photographic Essay* (Fort Worth, TX:
Amon Carter Museum, 1967). Meltzer has provided an exhaustive bibliography
and copious notes on this extraordinary artist.

474   Munsterberg, Hugo, 1916- . **A History of Women Artists.** New York:
        C. N. Potter; distr. New York: Crown, 1975. 150p. bibliog. index.
        $12.95. ISBN 0517523809. LC 75-19043.

Munsterberg's view is not a feminist one (e.g., "clearly the view held by Mill
[and implied by most feminists] that women were suppressed in early times
and are becoming more outstanding as artists as more opportunities are open
to them is a misrepresentation of the facts," p. 146). He suggests that the reason
for the dearth of women artists of greatness lies in the fact that women may be
more verbally than visually talented. Despite his analysis, Munsterberg has
produced a visually pleasing and interesting text about women artists ranging
from women artists in prehistoric times and primitive civilizations to women
graphic artists and women painters. For a more feminist interpretation in a
survey of women's art, see Karen Petersen and J. J. Wilson, *Women Artists*
(1976).

475   Nemser, Cindy. **Art Talk: Conversations with 12 Women Artists.** New
        York: Scribner, 1975. 367p. bibliog. $14.95. ISBN 0684139847.
        LC 74-11302.

Cindy Nemser, former editor of the now defunct *Feminist Art Journal*, speaks
with twelve women artists about their lives and work. The artists are: Barbara
Hepworth, sculptor (b. 1903); Sonia Delaunay, painter (b. 1885); Louise
Nevelson, sculptor (b. 1899); Lee Krasner, painter (b. 1908); Alice Neel, painter
(b. 1900); Grace Hartigan, painter (b. 1922); Marisol Escobar, sculptor (b. 1930);
Eva Hesse, sculptor (1936-1970); Lila Katzen, sculptor (b. 1932); Eleanor Antin,
conceptual artist (b. 1935); Audrey Flack, painter (b. 1931); and Nancy Gross-
man, painter/lithographer/sculptor (b. 1940). The interviews are personal,
confronting such issues as the conflict between traditional woman's role and
that of the artist, and whether or not the artist felt discriminated against because

of gender. Nemser is very interested in art and the individual artist's approach to her art. Nemser asserts that she finds no "over-all female sensibility" in the work of women artists. She does believe, however that, "physical traits, race, class, ethnic background, social circle, philosophical milieu, as well as gender, are all inseparably intertwined in the finished aesthetic product." Many photographs of the artists' works illustrate the text, and Nemser has provided a selected bibliography of exhibitions, catalogs, and monographs for each artist.

476   O'Keeffe, Georgia, 1887- . **Georgia O'Keeffe.** New York: Viking Press, 1976. 200p. $35.00. ISBN 0670337102. LC 76-23452.
Georgia O'Keeffe presided over every aspect of the creation of this stunning collection of her work. She chose the paintings (108 reproduced in color) and wrote the accompanying text. Little has been published on this significant woman artist. This volume is a must.

477   Petersen, Karen, 1943- , and J. J. Wilson, 1936- . **Women Artists: Recognition and Reappraisal from the Early Middle Ages to the Twentieth Century.** New York: Harper and Row, 1976. 212p. bibliog. index. $5.95. ISBN 0060903872. LC 75-39543.
In this general historic treatment of women artists in Western civilization, Peterson and Wilson have begun to remedy the fact that little has been done to record the work of women artists. This gap is reflected in the dearth of reproductions of the work and bibliographies about the work and lives of women artists. "Our aim is to accumulate in one place as much information as we have found thus far on the lives of women artists, realizing how much has been lost or distorted. The illustrations must speak for themselves, as we are not able to give them the formal analysis of trained art historians," write the authors. In pointing out the difficulties encountered by students in doing research on women artists, Petersen and Wilson hit upon the general problems inherent in women's studies. They lament the lack of reference books that document the achievements of women artists and explain that often students would rather do work on an established male artist "because their teachers, librarians, and fellow students given them more support in these well-trodden areas." Outstanding features of this book include painstakingly researched notes, the best bibliography to date on women artists, and an appendix on Chinese women artists. Complementing the text are 340 black and white illustrations. It should be noted that Harper and Row has produced three slide sets from the materials that Petersen and Wilson developed in their initial researching of women artists. (For more information on the Women Artists slide series, contact Harper and Row Media Department, 10 East 53rd St., New York, NY 10022).

478*   Pool, Jeannie G. **Women in Music History: A Research Guide.** Ansonia Station, NY: Pool, 1977. 42p. bibliog. $3.00.
Jeannie Pool has written and published an excellent introduction and research guide to women in music history. She sees her pamphlet as a tool for the ongoing project of retrieving the work and information about the lives of women musicians who have been ignored; her pamphlet does this by identifying existing resources and work that needs doing. Included here are: "An Essay on the History of Women in Music," by Pool; a bibliography of little known sources

(books, articles and periodicals) and of bibliographies of common sources; lists of organizations, record companies, and recordings of music by women for women; a list of women composers before 1900; a discography of recordings of music by women composers available as of September, 1977; and a list of possible research topics. *Women in Music History* is being distributed by the author: P.O. Box 436, Ansonia Station, New York, NY 10023. Pool intends to issue an updated version in the future.

479   Rosen, Marjorie. **Popcorn Venus: Women, Movies and the American Dream.** New York: Avon Books, 1973. 448p. bibliog. index. $1.95. ISBN 0380001772.

Rosen has great enthusiasm for her subject and writes with authority about the major eras of film and the images of the women projected on the screen from the beginning of the twentieth century to the '70s. Her subject is a vast one— women in the movies, women who made the movies, stereotyped images of women on film, dominant cultural images of women in the society of each decade, themes in major films. Because of the scope of the project, Rosen tends to focus on big names and big pictures only—Mary Pickford, Lillian and Dorothy Gish, Clara Bow, Joan Crawford, Garbo, Harlow, Mae West, Rita Hayworth, Marilyn Monroe, Ingrid Bergman, Lauren Bacall, and Jane Fonda, of the actresses; Ida Lupino, Frances Marion, Anita Loos, Lois Weber, and Dorothy Arzner, of the writers and directors. Rosen's major point is that the mass media have wielded enormous influence on the images men hold of women and women hold of themselves. Victorian heroines, vamps, flappers, the mysterious women, babes, pinups, independent women, sensualists, spinsters, goddesses—each of these stereotypes has at once been born of the culture and has proliferated its kind in societal reality. The index is especially important in an encyclopedic treatment of this type, and Rosen's is competently done.

480   Seibert, Ilse. **Women in the Ancient Near East.** New York: A. Schram, 1974. 66p. bibliog. $20.00. ISBN 0839001495.

Even though the history of woman in the ancient Near East is sketched here along with details of her status, legal rights, and position in the family, in the main this is a beautiful artbook illustrating the brief text. Although women occupied a high position as cult figures of worship and were appreciated as erotic partners in ancient art, their inequality was and is apparent in almost every other aspect of the society. Chapters detail women rulers and life in the harem as well as woman's position in matrimony and family life. Seibert constructs a useful chronological table up to 660 A.D., rendering events in the political history, civilization, and important documents of the Near East. The 112 plates depict images of women on stamps, seals, cups, tablets, temples, jewelry, tombs, and a variety of other artifacts and media.

481   Smith, Sharon. **Women Who Make Movies.** New York: Hopkinson and Blake, 1975. 307p. bibliog. index. $9.95. ISBN 0911974091. LC 74-79562.

Smith's study has two aims: to be a history of women filmmakers and to name the new women filmmakers. On both counts, she is successful. In addition to providing a visually augmented overview of filmmakers of the world from 1896 to contemporary times, Smith analyzes specific filmmakers: Lois Weber, Dorothy Arzner, filmmakers of the avant-garde movement of the '40s and '50s, Ida Lupino, Shirley Clarke, Elaine May, Susan Sontag, Barbara Loden, Stephanie Rothman, Faith Hubley, Germain Dulac, Lina Wertmuller, Liliana Cavani, Leni Riefenstahl, and many others. The author asserts that "there is nothing connected with the making of a motion picture that a woman cannot do as easily as a man, and there is no reason why she cannot master every technicality of the art." Fine photographs accompany the text, which is international in scope. The third section of the book is a directory of women filmmakers in the United States and a listing of relevant organizations and distributors. Though this book on women and film may lack certain eloquent critical insights, its practical features are a welcome addition to the literature.

482   Sontag, Susan, 1933- . **On Photography.** New York: Farrar, Straus and Giroux, 1977. 207p. $7.95. ISBN 0374226261. LC 77-11916. Originally published as a series of six essays in the *New York Review of Books*, the titles of these pieces are: "In Plato's Cave"; "America, Seen Through Photographs, Darkly"; "Melancholy Objects"; "The Heroism of Vision"; "Photographic Evangels"; and "The Image World." A brief anthology of quotations at the end expresses the definitions of photography held by a number of notable individuals—Julia Margaret Cameron, Diane Arbus, and Margaret Bourke-White are among the photographers represented. Sontag brilliantly argues for the power of the photographic image (e.g., our attachment to personal photographs; the way we defer to the presence of a camera in a social setting) even as she rejects photography as fine art, comparing the photograph to a "visual crumb." Instead of heightening emotional sensitivity, Sontag comments that the realism of the photographic image can be responsible for emotional detachment and distancing. Her final analysis is that photography is a sort of ultimate consumption. "As we make images and consume them, we need still more images; and still more." She compares this consumption of the visual to a lust that can never be satisfied. "Cameras are the antidote and the disease, a means of appropriating reality and a means of making it obsolete."

483   Sophia Smith Collection. **Picture Catalog of the Sophia Smith Collection.** Northampton, MA: Smith College, 1972. 128p. index. $6.00. This pamphlet reproduces selected photographs held by Sophia Smith and covering the following areas: abolition-slavery; arts-humanities; biography; countries; frontier; miscellaneous; social reform; war; and women's rights. Each photograph is fully identified, dated, and its dimensions noted. Ordering information is included at the back. See the description of the overall collection held by Sophia Smith and a note on the G. K. Hall edition of the full holdings under: Sophia Smith Collection. **Catalog of the Sophia Smith Collection Women's History Archive** (1976).

484   Swan, Susan Burrows. **Plain and Fancy: American Women and Their Needlework, 1700-1850.** New York: Holt, Rinehart and Winston, 1977. 240p. bibliog. index. $14.95. ISBN 003015121X. LC 77-1627. "This book's purpose is to show the integral part needlework played in the lives of these women [of early America], particularly how it allowed them to express

themselves in an almost completely male-dominated society. For needlework, in addition to being the most important contribution made by early American women to the decorative arts, was also their most acceptable outlet for creative expression and, indeed, in many instances the only concrete evidence of their endeavors. Needlework tells us a good deal about what it was like to be a woman in early America" (Swan's introduction). Swan's credentials for writing this superbly illustrated volume on needlework and social history are her association with the Winterthur Museum and her teaching in the area of needlework in the museum's program. She began her research by arranging more than 600 pieces of American needlework by technique and by date, noting that between 1825 and 1875, "a marked deterioration in needlework skills became apparent." To comprehend trends, Swan examined eighteenth-century periodical sources for information on techniques as well as for the philosophical currents of the times concerning women. Included are 165 photographs, extensive notes and bibliography, and a concise glossary of terms.

485　Synder-Ott, Joelynn, 1940- . **Women and Creativity.** Millbrae, CA: Les Femmes, 1977. 144p. bibliog. index. $5.95. ISBN 0890879265. LC 77-77954.

Synder-Ott is both teacher of art and art history and an artist herself. Here she is concerned with assessing women's historic contributions to art and with retrieving contributions that have been neglected, buried, or completely unrecognized. Her two chapters on women's art pedagogy may be of particular interest to women's studies: "A Dialogue with Women Art Students and Women Faculty Members at the Oldest Art School for Women in the U.S. (Moore College of Art, Philadelphia)" and "Starting a Feminist Art Program at Community Level, University Level."

486　Tucker, Anne, comp. **The Woman's Eye.** New York: Knopf; distr. New York: Random House, 1973. 169p. bibliog. $15.00. ISBN 0394486781. LC 73-7283.

Chosen from the work of ten photographers, with biographical introductions to each, this anthology provides a fairly inclusive, historical treatment of women photographers and their work: Gertrude Kasebier (1852-1934), Frances Benjamin Johnston (1864-1952), Margaret Bourke-White (1904-1971), Dorothea Lange (1895-1965), Bernice Abbott (1898-), Barbara Morgan (1900-), Diane Arbus (1923-1971), Alisa Wells (1929-), Judy Dater (1941-), and Bea Nettles (1946-).

487　Tufts, Eleanor. **Our Hidden Heritage: Five Centuries of Women Artists.** New York: Paddington Press, 1974. 256p. bibliog. index. $12.95. ISBN 0846700263. LC 73-20955.

"The basic art survey books used today only rarely allude to the names of women artists, and even most histories dealing with specific periods of art do not seriously consider their work. And yet in the past women were appointed as court painters, were accepted as professionals, and were unstintingly appreciated by their contemporaries." Tufts suggests that silence about the contributions of women artists is a recent phenomenon that took root in the Victorian period, when art history became a recognized discipline. Her exposure of neglected women artists from the sixteenth to the twentieth centuries brings 22 artists to light, each biographical piece accompanied by a portrait or self-portrait of the artist with a bountiful selection of full-page black and white plates of her work (136 plates in all). The artists: Sofonisba Anguissola (1535/40-1625); Lavinia Fontana (1552-1614); Levina Teerling (c1515-1576); Catharina Van Hemessen (1528-after 1587); Artemisia Gentileschi (1593-c1652); Judith Leyster (1609-1660); Elisabetta Sirani (1638-1665); Maria Sibylla Merian (1647-1717); Rachel Ruysch (1664-1750); Rosalba Carriera (1675-1757); Angelica Kauffmann (1741-1807); Elisabeth Vigée Lebrun (1755-1842); Sarah Peale (1800-1885); Rosa Bonheur (1822-1899); Edmonia Lewis (1843-?); Suzanne Valadon (1865-1938); Käthe Kollwitz (1867-1945); Paula Modersohn-Becker (1876-1907); Gwendolyn John (1876-1939); Natalia Goncharova (1881-1962); Germaine Richier (1904-1959); I. Rice Pereira (1907-1971). Tufts has consciously omitted names of well-known artists from her book—Mary Cassatt and Romaine Brooks, for example—in order to give more attention to lesser known women. An excellent bibliography is included as well.

488   Vequaud, Yves. **Women Painters of Mathila.** New York: Thames and Hudson, 1977. 112p. $8.95. ISBN 0500270937.

This is a translation of *L'Art du Mathila*. Mathila is a matriarchal community located in the Bihari province in northeast India. The women of Mathila create paintings illustrative of the important Indian folk art tradition. The work centers around the ritual depiction of marriage. These paintings take two specific forms, indicating the spiritual and sociological significance of the marriage relationship— the *Kohbar*, which represents the marriage proposal, and the *Aripana*, which depicts the magic circle. The tradition of these very colorful, geometrically precise paintings is 3,000 years old. Vequaud's book addresses the longevity of the tradition and traces its development through the text.

489   Wiesenfeld, Cheryl, et al., eds. **Women See Woman.** New York: Thomas Y. Crowell, 1976. 145p. $12.50. ISBN 0690009658. LC 75-16410.

This is an exciting collection of photographs by contemporary women photographers. The editors initiated the project with the dual purpose of showcasing work by women photographers, who are all too often not represented in photographic collections, and of developing visually the theme of how women see women. The initial press release inviting submissions attracted over 10,000 photographs from all over the United States, which were eventually edited down into the 135 pages of this book. A section at the end gives brief biographies of the photographers whose work is displayed.

490*   Wilding, Faith. **By Our Own Hands: The Woman Artist's Movement, Southern California, 1970-1976.** Santa Monica, CA: Double X, 1977. 111p. bibliog. LC 77-365980.

This important book traces the genesis and development of the Woman's Art Movement in California and complements Judy Chicago's account in *Through the Flower*. The illustrations give ample evidence of the works of art produced by such California feminist art groups as the Feminist Studio Workshop, Womanspace, the Feminist Art Program at CalArts, and the Fresno Feminist Art Program.

491   Wilson, Michael, 1914-1978. **Salt of the Earth: A Screenplay**. Old Westbury, NY: Feminist Press, 1978. 187p. bibliog. $4.95. ISBN 0912670452. LC 78-4212.

Salt of the Earth is a film written by Michael Wilson (shot in New Mexico in 1953, premiered in New York in 1954) which has been rediscovered by the contemporary women's movement after years of obscurity. Feminists have been astonished by the way this film of the McCarthy era portrays the realities of class, ethnic, and feminist struggle in people's lives. The film is based on an actual strike which took place in Hanover, New Mexico, from October 1950 to January 1952, at a mine owned by Empire Zinc, a subsidiary of New Jersey Zinc. The history of this area of New Mexico has been shaped by the exploitation of its resources and of Mexican-American labor by big mining corporations (today Kennecott Copper is one of the chief of these). The film conveys vividly the way that racism was used as a weapon against the strikers and the way the strikers resisted these attacks. It also highlights the centrality of the women to the entire struggle. When an injunction prevented the men from walking the picket line, the women took over and stood firm against all attempts to move them—against violence, provocation, and mass arrest. The film shows the way this mobilization by the women brought in its wake a series of struggles over the men's attitudes toward them and over their responsibility for home and children. This volume presents the screenplay by Michael Wilson, illustrated with some excellent stills, and a lengthy commentary by Deborah Silverton Rosenfelt on the making of the film—a story at least as extraordinary as that of the strike itself. The film was the result of collaboration between blacklisted Hollywood people and the members of New Mexico Local 890 of the International Union of Mine, Mill, and Smelter Workers. Women and men of the mining community played most of the major roles. Also included in this volume are contemporary accounts of the making of the film and a chronology of events.

492   Zinserling, Verena. **Women in Greece and Rome**. New York: A. Schram, 1973; distr. New York: Universe Books. 85p. bibliog. $20.00. ISBN 0876631812. LC 72-91539.

This translation of *Die Frau in Hellas und Rom*, with more than a hundred plates illustrating the representation of women in Graeco-Roman art, follows a similar format to other Schram publications treating various cultural representations of women in art. The short text treats Greece and Rome separately. For Greece, the following topics are treated: Crete and Mycenae; The Trojan War and After; Classical Period: Women of Athens; Classical Period: Spartan Life; The Hellenistic Period: A Cosmopolitan Age; The Hetaerae; Fashion and Beauty. Zinserling notes that woman's basic position was one of servitude though she received significant representation in the arts. The text for the Roman section covers: Women and the Law; The Roman Woman; Religion and Cult; Heroines in Myth and History; The Empresses; Fashion, Ornament, and Cosmetics. The bibliography draws on sources in English, German, Italian, and French.

Works listed here tend to be works on the United States, with some European and British emphasis clustering around major organizations and movements (see Jane Addams), revisionist feminist history (see Boulding), or primary collections of documents (see Lerner). Thus, materials on temperance, suffrage, socialist and labor movements, abolitionism, and the women's club movement are likely to appear in this section. Feminist historiography (see Rowbotham) and the works of first-wave feminist historians, such as Beard's *Woman as a Force in History*, are essential to history collections supporting women's studies as are historical studies documenting the experiences of minority women in a racist culture (see Vasquez). Works on family history appear in this chapter. Look for historical works on education, economics, anthropology, medicine, sexuality, health, sports, and the fine arts under those specific chapter headings. The work of feminist historians is a particularly rich area, with much periodical literature available in women's studies journals as well as in the interdisciplinary and social historical journals (e.g., *Journal of Family History, Journal of Psychohistory, Journal of Interdisciplinary History,* and *Journal of Social History*). Again, the *Canadian Newsletter of Research on Women* bibliographies of special issues identify important scholarly periodical literature on women's history.

493   Adam, Ruth. **A Woman's Place, 1910-1975.** New York: Norton, 1977. 224p. bibliog. index. $8.95. ISBN 0393056228. LC 76-51803.
This is a briskly written account of women's liberation in Great Britain. Topics covered include an overview of women's status in the Empire; the Suffragettes; the position of women at home, in the military, and in industry during the First World War; post-World War I changes in women's status; the sexual revolution of the '20s; economic and marital trends affecting women during the Depression; World War II and the effects of evacuation and conscription; the affluent working wives and failed marriages of the '50s; the emancipation of women, sexually and societally, of the '60s; the situation of the woman alone in the '70s and the attendant social movements of permissiveness and women's liberation. Though many may disagree with Adam's analysis of cause and effect, her capsulization of social history is useful. Twenty photographs illustrate the changing status of women—from bicycle riding to fashion trends.

494   Addams, Jane, 1860-1935. **Peace and Bread in Time of War.** New York: Macmillan, 1922; repr. New York: J. S. Ozer, 1972. 257p. $10.95. ISBN 0891980512. LC 75-137524.
This is a history of the pacifist movement during World War I, particularly of the Woman's Peace Party and the Women's International League for Peace and Freedom, by the great social critic, activist, and founder of Hull House, Jane Addams. As this history is also part of her personal history, she integrates her own experience, interpretation, and assessment into the account. Throughout the book, but especially in the chapter entitled "A Review of Bread Rations and Woman's Traditions," Addams is concerned with ways in which women's traditional roles as mothers and providers of food could be extended into a

political activism around the cause of peace and bread. Readers with a further interest in the pacifist movement of this period would do well to consult Marie Louise Degen's *The History of the Woman's Peace Party* (orig. 1939; repr. B. Franklin, 1974).

495   Addams, Jane, 1860-1935, et al. **Women at the Hague: The International Congress of Women and Its Results.** New York: Macmillan, 1915; repr. New York: Garland, 1972. 171p. $29.50. ISBN 0824002466. LC 73-147452.

The Hague International Congress of Women opened on April 28, 1915, bringing together 1,136 voting delegates from twelve different countries, neutral and belligerent, to voice their opposition to World War I and their faith in internationalism. This step into the arena of international politics was remarkable at a time when women from most countries remained disenfranchised and when nationalism was the prevailing sentiment, having even undermined the internationalist commitments of the socialist Second International. Many of the women were suffragists, and the Hague Congress had in fact been called in place of the congress of the International Woman Suffrage Association, which was to have been held in Berlin in June 1915, but was called off because of the war. This volume contains an account of the Hague Congress by Jane Addams, who presided over the gathering; Professor Emily G. Balch, economist from Wellesley College; and Dr. Alice Hamilton, Special Investigator of Dangerous Trades for the U.S. Dept. of Labor. The Garland reprint edition includes a brief introduction by Mercedes M. Randall.

496   Altbach, Edith Hoshino. **Women in America.** Lexington, MA: D. C. Heath, 1974. 204p. bibliog. index. $2.95. ISBN 0669634530. LC 73-8185.

Women in America is intended as a general introduction to the history of women in the United States, but Altbach is clear about her particular focus. She is concerned about a bias she sees as prevalent in the new writing on women by women: "the plain fact is that most women writing about women have forgotten or never knew what being a woman means for most women." Altbach shies away from the common emphasis upon "exceptional" women, choosing instead to highlight the experience of the housewife, both middle and working class, and the wage-earning woman. The book is divided into four major sections: Domestic Life, The Labor Force, The Woman Movement (i.e., the nineteenth and early twentieth century movements), and The New Feminism. Altbach includes as an appendix a timeline of women's history in the U.S. ("Events of Note in the History of American Women"), which traces side by side, from 1617 to 1973, changes in a) employment, technology, inventions, health, home, morals, fashion, and education; and b) achievements and events, Women's Movement, Women's Liberation Movement, and miscellaneous.

497   Andrews, John Bertram, 1880-1943, and William Dwight Porter Bliss, 1856-1926. **History of Women in Trade Unions.** New York: Arno Press, 1974. (Repr. of 1911 ed.). 236p. bibliog. $14.00. ISBN 0405060718. LC 74-3925.

A comprehensive history of women and trade unions, originally published in 1911, this is organized into two major parts—"1825 Through the Knights of Labor" and "From Organization of American Federation of Labor." The history is approached both by geographic region and by occupation. Attitudes of men unionists toward women's employment and organization and the gains made by unions are considered, in addition to strikes, organizations and legislation.

498   Aries, Philippe. **Centuries of Childhood: A Social History of Family Life.** New York: Random House, 1965. 447p. bibliog. index. $3.45. ISBN 0394702867.

Written by a demographic historian, this is one of the real classics acclaimed by historians, women's studies scholars, and general readers within the contemporary women's movement. Its importance lies in its inquiry into the historical and changing (rather than purely instinctual) nature of the institutions of childhood and the family, as revealed through changes in the *ideas* that people hold of these institutions. A key question informing the study is "whether the idea of the family had not been born comparatively recently, at a time when the family had freed itself from both biology and law to become a value, a theme of expression, an occasion of emotion." (This is a translation of *L'Enfant et la vie familiale sous l'Ancien Régime.*)

499   Backer, Dorothy Anne Liot. **Precious Women.** New York: Basic Books, 1974. 308p. bibliog. index. $12.00. ISBN 0465061931. LC 73-90137.

Backer explores the phenomenon of the *précieuse* in seventeenth-century society and sees this woman of society as much more than a passive and silly coquette. "They were the magical secret feminine center of early seventeenth-century society . . . and their aim in life was nothing less than the creation of worldliness, the imposition of form and ritual on a community that was wallowing in lust, blood, and dirt." The author explores the faults of this group of self-absorbed women, but recognizes the good aspects of *préciosité* that ushered in the New Woman as a substantial intellectual force in the eighteenth century.

500   Bainton, Roland Herbert, 1894- . **Women of the Reformation, from Spain to Scandinavia.** Minneapolis, MN: Augsburg, 1977. 240p. bibliog. index. $9.95. ISBN 0806615680. LC 76-27089.

This is the final volume of Bainton's three-volume work on women prominent in the Reformation. Bibliographies for further reading and research follow each brief biography. This volume looks at women from Spain, Portugal, Scotland, England, Denmark, Norway, Poland, Sweden, Hungary, and Transylvania.

501   Bainton, Roland Herbert, 1894- . **Women of the Reformation in France and England.** Minneapolis, MN: Augsburg, 1973. 287p. bibliog. index. $8.95. ISBN 0806613335. LC 73-78269.

This is the second volume in Bainton's three-volume work on women prominent in the Reformation. Bibliographies for further reading and research follow each brief biography.

502   Bainton, Roland Herbert, 1894- . **Women of the Reformation in Germany and Italy.** Minneapolis, MN: Augsburg, 1971. 279p. bibliog. index. $7.95. ISBN 08066111612. LC 70-135235.

This is the first part of a three-volume work that "aims to give brief biographical sketches of women who played a prominent role in the Catholic and Protestant reform movements in the early years of the sixteenth century" (from the author's preface). The sketches are very short, but followed by bibliographies for further reading.

503   Banks, Joseph Ambrose, and Olive Banks. **Feminism and Family Planning in Victorian England.** New York: Schocken Books, 1964. 142p. bibliog. index. $4.75. ISBN 0805200622. LC 63-18387.

This is a historical and theoretical discussion of feminism and family planning in Victorian England—of the apparent simple connection between the two (the rise of feminism coincident with the decline in the birth rate), and the actual ambiguity of their historical relationship. Readers might want to compare this study with Linda Gordon's more recent book, *Woman's Body, Woman's Right: A Social History of Birth Control in America* (1976).

504   Banner, Lois W. **Women in Modern America: A Brief History.** New York: Harcourt, Brace, Jovanovich, 1974. 276p. bibliog. index. $5.95. ISBN 0155961934. LC 73-20976.

This is an excellent basic text in the social history of women in the United States from 1890 to the 1970s. Banner explains in her preface that her primary aims were threefold: "to explore the reasons why feminism rose and fell and rose again; to examine the history of various groups of women, including the working class, blacks, immigrants, farm women, and the middle class, each of which responded to the pressures and opportunities of the times in a different way; and, finally, to focus on the dramatic and continuing struggle waged by determined, innovative women to achieve their rights." The book is written in an accessible style, is amply illustrated, and a critical bibliography is appended to each chapter.

505   Barker-Benfield, G. J. **The Horrors of the Half-Known Life: Male Attitudes Toward Women and Sexuality in Nineteenth-Century America.** New York: Harper and Row, 1976. 352p. bibliog. index. $15.00. ISBN 0060102241. LC 75-6327.

This is an important cultural history, largely psychoanalytic in method, of nineteenth-century men's views on women and sexuality in the United States. Divided into four parts, the first examines and develops de Tocqueville's analysis "of the uniquely extreme separation of the sexes in America"; the second tells the tale of the appropriation of control over reproduction by physicians and the suppression of midwifery; part three discusses the Reverend John Todd's advice to young men on behavior appropriate to the competitive economy and relates this to men's fears about sexuality, especially women's sexuality; finally, in part four, the author analyzes the writings of an obstetrician and gynecologist, Augustus Kinsley Gardner, and in particular his views on "the social and political meaning of reproduction."

506   Baxandall, Rosalyn, et al., comps. **America's Working Women: A Documentary History, 1600 to the Present.** New York: Random House, 1976. 408p. bibliog. index. $15.00. ISBN 0394491505. LC 76-10575.

Rosalyn Baxandall, Linda Gordon, and Susan Reverby have put together a wonderful collection of primary source material on women's history in the United States. Despite the ambitious scope and diverse sources, the book flows well and makes for very enjoyable reading. The compilers have written an excellent introduction, plus short introductions to each piece and lengthier comments on each historical period covered. The selections include union records, short stories, poems, songs, social workers' reports, statistical studies, and more. The reader interested in such primary source material on women's history in the U.S. might also want to consult two collections by Gerda Lerner, *The Female Experience* (1977) and *Black Women in White America* (1972).

507   Beard, Mary (Ritter), 1876-1958, ed. **America Through Women's Eyes.** New York: Macmillan, 1933; repr. New York: Greenwood Press, 1968. 558p. bibliog. index. $21.50. LC 68-54772.

Beard's intention in this book is "to illustrate, if in a fragmentary way, the share of women in the development of American society—their activity, their thought about their labor, and their thought about the history they have helped to make or have observed in the making" (from the introduction). The book looks at American history from the period of colonization to the early 1930s.

508   Beard, Mary (Ritter), 1876-1958. **Mary Ritter Beard: A Sourcebook.** Edited by Ann J. Lane. New York: Schocken Books, 1977. 252p. bibliog. index. $15.00. ISBN 0805236686. LC 77-3135.

Ann Lane set out to write a biography of Mary Beard, but modified her aims when she discovered how successful Mary and her husband Charles Beard—both historians—had been at destroying their own records. In place of a biography, Lane wrote a 75-page appraisal of Mary Beard's life and work, which is fascinating and tantalizing in its sketchy portrait of a most unusual woman; also presented are collected excerpts from her writings and speeches. These writings reflect her lifelong work as a feminist historian and activist. Section 1 of her writings (Political Activism—The Early Years) includes, among other pieces, "Mothercraft," "Votes for Workingwomen," and "The Legislative Influence of Unenfranchised Women." Part 2 (Feminism as a World View—Theory) includes selections from *On Understanding Women* and *Woman as Force in History*, plus a lesser-known article, "Feminism as a Social Phenomenon," which "examines nineteenth-century feminism in its relationship to the ideas of the Enlightenment and the development of capitalism." Part 3 (Feminism as a World View—Practice) includes "A Changing Political Economy as It Affects Women" and "The Economic Background of the Sex Life of the Unmarried Adult." Lane has written brief introductions to each major section and to each selection. Mary Beard's life and work are essential background for the new women's history.

509   Beard, Mary (Ritter), 1876-1958. **Woman as a Force in History: A Study in Traditions and Realities.** New York: Macmillan, 1946; repr. New York: Octagon Books, 1976. 382p. bibliog. index. $15.00. ISBN 0374905037. LC 76-39976.

"Women have done far more than exist and bear and rear children. They have played a great role in directing human events as thought and action. Women have been a force in making all the history that has been made" (from the preface). This book has been a very important discovery for women in the contemporary women's movement who are trying to learn about and create women's history. Most important is the effort that Mary Beard made to confront and contradict "the tradition that women were members of a subject sex throughout history."

510   Beard, Mary (Ritter), 1876-1958. **Woman's Work in Municipalities.**
      New York: Arno Press, 1972. (Repr. of 1915 ed.). 344p. $15.00.
      ISBN 0405044461. LC 72-2588.

In this lesser-known work by the feminist historian, Mary Beard, material is presented that documents "the extent and variety" of women's volunteer work in the United States at the turn of the century. Much of this work has since been professionalized within the field of social work. Topics discussed: Education; Public Health; "The Social Evil" (prostitution); Recreation; The Assimilation of Races; Housing; Social Service; Corrections; Public Safety; Civic Improvement; and Government and Administration. Beard's analysis is frequently buttressed with excerpts from women's own accounts of their work and from records of women's organizations.

511   Bell, Susan G., comp. **Women: From the Greeks to the French Revolu-**
      tion. Belmont, CA: Wadsworth, 1973. 313p. bibliog. index. $5.95.
      ISBN 0534002846. LC 72-93472.

This is an anthology of writings on the position of women in Western civilization from the classical Greek era to the end of the eighteenth century. Included are both writings from antiquity (e.g., Plato, Aristotle, The Bible) and from more contemporary historical works. The material is divided into seven sections: Women in the Ancient World: Greece and Rome; Early Christian Attitudes toward Femininity; Nunneries as the Medieval Alternative to Marriage; Varieties of Womanhood in the Middle Ages; Humanism and the Renaissance Education of Women; Renaissance Women and Reformation Influences; and Women in the Century of the French Revolution. A lengthy bibliography follows. This collection should be of value for introductory courses on the position of women in Western society, for general courses on the history of Western civilization, and as a reference tool. It is a good introductory guide to sources.

512   Benson, Mary Sumner, 1903- . **Women in Eighteenth-Century America:**
      A Study of Opinion and Social Usage. New York: Columbia University
      Press, 1935; repr. New York: AMS Press, 1976. 343p. bibliog. index.
      $18.50. ISBN 04041514057. LC 75-41025.

Originally published as the author's Ph.D. thesis (Columbia University, 1935), this is primarily a study of what Benson calls "theoretical aspects of women's position" in eighteenth-century America. She considers both American writers of the period and the key European influences. As she notes, "such a treatment of theoretical material is almost of necessity confined to women of the upper and middle classes." Aware of the necessary gap between theory and practice,